Approaches to

Global Governance Theory

SUNY series in

Global Politics

James N. Rosenau, editor

APPROACHES TO GLOBAL GOVERNANCE THEORY

Edited by

MARTIN HEWSON
TIMOTHY J. SINCLAIR

STATE UNIVERSITY OF NEW YORK PRESS

Published by
State University of New York Press, Albany

For information, address State University of New York Press,
State University Plaza, Albany, NY 12246

Production, Laurie Searl
Marketing, Nancy Farrell

Library of Congress Cataloging-in-Publication Data

Approaches to global governance theory / edited by Martin Hewson and Timothy J. Sinclair.
    p. cm.
Includes bibliographical references and index.
ISBN 0-7914-4307-8 (hardcover : alk. paper). — ISBN 0-7914-4308-6 (pbk. : alk. paper)
    1. International cooperation. 2. International relations––Philosophy. I. Hewson, Martin, 1965– . II. Sinclair, Timothy.
JZ1318.A67 1999
327.1'7'01—dc21   99-17095
                                                    CIP

10 9 8 7 6 5 4 3 2 1

Contents

PART THREE
KNOWLEDGE, MARKETIZATION, AND GLOBAL GOVERNANCE

PART FOUR
POLITICAL IDENTITY, CIVIL SOCIETY, AND GLOBAL GOVERNANCE

PART FIVE
CONCLUSION

Acknowledgments

An earlier version of chapter 6 was published as "Governance and the 'Commoditization' of Information" in *Global Governance: A Review of Multilateralism and International Organization* vol. 4 no. 2 (April–June 1998), copyright © 1998 by Lynne Rienner Publishers. Reprinted with permission.

An earlier version of of chapter 12 was published as "From Place to Planet: Local Knowledge and Global Environmental Governance" in *Global Governance: A Review of Multilateralism and International Organization* vol. 3 no 1 (Jan.–April 1997), copyright © 1997 by Lynne Rienner Publishers. Reprinted with permission.

Preface

This book is concerned with global governance as it has been, is, and may become. The studies presented here ask how patterns of global governance have changed and are changing. We want to emphasize that real global governance should not to be regarded as either necessary or beneficent. Real global governance is not in itself a political good or a solvent for the world's problems. In other words, this volume adopts a critical and realist attitude towards the phenomenon.

Understanding change from the vantage point of real global governance means taking a broad and bold view. It certainly means breaking with orthodoxy as far as realism is concerned. The studies here bring in such innovative issues as territoriality and globalization, knowledge and communications, identity and civil society, credit and technology. They show that real global governance is composed of multiple sources of power.

A first step toward understanding changing global governance is to focus upon ontology. The bringing of ontology into global governance theory is at the core of this book. For some people, of course, mention of ontology is liable to provoke unease. They will object: surely the stuff of global governance is about finding practicable ways of coping with global problems? Important as this is, there is nonetheless an implicit confusion generating this kind of objection. It supposes that an ontological approach is necessarily abstract and perhaps even metaphysical. This book aims to demonstrate that the objection is misplaced.

To start with ontology is to be explicit about the structure of reality and the entities that compose existing forms of global governance. Ontology leads to realism, though not necessarily of the kind that became dominant in the postwar discipline of International Relations. Postwar realism acknowledged the existence of only a narrow band of entities. Reexamining ontology is a challenge to raise anew the question of what kind of entities and forces are pertinent to change in global governance today and in the future.

The conversations within this book are about what entities to acknowledge as involved in changing global governance. Questions that arise include the following: What is the balance of apparently universalistic forces, such as globalization, with localized forces? What implications do changing forms of knowledge have for configurations of global governance? What is the status of collective political identities and of civil society in global governance? At the level of actors, what is the relative importance of states and nonstate actors? The concluding chapter by James Rosenau draws together many of these issues into a framework for posing these and other ontological questions.

A second step in the present project has been to select a set of salient issues that urgently require clarification in the context of global governance theory. First and foremost are the meaning and value of the global governance concept itself. The chapters by Robert Latham and Ronen Palan are explicitly skeptical of the way in which the global governance concept is characteristically employed.

An additional salient theme concerns the hypothesis that knowledge and the "world information order" are a mainspring of change in global governance. This issue is explored by examining several key forms of knowledge. Karen Litfin inquires into the implications of environmental remote sensing by satellite. Timothy Sinclair's analysis of what he argues is the dominant form of global governance makes use of examples from disintermediated financial markets, budget deficit debates, and the "Global Information Economy" (GIE). Edward Comor looks at the issue from the perspective of the current trend toward a globalizing of the media industries. Martin Hewson discusses the history of globally oriented intellectual technologies. Mark Amen traces the influence of innovations in credit instruments on governance in everyday life.

A third theme is that civil society and political identity are key sources of changing global governance. Yale Ferguson and Richard Mansbach provide a comprehensive mapping of the historical significance of political identities. Michael Schechter gives a critique of what is the most prominent statement of global governance thinking – the report by the Commission on Global Governance – for its inadequacies as regards civil society forces. Ronnie Lipschutz explores the space for local knowledge and local agency in the context of global environmental governance.

An ongoing debate in these pages concerns how best to conceive global governance, or indeed whether the notion is helpful at all. But more substantive controversies and conversations are also at play. Three issues are at the forefront. First, there is the changing status of the nation-state and of territoriality. While avoiding the simplistic extremes of either proclaiming the coming end of the state or its immutable centrality, a central problem is nonetheless to pinpoint alterations in the saliency of the Westphalian state system as an ingredient of global governance. Second, there is the question of power. What kinds of domination and determination are involved in global governance? Simplistic models of a unitary hierarchy must be discounted. Nonetheless, these pages reveal a debate over the principal loci and sources of power. Finally, the issue of continuity, change, and timing is central. The analysis of global change is one of the greatest intellectual challenges of the present. Yet that has to be complemented with a sense of the differing time scales and continuities that different aspects of the world order exhibit. In sum, the chapters below offer contrasting approaches to these central dilemmas of global governance theory.

The first part of this collection approaches global governance from a conceptual and theoretical vantage point. The initial chapter by Martin Hewson and Timothy Sinclair provides an overview of why so many commentators are now using the term *global governance*. Since the fall of the Berlin Wall, the study of global governance has become a growth sector. The least innovative aspects of this phenomenon, Hewson and Sinclair argue, have emerged from international regime theory and from reflections on the present and potential status of the world organizations. The more innovative side of global governance theory has come from attempts to create comprehensive and integral accounts of globalization and global change.

Robert Latham's chapter offers a critique of the global governance concept in general and Rosenau's work in particular. For Latham, the global governance discourse is seductive because of its openness. It seeks to break with the rigidities of the 'domestic/foreign' dichotomy. It seems to view world politics as if in a "floating world" of flux and uncertainty. Nonetheless, Latham doubts whether the discourse can live up to this potential. There is, he argues, an undertone of modernization thinking and a concomitant silence as regards 'dysgovernance', by which he means negations of, and resistances to, global governance. In addition, there is a tendency to downplay the significance of state power in constituting political action by assuming a single fabric of global life, a "great hum of quotidian governance."

Ronen Palan too casts a dubious eye over the global governance discourse. Palan's critique seeks to situate contemporary attempts to imagine global governance in the longer context of attempts to imagine society and the nation-state in social and political theory. According to Palan, each of these imagines a shared space. There is more continuity than global governance theorists are willing to acknowledge. In addition, Palan argues that the imagined is an important source of social construction. Just as nineteenth-century attempts to imagine society and the nation-state constructed social closure, so today's attempts to imagine global governance are also constructing new types of social closure. The point, implies Palan, is not to imagine a global governance, but to imagine social openness.

The second part of this collection approaches global governance from the vantage point of the communications globalization trend, examining how both technology and discourse are implicated in changing patterns of global governance. Fifty earth-observation satellites are due to be launched during the 1990s. In chapter 4, Karen Litfin examines the social and political implications of this new, high-technology, ecology-oriented global gaze. What kind of global governance is implicated in satellite earth observation? According to Litfin, the globality of environmental remote sensing creates a disjuncture with territorially-based statehood. Yet it may also serve to bolster the territoriality of relatively unmapped states. Similarly, earth observation reinforces the power of technocratic science while at the same time offering opportunities for more localized and participatory forms of environmental governance.

The chapter by Martin Hewson puts the focus on the significance of relocations of governance in the making of the modern world order. This approach he calls a neo-Weberian style of global governance analysis. In elaborating it, Hewson asks how informational globalism emerged. His answer traces the part played by the main world organizations, since the late nineteenth century, in globalizing communications and information. Hewson argues that periodic attempts to create a global governance in practice served to stimulate the extension of key practices of informationalism.

The current thrust toward a globalizing of media industries has frequently been taken as implying a decline of the state and a diminution of the state system as a structure of global governance. Edward Comor's essay challenges this idea—at least as regards the salience of American power. He traces how the US government has vigorously promoted the globalization of communications in a form that entails the commodification of knowledge. Comor regards the implications of this development to be above all the creation of new "monopolies of knowledge." This term, borrowed from the political economy of Harold A. Innis, is intended to convey the significance of the increasing concentration of the media of communications under the control of global media and technology firms.

The third part of this book approaches global governance from the vantage point of the economic globalization trend, examining the interplay between knowledge and marketization as constituents of these economic dynamics. Tony Porter's chapter builds on Susan Strange's earlier work on knowledge structures, extending her concerns to the particular historical period of late-modernity, incorporating a longer-run sociohistorical analysis. He looks at the increased speed and intensity with which new codified knowledge is turned into routine ways of doing things and the distributional effects which follow. In doing so, Porter develops a new approach to global financial governance.

Timothy Sinclair also argues that global governance must be understood in historical terms. Different forms of global governance can be identified, just as we can talk of different forms of state. He distinguishes two contending forms and suggests one of these—what he sees following Cox and Piaget, as the static or synchronic form—as being in a commanding position. To understand this form, he argues, new tools of analysis will be needed. This international political economy of the commonplace (IPEC) will be concerned with habits and practices rather than more state-centric policy issues. Sinclair discusses three examples of global governance mechanisms which he sees exemplifying this synchronic form.

Mark Amen in chapter 9 offers a wide-ranging interpretation of the implications of innovatory credit instruments. The chapter includes a particularly clear and accessible explanation of derivatives, that most abstract and complex of credit instruments. He is concerned to highlight the impact of derivatives upon everyday life and the kind of governance found in the everyday arena. Amen argues that a pervasive uncertainty is the result, a condition that he maintains is unacknowledged in the currently influential approaches to the role of knowledge in world order.

Part four approaches global governance from the vantage point of political identities and civil society, showing how they can be considered as sources of change in global governance. A map of global governance that excludes political identities is surely quite incomplete. Yale Ferguson and Richard Mansbach provide just such a mapping in a comprehensive but concentrated way. Drawing on numerous contemporary and historical cases, the authors first consider political identities and their associated polities in the spatial dimension. Instead of being arranged in a discrete Westphalian pattern, polities are most often "nested" and overlapping. In addition, political identities interweave with ethnic, religious or other forms of collective identification. Ferguson and Mansbach then attend to the temporal dimension. Political identities are not fixed; they alter as they encounter one another. In certain historical periods there have been widespread mutations in political identity. The present period may in due course be viewed retrospectively as just such an era of change.

Since 1995, relatively wide journalistic comment has followed the report of the Commission on Global Governance on reforming the world organizations. As a result, the report has become the most widely known statement of global governance thinking. Michael Schechter provides a probing critique of the commission's approach. Although the report presents itself as radical and innovative, Schechter shows this to be not the case. Schechter argues for the policy advantage of adopting an approach that he terms a "critical policy-relevant theory." In particular, this would take a more long-term view of the potential for the reconstruction of civil society forces on a worldwide scale.

The issue is then taken-up by Ronnie Lipschutz in chapter 12. Lipschutz asks "whether it is possible to nurture a governance system that privileges local choice and, at the same time, takes into account global complexities, connections, and justice." The potentialities for this may come from a context of conjunction between integrating and fragmenting forces. But most of all, for Lipschutz, it entails a valuation and acknowledgement of the importance of local knowledge.

The final part of this book, and its concluding chapter, returns to the global governance concept. The discussion of an ontology for global governance is elaborated in the concluding chapter by James Rosenau. Proceeding from a nice distinction between an ontology and a paradigm, Rosenau describes ontology as inquiry into assumptions about reality and the basic elements in an order. The principal feature of Rosenau's ontology is its avowedly synthetic character. It seeks to highlight a certain coherence in the world order, which at the same time encompasses processes of change and disruption, conceived as both integrating and fragmenting forces. Analysts ought to acknowledge that "if a map of the world were drawn, it would depict global governance as highly disaggregated even as many of its spheres are overlapping." Rosenau therefore proposes that the key entities in global governance are distinct but intersecting "spheres of authority."

This book has been a long time in the making. The ideas behind it have evolved in conversations between the editors while at York University, Toronto, and subsequently among the contributors. The editors wish to express their appreciation to all of the contributors for their efforts and willingness to explore in a critical and realist spirit this centrally important concern. We thank in particular James Rosenau, without whom it would not have been possible.

PART ONE

THE GLOBAL GOVERNANCE CONCEPT

CHAPTER 1

The Emergence of
Global Governance Theory

MARTIN HEWSON and TIMOTHY J. SINCLAIR

During the 1990s many students of world politics began to use the concept of 'global governance'.[1] At the same time, the question of global change, its sources and implications, rose to become the preeminent issue in international relations theorizing. In this chapter we argue that global governance theory has emerged as a key vantage point on this central question of our times.

Global change is now the great debate in international relations. Yet the debate has tended to move along several parallel and rarely intersecting tracks. There is the issue of whether the end of the Cold War was a turning point or a moment of a longer continuity. There is also the dispute over the extent and implications of economic globalization. In addition, there are debates over the degree of change in relation to global civil society and the world's cultural arena. What is needed are more integral and comprehensive tools for understanding global change. The global governance concept may turn out to be one such tool.

The formal ending of the Cold War is the proximate source of the contemporary salience of the question of changing patterns of global governance. Realism came to supremacy in the Cold War by providing a potent way of accounting for the great contest between East and West. Subsequently, neorealism sought to universalize a Cold War conception of the state and the state-system. The pattern of global governance appeared to be essentially unchanging, and its organization around the territorial principle could therefore be safely left out of the study of world politics.

Times have changed. It has now become a matter of inquiry to explore how patterns of global governance developed in the past and how they may be transformed at present. A realism remains relevant in the sense that politics is a power struggle.[2] Nonetheless, the kinds of power and the organizing principles that form patterns of global governance need to be brought into any comprehensive account of global change. Today the powers deriving from global finance or information technologies as well as the organizing principle of globalization need to be taken into account.

In addition to the formal ending of the Cold War, the debate on globalization is an important source of the emergence of global governance theory.[3] Hitherto, economic globalization has been viewed primarily from the perspective of states and markets. As a factor of global change, economic globalization is seen from this perspective in terms of a worldwide tilt from the state to the market. The extent of that tilt is currently in dispute. We shall argue in the first section of this chapter that using the global governance concept offers one way beyond this dualistic and restrictive perspective on globalization.

In the second section we briefly review how the problem of global change has entered international regime theory. When this body of thought rose to prominence in the 1980s, attention to global change was not among its most salient characteristics. Subsequently, there have been regime theorists who have sought to account for broad shifts in the patterns of international regimes by using the governance concept. Meanwhile, the ending of the Cold War brought the expectation that the United Nations and its associated agencies would become more effective agencies of global governance. The third section discusses the uses of global governance in examining the relationship between the world organizations and global change.

It follows that the notion of global governance today has three main overlapping (and competing) meanings. In the final section, we shall defend the first of these as the most valuable contribution to an understanding of the significance of contemporary global change. This strand of global governance theory in particular is a potentially important resource for those who would seek a comprehensive assessment of the nature and extent, as well as the sources and implications, of the global changes of our times.

This chapter is about more than just the notion of global governance. It can be read as an examination of change in the study of international relations theory. What are the intellectual processes involved in the emergence of a new cluster of research problems? How does a new problematic come to prominence? As is by now widely accepted, the field of international relations is currently undergoing considerable change: the rise of global governance theory is one of the main aspects of those changes.[4]

PERSPECTIVES ON GLOBAL CHANGE

The most important use of the global governance concept—as a vantage point on the sources and political implications of global change—has come into prominence at the same time as the notion of economic globalization. The former stands in a critical relationship to the 'states and markets' theme which dominates the latter.

The economic globalization perspective on global change focuses, in conventional usage, on a worldwide tilt from states to markets. There is debate over the extent of this tilt. At one extreme is the myth of the world market levelling states to produce a "borderless world."[5] A more sophisticated view is that the internationalization of markets has more direct implications for coalitions of domestic interests than for states.[6] On the other side of the debate, others have mounted a vigorous challenge by arguing that because global markets are neither new nor form a single integrated world economic space, there is no substantial tilt away from the significance of autonomous national policy.[7]

As a perspective on global change, this sense of economic globalization is clearly a restricted one. By contrast, the first set of usages of the global governance concept point towards a more comprehensive and integral perspective on the politics of global change. We shall highlight four global governance perspectives on global change. Although interrelated, the four can be distinguished for the sake of exposition.

One feature of global change that the global governance concept highlights is a shifting of the location of authority in the context of both integration and fragmentation. This is the usage pioneered by James Rosenau. He brought the global governance concept into prominence in conjunction with a terminology designed to appreciate the ways in which global change is an encompassing phenomenon involving relocations of authority across multiple levels and areas. Rosenau describes the process as "a pervasive tendency . . . in which major shifts in the location of authority and the site of control mechanisms are under way on every continent, shifts that are as pronounced in economic and social systems as they are in political systems."[8]

In particular, Rosenau uses the term *global governance* in order to emphasize the implications of a widespread reorientation of individuals' political skills and horizons. One way of putting Rosenau's view is the thesis that changing patterns of global order are related to changing patterns of global life. At one point, Rosenau described the implication of new political skills and horizons as tending towards a "bifurcated" world composed of both state-centric and multi-centric realms.[9] Subsequently, he has suggested that this phenomenon implies a proliferation in many simultaneous directions: subnational, transnational, international, and global.[10] Either way, taking account of these shifting political horizons, contends Rosenau, means acknowledging the possibility of a global change from the primacy of "government" to that of "governance."

Rosenau's reflections on changing patterns of global governance at the end of the twentieth century first appeared in the volume *Governance without Government*. Many people would suppose that this book brought the phrase *global governance* onto the scholarly stage. But, in fact, the term is notable by its almost complete absence from the book. The preface speaks of "international governance," as do several of the contributors. Others speak of "systems of governance" or the "governance of the international political economy." Rosenau introduces the collection by referring, almost interchangeably, to the "governance of world politics," "governance on a worldwide scale," the "governance of international orders," or "governance in a global order."[11]

As a matter of fact, only when Rosenau began to explore global life, the intensive or micro-level dimension of global change, does he begin to use the phrase *global governance*.[12] This most pervasive of all sorts of governance emerges as if from the bottom up, from the increasing skills and capacities of individuals and from their altering horizons of identification in patterns of "global life." Few other analysts use the term *global life* as regularly as does Rosenau. Few others pay particular attention to the "micro-level"—the capacities and orientations of individuals and small groups—of the global order.[13] Indeed, much of Rosenau's current research agenda could be described as a sociology of global life. This notion may prove to be one of Rosenau's most significant contributions. It suggests an existential or ontological condition of daily life in thoroughly altered circumstances.[14] Or, to put it in different terms, it suggests that globalization is not just extensive, forming interconnections across space, but also intensive, reaching into the level of personal conduct.

Rosenau's writings on global governance effectively convey two basic principles of an analysis of global change from the perspective of shifting political skills and horizons of individuals. The first is that the analysis of global change has to depart from conventional international relations thinking by conceiving it in a holistic way. The global order is to be conceived, says Rosenau, "as all-encompassing" and, particularly from the point of view of universal dependence on the biosphere, as an "organic whole."[15] In consequence, analysis necessarily becomes rich and exploratory rather than parsimonious.

The second principle is that global change from this perspective is to be seen as composed not of one overarching trend but several dialectical and contradictory tendencies. According to Rosenau, there have emerged both integrating and fragmenting influences, both globalizing and localizing tendencies, both cohesive and conflictual dynamics. As a result, there have emerged an enormous variety of forms of global governance. Positing a shift from government to governance, Rosenau attempted an overview of the continuum of global governance arrangements that are becoming salient on the eve of the twenty-first century. This continuum stretches between the transnational and the subnational, the macro and the micro, the informal and the institutionalized, the state-centric and the multi-centric, the cooperative and the conflictual.[16] For example, if one were to consider the significance of the Internet from the perspective of global governance, then one would emphasize the dynamics of proliferation and informality, the micro-processes and multiplicity of choices it generates.

In sum, this way of using the global governance concept affirms an encompassing trend of authority being relocated in multiple directions. The Westphalian or territorial state system is no more that one form or element of contemporary global governance. Numerous other forms of governance seep through the fabric of global life, proliferating and diversifying. The global governance concept does not refer to a distinct sphere or level of global life. It is not monopolized in any special organizations. On the contrary, it is a perspective on global life, a vantage point designed to foster a regard for the immense complexity and diversity of global life.

A second feature of global change is the emergence—in actuality or in potential—of a global civil society.[17] This is a further phenomenon that the global governance concept highlights. Although the idea and practice of a specific terrain of civil society located in-between the economy and the state dates back to eighteenth-century liberalism, its contemporary return owes much to the activities of dissidents in Eastern Europe in the 1980s. In the West, social movements increasingly oriented to a worldwide scale of activity and organization came to adopt an understanding of global civil society as an arena of transnational ideological tendencies, worldwide movements, and international non-governmental associations.[18]

To take one example, since the middle of the 1970s a notable development is that indigenous peoples' movements have adopted a partly global orientation. This movement is rooted primarily in the countries of North and South America, though it extends also to indigenous groups in Australia and New Zealand, India and Indonesia. An element of global organization is provided by the umbrella group called the Working Council of Indigenous Peoples. The political focus of this reorientation is in large measure provided by the United Nations as a forum for publicizing the claims of indigenous people in the language of the international law of self-determination and human rights.[19]

From these developments has arisen a line of thinking that has sought to inquire into the normative and democratic potential of a diversified and enhanced realm of global civil society.[20] In the view of Richard Falk, the roots of a "humane global governance" are to be found in global civil society.[21] In the view of David Held, as the liberal democratic state is being bypassed by the forces of globalization, it becomes necessary to envisage an extension of democratic space. A "cosmopolitan democracy" therefore can be envisaged as arising from the development of a global public sphere.[22]

There is a third element in global change described by the global governance concept. In the current process of restructuring the global political economy, a key role is played by the reorientation of key intellectual, business and political elites in the G-7 zone. Robert W. Cox's usage of the global governance concept emphasizes the importance of these forces. Indeed, it is one of Robert W. Cox's main achievements to have brought the study of transnational coalitions of social forces into international relations in general.[23]

In Cox's historicist approach, the social forces of global governance are to be understood as taking different forms in different eras. A specific historical era will be shaped and defined by pervasive forms of ideology, economy, and state. In the mid 1980s, Cox described the two predominant sorts of social forces as those oriented toward a "hyper-liberalism" and those oriented towards a "state capitalism." The former, primarily Anglo-American, organized themselves according to the globalization principle. The latter organized on the territorial principle.

By the late 1990s, the intellectual, political, and economic leaders of hyper-liberalism appeared to have gained the upper hand. They shape the predominant form of global governance today. That shaping process Cox described as a *nebuleuse,* by which he meant the ideological influences fostering a realignment of thinking to the needs of the world economy. Its institutional focus is in the networks of key international financial institutions, finance ministries in G-7 governments, private international relations councils, and business schools. Its material capacities, it became clear during the Gulf War of 1990-1991 adds Cox, are nonetheless underpinned by territorially based US military power.[24]

The study of transnational political-ideological tendencies at the apex of global governance has been further advanced by Stephen Gill. Gill refers to these directive elements of global governance as "globalizing elites."[25] Acknowledging that they are by no means a homogenous bloc, and instead describing them as a "nexus" with its core in the G-7 area, Gill nonetheless emphasizes their growing power since the 1970s. A network of institutions has operated as a forum for consensus formation. These include the World Economic Forum held annually at Davos in Switzerland, the Trilateral Commission, and the broad G-7 process of meetings among officials.

The position of "globalizing elites" is based upon the renaissance of the power of money capital in the global political economy of the late twentieth century.[26] Their approach to politics centers on the creation of a market civilization by adjusting the norms and practices of everyday life. A feature of this approach is the "new constitutionalism" in which public institutions such as central banks are ring-fenced from political interference with anti-inflationary mandates. In addition, the greatly increased interlinkage of production, consumption, and tax bases has created new challenges for national communities seeking to shape the form of investment and thus influence the impact of economic benefits on their environment. The mobility of capital has increased, as holders of funds for either portfolio or direct investment are provided with more locational options. These options serve to constrain those of states and communities, and indeed force them into bidding wars that revolve around the establishment of deregulated business environments.[27]

The historicist approach also raises the question of opposition and negation of neoliberalism by social forces. According to Cox, one future project of global governance could coalesce around "post-globalization" forces which seek to re-embed the world economy in social norms. The environmental movement is one potential tendency of this kind. Another future project of global governance could cohere around the "post-Westphalian" movements of indigenous peoples or migrants. A third, which Cox refers to as "post-hegemonic," may come to be represented by the reemergence of civilizations as influential entities in world order.[28]

In addition, there is a fourth aspect of global change that merits attention from the viewpoint of global governance. It overlaps with those discussed above but is nonetheless of distinct importance. There is good reason to use the global governance concept in reference to the salience of globally oriented epistemic elites and authorities. These are the knowledge brokers or the high-level symbolic analysts who direct the emerging global information order. The editors of this volume have played a role in developing this strand of global governance theory. Inspired both by both Rosenau's and Cox's innovations in broadening perspectives on globalization, we began in 1994 to initiate a series of panels at meetings of the International Studies Association as an effort to bring together scholars working in ways we perceived as parallel. One aim was to encourage the kinds of mutual criticism and assessment we needed to develop global governance theory. The agenda we set was to bring the informational dimension of global governance into view.

This aspect of global governance arises in large part from the global changes associated with the technologies of the emerging worldwide knowledge order. Informational elites appear to be in the process of forming and organizing in a globalized fashion. Their institutional supports are the networks of innovation centres in major global cities, key private and public international institutions concerned with fostering the use of information, and professional agencies of global communications.[29]

From this perspective, the process of global governance can be thought of as elevating global knowledge, the sorts of intelligence and communication that contribute to and help to coordinate other aspects of globalization. This process can be thought of, first, as aimed at coordination and risk abatement in a context of intensified global competition and, second, as dependent on the creation of new forms of epistemic authority, that is, the ability to produce attention, respect, and trust at a distance, based on expertise and professional eminence.[30] The process of reorganizing relationships in this way gives rise to new transnational fields of authority. Proverbially, knowledge is power; today, it may now be said, inquiring into the globalization of knowledge is one of the best ways of understanding the power of globalization and governance.

To summarize, we have suggested that one set of usages of the global governance concept has emerged in the attempt to develop comprehensive and integral approaches to analyzing global change. By far the most comprehensive is that of James Rosenau as a result of his focus upon the relocations of governance that arise from the micro-level in the context of trends towards integration and fragmentation. Others have sought to use the global governance concept to highlight the implications of more specific global changes: the emergence of global civil society, the internationalization of the intellectual and political elites of hyperliberal (or neoliberal) capitalism, and the emergence of informational elites. Overall, the emergence of this strand of global governance theory thus should be seen as a feature of the debates in international relations and beyond on the question of global change.

GLOBAL CHANGE AND INTERNATIONAL REGIMES

A second source of global governance theory arose in the context of international regime theory, which had a significant impact on scholarly thinking in the 1980s. Some hailed it as a radical break from the past. Others regarded it as a passing fashion.[31] In one of the more probing and historically minded assessments, Friedrich Kratochwil and John Ruggie situated it within the twists and turns of the past fifty years of writing on international organization. They discerned neither radical break nor passing fashion but considerable continuity. According to Kratochwil and Ruggie, international regime theory represented a development of the same long-standing problematic: a concern with the "international governance" that occurs within the arena formed by multiple territorial states.[32]

Yet Kratochwil and Ruggie had relatively little to say regarding the meaning and importance of international governance. Richard Ashley was one of those who noticed this implication. In taking up this issue, Ashley in effect proposed to replace the term *international governance* with "international purpose." International purpose is formed of those discourses that produce continuity across time and space, that objectify enduring structures, that create the "effect of spatial and temporal continuity and collective direction," and that displace disturbances so as to create the continuous boundaries of sovereignty.[33] In short, Ashley puts the focus upon what might be called "discourses of continuity" in constituting the field of international governance. No doubt he had in mind the discourse of regime theory itself.

A different development of international regime theory emerged with the notion of a "system of international governance." In effect, this idea recognizes that regime theory's characteristic focus on narrow issue-areas has been a definite hindrance to the study of change in international governance. The notion of a system of governance relaxes the brackets around individual regimes to situate them within a context of multiple overlapping international regimes. This has the makings of an important shift in the international regimes research program. Changing focus from an "issue-area" to a "system" makes it much easier to spot changes in the condition of international governance.

Consider three examples. To begin with, over the past three decades, the number of international regimes for the environment has grown from virtually nothing to nearly one hundred (depending on the method of counting). Oran Young has analysed this body of policy arrangements as a system of international governance.[34] A second illustration is that as the Cold War proceeded, the two sides spawned a body of regimes that channelled international conflict and the arms race in directions tolerable to the two superpowers. For Ernst-Otto Czempiel, this can be understood as a system of international governance.[35] A final instance refers to the order established among the Great Powers during the "Long Peace" (1815–1914). It involved a willingness to develop such regimes as would reduce the risk of another major war that could undermine their own stability and power. K. J. Holsti points to this as a system of international governance.[36]

Beyond these clusters of regimes, what of the overall condition of *all* international regimes? Perhaps the entire body of international regimes—economic, security, environmental, and so on—could be considered a system of international governance. Mark Zacher suggests that the corpus of regimes is likely to enter a period of proliferation as the world experiences the effects of the declining effectiveness of major war, the increasing harm to the environment, the widening of economic interdependence, and the global spread of communications, democracy, and consumer culture. But Zacher concludes that this proliferation is nonetheless likely to take an uneven "patchwork pattern" rather than a planned and organized system of international governance.[37]

As these examples illustrate, the notion of international governance has provided an innovative way of clearing one of the major blockages within international regime theory of the 1980s. Rethinking regimes as enmeshed in broader systems of governance invites rethinking of perspectives on changing patterns of international policy coordination. But it is surely of considerable significance that this strand of global governance theory generally avoids the term *global governance* and lacks, by implication, a concern with the overall significance of global change. Nor is it primarily concerned with the position of the global organizations.

GLOBAL CHANGE AND THE WORLD ORGANIZATIONS

A third usage of the global governance concept is to point out that global change has transformed the environment of the world organizations. One source of this strand of global governance theory was the expectation that the formal ending of the Cold War would inaugurate a new era for the United Nations and the other world organizations.[38] In particular, expectations rose about the potential for humanitarian interventions through the UN once it was set free of superpower deadlock. A further source was the realization that key world organizations have come to play a critical role in fostering economic globalization. The G–7 began meeting in 1974; the International Monetary Fund assumed a prominent role in promoting economic liberalization during the debt crisis of the early 1980s; and the World Trade Organization was formed in 1995 to oversee expanded liberalization of the services and agriculture sectors. A third source of this usage of the global governance concept was the development that in shorthand is called the emergence of global civil society. After the first global environment conference in 1972, the activities of environmental, humanitarian, women's, and human rights movements increasingly intersected with the world organizations.

In this context, the global governance concept serves as a useful emblem for the program of reforming the world organizations. Although there have been several programmatic statements of how the world organizations should have global governance as their aim, by far the most influential is that of the Commission for Global Governance. In this process, the idea of global governance has gained some prominence beyond academia and into some sectors of public debate.

In response to the new prominence of the UN during the Gulf conflict (1990–1991), an initiative of the Swedish prime minister Ingvar Carlsson brought together a Commission on Global Governance to suggest ways of building upon and consolidating the apparent revival of the UN.[39] What resulted was a manifesto in the social democratic tradition of Willy Brandt's North-South report of 1980 and Gro Harlem Brundtland's sustainable development report of 1987.[40] However, there is one striking difference in tone between the earlier global reform reports and the global governance report. The earlier reports had focused on solving a particular problem facing the world. The global governance report is more concerned with conveying the argument that pervasive global changes have altered the terrain on which global problem solving is to take place.

On the one hand, the commission's report envisages that the ending of the Cold War enables a considerable strengthening of the world organizations. For instance, the report recommends the establishment of a standing military force, a facility for automatic taxation, and a tribunal to oversee global competition. On the other hand, the commission also envisages a situation in which the agencies of global civil society increasingly become involved in the functions of global governance. For example, it proposes a widening of the institutional forums in which Non-Governmental Organizations (NGOs) can gain an effective presence on the world stage.[41]

The view that the end of the Cold War, the rise of economic globalization, and the emergence of a transnational civil society have altered the stage on which global problem solving can take place is the key idea in several studies that employ the global governance concept. According to Mihaly Simai, for example, the world organizations' task of "managing risk and change in the international system" has entered a new era. Simai, an analyst associated with the UN Development Programme (UNDP), argues that any effective future for the global organizations would have to involve the leaders of the UN system and the main sponsoring governments recognizing the momentous changes of contemporary times.[42]

Groom and Powell have summarized the perspective arising from this usage of the global governance concept. As they put it, global governance concerns "the identification and management of those issues which necessarily have an impact on all parts of the globe." These issues include ecology, human rights, and development, as well as refugees, migration, drugs, and epidemics. As a result of increased awareness of such issues since the 1960s, there is "a heightened need for global governance." Yet the actual identification and management of such issues is amorphous and partial. This leads Groom and Powell to conclude that global governance is "a theme in need of a focus."[43]

By far the most theoretically and historically informed study of the relationship between global change and the world organizations is Craig Murphy's rich historical study of the development of the world organizations since 1850.[44] The dimension of global change that Murphy primarily focuses upon is the development of industrial capitalism from the origins of the second industrial revolution to the crisis of Fordism in the 1970s and 80s. In Murphy's usage, global governance refers to the activities of the world organizations. However, he argues that since 1850 these activities have derived from the ability of transnational coalitions of liberal social forces to invest the world organizations with the task of promoting the leading industries in successive phases of industrialism. This is what happened in Europe's "belle epoque" (1880–1914) and the Free World's "Golden Age" (1945–1970) of industrial capitalism. In each case, according to Murphy, world organizations helped to create the conditions that promoted a new and more inclusive phase of industrial capitalism.

A common theme throughout this strand of global governance theory is the importance of global civil society as a source of revitalization for global organizations. The social democratic programs for renewing global organizations envisage a redesign that turns them into networks embedded in global civil society. The global organizations would be more open to influences from global civil society (and in that sense more democratic); they would rely more upon the resources and expertise of global civil society (devolving responsibility onto firms and nonprofit agencies); and they would actively promote the spread of a global civil society (by encouraging democratic governance).

Part of this rethinking of the role of world organizations in terms of governance mirrors recent developments in their actual practice. In 1989, the World Bank diagnosed a "crisis of governance" as the source of Africa's development problems.[45] Later it began to redefine development as involving the promotion of governance, understood as better professional administration and the fostering of the capacities of civil society.[46] In so doing, it has set aside previous limitations on involving itself in "political affairs" in order to promote liberal democracy in its clients. In a parallel development, former UN Secretary General Boutros-Ghali has written that a new "imperative" for the UN system should be regarded as promoting democracy.[47]

In sum, the use of the global governance concept to refer to the activities of the world organizations is now well established. This is not just a matter of "old wine in new bottles," because the theme of global change has also become more prominent. This strand of global governance theory is perhaps the most widespread and prolific. Probably the impetus of the UN's fiftieth anniversary in 1995 made that year particularly fruitful for reflecting on the current status and potential future of global organizations.

CHANGE AND GLOBAL GOVERNANCE

How useful is the global governance concept for understanding patterns of global change? As we have seen, it has been called a theme in need of a focus. According to one critic, global governance "appears to be virtually everything."[48] By implication, it is useless: too broad and too complex to be of use as a conceptual tool. According to this view, what is needed is to fix a narrower and more parsimonious meaning upon the term.

We have sought to argue otherwise. A comprehensive account of global change is essential. Hence each of the usages of the global governance concept has the potential to illuminate an aspect of change. Nonetheless, the strand concerned with changing patterns of international regimes and that concerned with the changes affecting the world organizations are of more limited usefulness.

For the strand that focuses upon systems of international regimes, the broadening of international regime theory in this way has opened new puzzles concerning change in configurations of international regimes. Nonetheless, it remains open to criticisms that are by now fairly familiar.[49] These essentially revolve around the status of the state. The analysis of interstate policy coordination characteristically brackets the question of the changing salience of the territorial nation-state system as a form of global governance. So long as that remains the case, it is difficult to regard this strand of global governance theory as theoretically innovative.

For the strand concerned with world organizations, the theme of reforming the world organizations is paramount. As a result, it is less concerned with questions of fundamental change. Nonetheless, it reflects a sense that several of the activities of the world organizations have become more salient in the context of economic globalization and the end of the Cold War.

From the point of view of identifying the mainsprings of contemporary global change, the strand of global governance theory directly concerned with that question has much to recommend it. The criticism that it includes "virtually everything" is misplaced. We have sought to show that it points to a set of specific developments: the reorientation of individuals' political horizons, the weaving of a global civil society, the rising power of globalizing elites, and the emergence of global informational elites in particular. Each needs to be assessed. They are all multidimensional and comprehensive. An adequate understanding of the mainsprings of global change has to potentially consider virtually everything.

For understanding global change, we consider that an historicist epistemology and ontology are essential.[50] Historicist theory aims at proximate explanatory constructions which correspond to the changing forms which social life assumes as new challenges are faced by human communities, and as those communities are transformed by processes of hegemonic ascendance and decline. This does not mean that functional understandings of how things are organized in societies are without use, just that these are only useful within carefully specified historical and situational parameters.

The historicist approach is closely related to a critical purpose. As Cox has noted, and as many others have subsequently acknowledged, "Theory is always for someone and for some purpose. All theories have a perspective. Perspectives derive from a position in space and time, specifically social and political time and space."[51] Our purpose here is to understand the origins of forms of governance so as to anticipate their transformation into other forms over time, rather than the pragmatic concerns of most positivist or problem-solving work with making the existing system of global governance more effective.

Inquiry must begin with ontology or a statement of what seem to be the most salient features of our world at a particular time. Within the context of the contemporary ascendancy of globalization, we wish to offer the following specification of relevant forces. At the level of ideas, we identify the salience of what we have called epistemic authority, that is, the deference associated with professional, technical, or other specialized knowledge. This seems to be a defining feature of the epoch and a wellspring of global governance. The second feature is marketized institutions. These may not be market institutions in the narrow sense. However, even within public institutions the tendency is increasingly toward adopting market principles of organization and social intervention. The final element of our ontology is the complex of infrastructural technologies associated with the emerging knowledge economy. These material capabilities seem to be a developing locus of growth, setting the development dynamic of the age. We can represent their mutual interaction in the following way:[52]

Figure 1: Elements of Emerging Global Governance

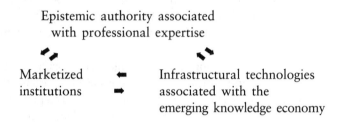

Epistemic authority associated
with professional expertise

Marketized   ←   Infrastructural technologies
institutions   →   associated with the
                         emerging knowledge economy

This ontology should be understood as a way of developing multilevel analyses of past and present (as well as potentially future) forms assumed by global governance.

CONCLUSIONS

One of the major features of the field of international relations in the late 1990s is a preoccupation with global change. The idea of a new era following upon the ending of the Cold War is at its heart. But so too is the debate on the nature and implications of global economic competition, as well as the tendency toward cultural globalization. We have sought to show that global governance theory has emerged in the context of this multilayer debate on the sources, extent, and consequences of global change. The global governance concept stands beside these other change-oriented concepts in aiding a more comprehensive understanding of global change.

Nonetheless, it has to be recognized that there are several distinct uses of the global governance concept. One arises from the attempt to trace broad changes in patterns of international regimes. A second is concerned with the implications of contemporary changes for the world organizations' capacities for addressing world problems. The third is concerned with identifying the ascendant political forces shaping the form of global governance. More inquiry is needed into shifts in the political horizons of individuals, into the increasing power of the transnational elites of the global political economy, into the emergence of a global civil society, and especially, we believe, into the rise of global informational elites. While each of the initial two approaches identifies an important dimension, the third approach of a political economy of forms of global governance is, we believe, most promising from the standpoint of a comprehensive view of global change.

NOTES

1. Perhaps the most visible example of this new focus is the scholarly journal *Global Governance*, which commenced publication in the winter of 1995.

2. See, for example, Robert W. Cox, ed., *The New Realism: Perspectives on Multilateralism and World Order* (London: Macmillan, 1997).

3. A pathbreaking discussion of globalization can be found in James H. Mittelman, ed., *Globalization: Critical Reflections* (Boulder, CO: Lynne Rienner, 1997).

4. An interesting discussion of the changing ways of thinking about international relations can be found in James N. Rosenau, ed., *Global Voices: Dialogues in International Relations* (Boulder, CO: Westview, 1993).

5. Kenichi Ohmae, *The Borderless World: Power and Strategy in the Interlinked Economy* (London: Harper Collins, 1990).

6. See, for example, Robert O. Keohane and Helen V. Milner, eds. *Internationalization and Domestic Politics* (New York: Cambridge University Press, 1996).

7. See Paul Q. Hirst and Grahame Thompson, *Globalization in Question: The International Economy and the Possibilities of Governance* (Cambridge, MA: Blackwell, 1996).

8. Rosenau, "Governance in the Twenty-First Century" in *Global Governance: A Review of Multilateralism and International Organizations* 1, 1 (1995) p. 18. Rosenau has elaborated on this in *Along the Domestic-Foreign Frontier: Exploring Governance in a Turbulent World* (Cambridge: Cambrdge University Press, 1997).

9. James N. Rosenau, *Turbulence in World Politics* (Princeton, NJ: Princeton University Press, 1990).

10. James N. Rosenau, "Distant Proximities: Dynamics and Dialectics of Globalization" in B. Hettne, ed., *International Political Economy: Understanding Global Disorder* (London: Zed, 1995).

11. James N. Rosenau, "Governance, Order, and Change in World Politics" in James N. Rosenau and Ernst-Otto Czempiel, eds., *Governance without Government: Order and Change in World Politics* (Cambridge: Cambridge University Press, 1992).

12. Rosenau, "Governance, Order, and Change in World Politics," p. 28, and "Citizenship in a Changing Global Order," esp. pp. 272–73.

13. A related literature has developed in sociology around individual capacities. See, for example, Ulrich Beck, Anthony Giddens, and Scott Lash, *Reflexive Modernization* (Cambridge: Polity, 1994) and Scott Lash and John Urry, *Economies of Signs and Space* (London: Sage, 1994).

14. Also see Fernand Braudel's treatment of "material life" in his *Capitalism and Material Life, 1400–1800,* translated by Miriam Kochan (London: Fontana, 1974).

15. James N. Rosenau, "Governance, Order, and Change in World Politics," pp. 12–14.

16. Rosenau, "Governance to the Twenty-First Century" in *Global Governance: A Review of Multilateralism and International Organizations* 1, 1 (1995) pp. 13–43.

17. The idea of a global civil society is one subject to much dispute in the literature of international relations. See Ronnie D. Lipschutz, "Reconstructing World Politics: The Emergence of Global Civil Society," *Millennium: Journal of International Studies* 21, 3 (1992) pp. 389–420. See also Ronnie D. Lipschutz with Judith Mayer, *Global Civil Society and Global Economic Governance: The Politics of Nature from Place to Planet* (Albany: State University of New York Press, 1996).

18. See Yoshikazu Sakamoto, "Democratization, Social Movements and World Order," in B. Hettne, ed., *International Political Economy: Understanding Global Disorder* (London: Zed, 1996).

19. See Bice Maiguashca, "Transnational Indigenous Movement in a Changing World Order," in Yoshikazu Sakamoto, ed., *Global Transformaton: Challenges to the State System* (Tokyo: UN University Press, 1995).

20. A collection on this theme is Meghand Desai and Paul Redfern, eds., *Global Governance: Ethics and Economics of the World Order* (London: Pinter, 1995).

21. Richard A. Falk, *On Humane Governance* (University Park, PA: Penn State Press, 1995).

22. David Held, *Democracy and the Global Order* (Stanford: Stanford University Press, 1996).

23. Robert W. Cox, *Production, Power, and World Order: Social Forces in the Making of History* (New York: Columbia University Press, 1987).

24. See especially the essay "Structural Issues of Global Governance: Implications for Europe," in Robert W. Cox with Timothy J. Sinclair, *Approaches to World Order* (Cambridge: Cambridge University Press, 1996).

25. Stephen Gill, "Structural Change and Global Political Economy: Globalizing Elites and the Emerging World Order," in *Global Transformation: Challenges to the State System,* edited by Yoshikazu Sakamoto (Tokyo: United Nations University Press, 1994).

26. Kees van der Pijl, "The Second Glorious Revolution: Globalizing Elites and Historical Change," in Björn Hettne, ed., *International Political Economy: Understanding Global Disorder* (London: Zed Press, 1995).

27. A good discussion of the dynamics at play here can be found in Stephen Gill and David Law, "Global Hegemony and the Structural Power of Capital" in *Gramsci, Historical Materialism and International Relations*, edited by Stephen Gill (Cambridge: Cambridge University Press, 1993). Also see *Structure and Agency in International Capital Mobility*, edited by Timothy J. Sinclair and Kenneth P. Thomas (New York: St. Martin's Press, forthcoming).

28. Robert W. Cox, "Towards a Post-Hegemonic Conceptualization of World Order: Reflections on the Relevancy of Ibn Khaldun" in Cox with Sinclair, *Approaches to World Order*.

29. For background, see Edward A. Comor, ed., *The Global Political Economy of Communication* (London: Macmillan, 1994). Also see Frank Webster, *Theories of the Information Society* (London: Routledge, 1995).

30. Bruce Lincoln, *Authority: Construction and Corrosion* (Chicago: The University of Chicago Press, 1994) pp. 3–4.

31. See, for example, Susan Strange's views, as expressed in her essay "*Cave! hic dragones*: A Critique of Regime Analysis," in *International Regimes*, edited by Stephen D. Krasner (Ithaca, NY: Cornell University Press, 1983).

32. Friedrich Kratochwil and John G. Ruggie, "International Organization: A State of the Art on an Art of the State," *International Organization* 40, 4 (1986) p. 754.

33. Richard K. Ashley, "Imposing International Purpose: Notes on the Problematic of Governance," in Ernst-Otto Czempiel and James N. Rosenau, eds., *Global Changes and Theoretical Challenges* (Lexington, MA: D.C. Heath, 1989).

34. See Oran R. Young, "Global Environmental Change and International Governance," *Millennium* 19, 3 (1990) pp. 337–46; Oran R. Young, *International Governance: Protecting the Environment in a Stateless Society* (Ithaca, NY: Cornell University Press, 1994); Oran R. Young, George J. Demko, and Kilaparti Ramakrishna, eds., *Global Environmental Change and International Governance* (Hanover, NH: University Press of New England, 1996); and Oran R. Young, ed., *Global Governance: Drawing Insights from the Environmental Experience* (Cambridge, MA: MIT Press, 1997).

35. Ernst-Otto Czempiel, "Governance and Democratization," in Rosenau and Czempiel, eds., *Governance without Government*. For a more detailed analysis of Cold War arms control as a system of governance, see Bruce D. Larkin, *Nuclear Designs: Great Britain, France, and China in the Global Governance of Nuclear Arms* (New Brunswick NJ: Transaction, 1996).

36. K.J. Holsti, "Governance without Government: Polyarchy in Nineteenth Century European International Politics," in Rosenau and Czempiel, eds., *Governance without Government*.

37. Mark W. Zacher, "The Decaying Pillars of the Westphalian Temple: Implications for International Order and Governance," in Rosenau and Czempiel, eds., *Governance without Government,* p. 99.

38. A useful review essay on this theme is W. Howard Wriggins, "Prospects for International Order and Governance," *Journal of International Affairs* 46 (1993) pp. 525–37.

39. Commission on Global Governance, *Our Global Neighborhood* (New York: Oxford University Press, 1995).

40. Independent Commission on International Development Issues, *North-South: A Program for Survival* (London: Pan, 1980); World Commission on Environment and Development, *Our Common Future* (New York: Oxford University Press, 1987).

41. The relation between NGOs and the UN is addressed in Thomas G. Weiss and Leon Gordenker, eds., *NGOs, the UN, and Global Governance* (Boulder, CO: Lynne Rienner, 1996). For a critical assessment of the Commission's program, see the chapter by Michael G. Schechter in this volume.

42. Mihaly Simai, *The Future of Global Governance: Managing Risk and Change in the International System* (New York: Twentieth Century Fund Press, 1995).

43. A.J.R. Groom and Dominic Powell, "From World Politics to Global Governance: A Theme in Need of a Focus," in A. J. R. Groom and Margot Light, eds., *Contemporary International Relations* (London: Pinter, 1994) pp. 81 and 82.

44. Craig N. Murphy, *International Organization and Industrial Change: Global Governance since 1850* (New York: Oxford University Press, 1994).

45. World Bank, *Sub-Saharan Africa: From Crisis to Sustainable Growth* (Washington, DC: World Bank, 1989).

46. World Bank, *Governance and Development* (Washington, DC: World Bank, 1992).

47. Boutros Boutros-Ghali, "Democracy: A Newly Recognized Imperative," *Global Governance: A Review of Multilateralism and International Organizations* 1, 1 (1995) pp. 3–12.

48. Lawrence S. Finkelstein, "What Is Global Governance?" *Global Governance* 1, 3 (1995) pp. 367–72 at p. 368.

49. See Alexander Wendt and Raymond Duvall, "Institutions and International Order," in Ernst-Otto Czempiel and James N. Rosenau, eds., *Global Changes and Theoretical Challenges* (Lexington, MA: D.C. Heath, 1989).

50. For a series of discussions and applicatons of historicist assumptions in international relations, see Cox with Sinclair, *Approaches to World Order.*

51. Cox, "Social Forces, States, and World Orders: Beyond International Relations Theory," in Cox with Sinclair, *Approaches to World Order,* p. 87.

52. This trinity draws on Cox, p. 98.

CHAPTER 2

Politics in a Floating World

Toward a Critique of Global Governance

ROBERT LATHAM

> [I]t is a feeling of an indissoluble bond, of being one with the external world as a whole. I may remark that to me this seems something rather in the nature of an intellectual perception, which is not, it is true, without an accompanying feeling-tone, but only such as would be present with any other act of thought of equal range.
>
> —Sigmund Freud, *Civilization and Its Discontents*

In 1930, Freud described what was termed an "oceanic feeling," a sense of "something limitless, unbounded." This sensation, it was suggested to him, was the basis of all religious feeling. Freud himself was skeptical of this claim. He saw a "feeling of infantile helplessness" as a far more likely "origin of the religious attitude."[1] For some reason he did not make the connection between the two sensations. Feeling that one is caught in an ocean of totality may flow from a sense of helplessness. The reverse might also hold, and together both sensations may represent a reinforcing dialectic of the overwhelmed.

I could not help wondering whether international relations scholars have entered into their own dialectic of the overwhelmed as they have attempted to describe and analyze global order and life at the end of the twentieth century. On the one hand, an oceanic feeling is experienced as a single global social and political fabric—or community of

23

humankind—is contemplated. On the other hand, a sense of helplessness emerges in the face of the sheer scope, diversity, and fragmentation
that mark the global, to say nothing of the coterminous processes of
integration and globalization that ebb and flow within it. State policymakers cannot articulate coherent foreign policies, international organizations flounder, and scholars look back to the wisdom of Gramsci's
adage about how old orders die but new ones come only slowly into
view.

Might the growing popularity of the concept of global governance
have something to do with this dialectic of the overwhelmed? James
Rosenau, who seems aware of the power of this dialectic and yet seems
to refuse to give in to it, begins one essay on global governance by
claiming:

> To anticipate the prospects for global governance in the decades ahead
> is to discern powerful tensions, profound contradictions, and perplex-
> ing paradoxes. It is to search for order in disorder, for coherence in
> contradiction, and for continuity in change. It is to confront processes
> that mask both growth and decay. It is to look for authorities that are
> obscure, boundaries that are in flux, and systems of rule that are
> emergent. And it is to experience hope embedded in despair.[2]

Perhaps governance is a way to retain the oceanic sensibility without
feeling so helpless. In the face of a global life that is profoundly complex and variegated and a global order whose contours and structures
have either not yet emerged or are not yet discernible, one can still
perceive—if not also argue for—attempts to govern relations, processes,
and practices on a global basis.[3] We may not have a world that coheres
for us in a given order, but we can still fashion—or watch the fashion-
ing of—dimensions of global life through governance. More than this,
governance conveniently allows us to avoid articulating a single vision
of order for fear of being taken for naive rationalists or, worse, ethno-
centric techno-imperialists. It offers international policymakers, bureaucrats, and corporate "custodians" a means for pursuing a well-mannered
multilateralism without having to proffer a globalized project of grand
order-making.[4] Global governance has the benefit of appearing open
and diffuse, if not a little noncommittal. Those are attractive qualities
in an era of ambiguity, uncertainty, and flux.

But I wonder if there is a seduction going on here.[5] The imagined
seduction by global governance takes place along two edges: first, as a
category for analyzing something happening in the world, and second,

as a call to envision new forms of agency that challenge the limits of what has hitherto been an unduly confined global politics. The question I will pursue in this essay is whether global governance is a too-comfortable vessel for both analysis and advocacy. Global governance may just fit too neatly into the global *Stimmung*, or mood of the times, match too closely the rhetoric of policymakers and bureaucrats, and make us too complacent about what is at stake in structures and practices that can sometimes be oppressive. The latter include those associated with predatory states and TNCs, repressive social relations and local power holders, or international economic regulatory agencies, such as the IMF, advocating structural adjustment programs.

Considered in a first section is what it means to globalize *governance*, a term typically associated with what states do or should do. A second section will explore how the discourse on global governance resembles midcentury structural-functionalist sociology, sharing with it its limitations as a mode of analysis and as starting point for asking important political questions about contesting and configuring forms of social existence. A third section probes the implications of the relative silence in the literature on what might count as negations of governance, based on two questions: what works against governance, and what is not subject to governance. The relationship between global governance and politics is pursued in a fourth section, where it is argued that governance can be understood as a postpolitical phenomenon, not unlike the way planning was at midcentury. A fifth section attempts to show that the peculiar relationship between governance and the political stems from the problematic way that states and societies— where so much of political life has been inscribed—are treated in the literature. Finally, the possibilities of critically bringing politics into global governance studies will be considered.

THE GLOBALIZATION OF GOVERNANCE

Governance, unlike *power* for instance, has not been a central term of contestation and analysis in political science or the social sciences more generally. Its meaning has basically been taken for granted. It is taken to be what decisionmakers, administrators, or steering committees generate as they manage or administer the activities of their organizations or those of the people and things for which they assume responsibility. Michel Foucault woke some of us up from our slumber regarding governance through his discussion of what he called "governmentality."[6]

Among other things, he distinguished the Sovereign lording *over* society (e.g., extracting resources, human and material, and settling disputes) from the ensemble of state organs (and allied agents in civil society) steering, defining, and administering relations *within* society (e.g., regulating and even constituting markets, bodies, and households).[7] The legitimation of and absorption in the latter practices and activities is what Foucault means by governmentality. Foucault historicizes governance for us, showing that the administration of people and things was not always a recognizable prerogative of the state.

But Foucault never really considered governmentality from a perspective other than the individual states and societies that have historically populated western modernity. Since his death in 1984 it has become *de rigueur* for a contemporary field of scholarship to note the globalization of one social form or another. Identity, culture, economy, security, society, and literature are just a few of the forms which are seen as either taking on global dimensions in themselves or feeding into a more general process of the globalization of nearly everything in the last decades of the twentieth century. Why should not governance—so neatly bound historically by political and social scientists in a discrete institution, organization, state, or society—be globalized as well?

What does it mean to globalize governance, to speak of global governance the way we speak of global culture, global economy, or global security? A Foucauldian scholar might argue that populations, structures of production and consumption, political relations, and so on are somehow increasingly being governed on a global scale. The proliferation of regulatory and "surveillatory" organizations and regimes whose purviews are international or global in scope, which as Craig Murphy ably shows has a robust lineage going back nearly two centuries, certainly lends credence to this view.[8]

We might also begin thinking about global governance by focusing on phenomena or issues that seem to have special salience from a global perspective. Some are simply reiterative across many if not all states and societies (e.g., fiscal crises). Others are discernible as issues or phenomena really only on a global basis (e.g., global warming).[9] For analysts such as Mihaly Simai, finding ways of dealing effectively with these issues and phenomena, that is, of managing "those factors of instability and risk," inevitably means embracing "collective multilateral governance."[10] One could indeed imagine a whole taxonomy of factors, issues, and the appropriate mode of global response, management, or problem solving. Murphy's prodigious research and analysis not only offers us a glimpse of this taxonomy, it provides a strong sense of the historical and ideational forces underlying its myriad elements.

Such a taxonomy would be confined mostly to governing that flows from institutions that regulate or surveil relations and practices on an international basis, that is, across a plurality of state and society spaces (a rule applied universally or a satellite eyeballing the planet). Rosenau innovatively challenges this more restricted sense of global governance with a far more open, fluid, and comprehensive understanding.[11] He sets up what appears to be a continuum. On one end are the formal and conscious efforts to construct rules and institutions to order aspects of global life as just described. On the other end are the far less formalized and less metaconscious forms of governance that emerge in the narrow and broad arrangements arrived at locally, regionally, or nationally through intersubjective understandings or patterns of practice. This continuum forms the great planetary hum of arrangements and regulated patterns that cohere into a global order. It refers to the way that, to varying degrees, global life is orchestrated by the myriad agents that inhabit it across different spatial levels: local, national, regional, and global. Whether through regimes, broad political accommodations, or discrete regulatory actions reiterated across the globe, governance is a ruling over, steering, or, more softly, a channeling or shaping of relations and practices.

How deeply into the totality of human existence does governance go? How much of humanity is part of the global governance grid? I find Rosenau somewhat ambiguous on this issue. In his most comprehensive statement on what comprises the global order subject to governance, Rosenau equates it with an understanding of "world politics . . . conceived as all-encompassing, as embracing every region, country, international relationship, social movement, and private organization that engages in activities across national boundaries."[12] Thus it appears that what is subject to governance is the transnational and international face of modern social existence. This view is consistent with a distinction made by the English School. Hedley Bull differentiated international order from world order, the latter denoting "those patterns and dispositions of human activity that sustain the elementary or primary goals of social life among mankind as a whole."[13] And Barry Buzan contrasted the interstate system with the interhuman system, that is, "the totality of human interaction on the planet."[14] In both Rosenau's understanding and the English School's, the status of the myriad domestic realms that ultimately populate the global order is not clear. Are we only interested in how they interact with one another? Or, relatedly, is it how they are drawn up into a system that is of concern (such as when we view the individual domestic economies joined together through rules and transactions to form the international economic system and global market)? I do not see how we can draw a line in any meaningful sense, since nearly every domestic transaction has global implications and every transnational interaction has domestic implications. Should we just clear the decks on this issue and identify the totality of human existence as subject to global governance?

Clarifying how deeply we go matters because, under Rosenau's pen, there is a powerful shift in the meaning of "global" in the phrase *global governance*. We move from governance that is global to governance in the global, with the latter meaning subsuming the former. Governance that is global refers to the steering at the global level. Governance in the global refers to all the governance that occurs throughout the global order. But, then, what is 'the global'? Is it the transnational face of the global totality, or the totality itself? What are the implications of emphasizing one over the other? Does global governance have a boundary? Is it economies but not households? It is not just that Rosenau faces a theoretical choice that those who are only concerned with "governance that is global" do not. For the latter, the issue is simply pushed one degree back. It is hidden by a general complacency or even silence regarding questions about what planetary context their governing operates in, and how much of the totality of human existence is subject to global governance. Of course, what is typically taken for granted in "governance that is global" approaches is an understanding of this context as an international or global system of states, their citizens, and a set of spheres of life inscribed across this expanse (e.g., the global economy or the environment).[15]

It is not immediately clear that having no ready sense of what the global is actually is a serious problem. After all, it is exactly this amorphous and elusive openness that can help generate a sense of possibilities for reconstituting forms of life across the great global totality. It is indeed tempting to look out across the global and find so many new forms of contest (new social movements) and of movements across borders, and pronounce that they are not contained within the confines of the interstate system. Critical scholars such as Rosenau, Richard Mansbach, Yale Ferguson, and Richard Falk want to think beyond the limits of the interstate system as such, a system which ultimately rests on "statist" assumptions that are no longer sufficient to contend with human needs and problems.[16]

But the very openness of 'the global' has some weighty implications when we speak of governance within it. Governance rests on a move toward closure, a move toward things being controlled or steered this way and not that way. It is an assignment of places, values, and options. If, as Rosenau claims, the global is full of governance of all sorts, then things are not really so open after all. In fact, it is closed by all the governance going on. The appearance of openness amid all this closure really stems from a lack. There is no political signified for the global, that is, no readily recognized political community or political society on whose behalf governance is executed. Scholars can theorize the formation or becoming of one—a global civil society for instance. Or they can argue for obligations extending to a moral community of humankind.[17] But until such a community becomes known to itself as a community, and also forges the social and political bounds around that identity, scholars are left in the uncomfortable position of arguing that there is a "knowable community" in existence, while those in the community (the bulk of humankind) hardly know it yet (the exceptions being some scholars, NGO activists, and social movement leaders).[18] As a result, appeals to the community, its welfare, its sinews of responsibility, and its forms of life as a field against which to evaluate and shape—rather than wait to be shaped by—governance are not readily accessible to the billions of human beings who otherwise might populate it. (I am assuming that it is not meant only to include leaders, activists, and scholars.) Of course, there are appeals by activists to the international community (mainly governmental and opinion leaders) regarding injustices; there are important links being forged by allied social movements across borders; and there are some scholars struggling to fashion meaningful normative bases for transborder and global claims of all sorts. But in the context of the great hum of quotidian governance (governance in the global) these efforts are either exceptional or are tightly grounded in the life of national communities associated with states. The embedding of human rights and their enforcement in the juristic community of the state is perhaps the most notable example of this.

I am not arguing for a nominalism about 'the global' or 'the international.' I readily recognize how important these dimensions are in areas such as human rights and environmental activism.[19] Nor do I want to argue against the possibility of global civil society. Rather, I want to point to some of the risks in crafting our analyses around a concept such as 'global governance,' even one that takes the possibilities of new social forms such as global civil society for granted. I believe we need to be more cautious about spending our limited intellectual capital without more careful reflection on related political questions about how groups, collectivities, and individuals would contest one structure or governance versus another, how they would fashion workable projects to gain power, exercise it, or prevent others from doing so over them, and how they would begin to know what the substance and implications of projects being proffered are? In the context of a national community there is a history of advocated forms of life, contested issues, and political actors who, at least in principle, are bound by some norms, if not juristic requisites, of collective responsibility. Does a focus on global governance risk, however well intended, legitimizing and thereby further empowering actors leading existing international institutions simply because they are the best placed and most capable governors? In other words, we want global governance to be effective, and we want it to be just, to lead to a just world order and the possibility of governing well. Yet we have only an open, fluid (if not nascent) social context ("the global community") against which to hold governors. This is not just a question of there being a democratic deficit, since that assumes some kind of democratic system (typically representative) waiting in the wings that is only deficiently applied. The issue here is far deeper. It is a matter of in what ways a political society—a community that knows itself as a field or space for political action and contest (a "knowledgeable community") that can, in a sense, govern governance—could come into being. Democracy may or may not be part of the answer, although scholars such as David Held are beginning to offer substantive theoretical arguments for why it is.[20]

Of course, in the broad sense of governance that Rosenau proffers, there are many governors operating across all walks of life in the global—in its farms, factories, families, and city governments. But there is big governance—the target of the Gramscians such as Robert Cox, Stephen Gill, and Murphy—that shapes the big financial and political relations of global order, and there is small governance—the shaping of life in local or national contexts, often in response or as an adjustment to the moves of big governance. The proliferation of governors and mechanisms, including NGOs, does not right this inequity. Many adjustments do not necessarily add up to big governance. Small is not always beautiful or powerful.

Despite all this, the concept of global governance can still be very valuable, and not just to point a finger at global regulators and powerful state actors from the west imposing unfair terms of trade and structural adjustment programs on vulnerable developing states and societies. To gain a sense of that value, it is necessary to probe its conceptual underpinnings and to flesh out further the still very cursory claims about it made above.

GOVERNANCE IN A FLOATING WORLD

> The development of global governance is part of the evolution of human efforts to organize life on the planet. . . . [W]e are convinced that it is time for the world to move on from the designs evolved over the centuries and given new form in the establishment of the United Nations nearly fifty years ago. We are in a time that demands freshness and innovation in global governance.[21]

When the language of global governance is evoked, typically lurking somewhere nearby is an implicit sense that what we are all living through is the modernization of international relations and global life more generally. This script is not centered on the impact on international relations of the "modernization" of states and societies, a theme stressed by Edward Morse twenty years ago.[22] Rather, what makes the new script unique is the emphasis on the modernization of the global per se. Not only are we becoming more "mature" in the way that the global is organized and governed,[23] but the very elements that sociologists from the nineteenth century on have been telling us mark a modern society, now mark the global (or shall I say global society). It is far more differentiated in terms of tasks, institutions, and social spaces, far denser in population and organizations (especially NGOs), and generally "more complex than ever before in history."[24]

I do not wish here to dispute the legitimacy of this script of the modernization of the global. Instead, I want to argue that through that script we might be retreading on some of the same questionable ground of mid-twentieth century structural-functionalist sociologists, especially Talcott Parsons, only this time regarding global rather than national society. Parsons and structural-functionalism stressed the integration and maintenance of given societies over the terms and bases of conflict and contradiction within them.[25] Crucial to Parsonian theory was the notion that "[s]ocietal order requires clear and definite integration in the sense, on the one hand, of normative coherence and, on the other hand, of societal 'harmony' and 'coordination'."[26] Parsons was responding to what he saw as a key challenge for sociological theory: why is there social order rather than a Hobbesian disorderly war of each against all?

How is it that highly complex and differentiated societies—persist, maintain, and reproduce themselves even as they face change and undergo transformation? If we substitute, for social order, governance and global order, we can read the same logic in Rosenau's thinking. He claims that "governance is always effective in performing the functions necessary to systemic persistence, else it is not conceived to exist (since instead of referring to ineffective governance, one speaks of anarchy and chaos)."[27] Elsewhere he argues for the importance of "intersubjective consensuses," bottom-up consent, and widespread legitimacy for mechanisms of governance.[28] The Commission on Global Governance also believes "the world's arrangements for the conduct of its affairs must be underpinned by certain common values." Organizations and laws must "rest on a foundation made strong by shared values."[29]

To my mind what drives the commonality between Parsonian theory and the global governance approach is the latter's effort to find patterns of authority and governance in the absence of a formal system of authoritative government. For Parsons government was part of the more fundamental political system which "could be viewed in the broader analytical setting of the 'political factor' of collective goal attainment, regardless of the status of the referent collectivity."[30] In other words, what was important, as David Easton had emphasized, was the functioning of the political system, rather than a state per se, to achieve the goals of a given society. Similarly, a system of governance, rather than a government, would operate to achieve goals in and of the global. Underlying that operation must be, if not a consensus on the actual goals, at least a consensus on the operation and existence of the governance system. Thus order emerges out of consensuses regarding governing rather than the legitimation of a top-down authoritative government. It is not necessary that this order be "grand" or globally coherent,[31] only that it be order rather than chaos.

The commonality between governance and structural-functionalist approaches does not end there. By pointing to not just political but also economic and societal systems, Parsons was abstracting out from society the various functional structures and their mechanisms, showing how they effected integration, pattern maintenance, goal attainment, and adaptation. By pointing to the various mechanisms and institutions of governance, the advocates of a global governance analytic (or global governists) make a similar move. To achieve the function of governance, 'rule systems and control mechanisms' must operate. However much this abstraction was problematic for Parsons, he could afford to make it far more than global governists. There was little hiding that for Parsons the society from which he abstracted was the American one. The norms that populated the consensuses he pointed to, *for him*, had a relatively substantive and delimited referent. Global governists, however, have no relatively contained socio-cultural context as a referent. The consensus around new global civic values argued for by the Commission on Global Governance must circulate in a global realm whose diversity, even by their own recognition, far exceeds that of Parsons's more delimited single society. Its consensus is therefore that much more problematic. Again, the point is not to be nominalistic about international norms surrounding phenomena such as democratization or human rights. Rather, it is to question whether we would want to assume that their circulation would undergird 'rule systems and control mechanisms,' that is, whether the specific and differentiated ways such norms have been interpreted and put into practice and even resisted within myriad societies and normative contexts constitutes a foundation for governance. Thinking it does may make us feel better that governance is a bottom-up phenomenon, but such a sense may be somewhat self-deceiving.

Some might see this simply as an empirical issue. Perhaps that is so. But there is a more basic issue stemming from the way governists—like structural-functionalists—abstract out mechanisms from their context. Although the problems and variegated forms of life of the global can be partially sensed, measured, and responded to with governance measures, the global is taken to be a sort of infinite repository of social identities (e.g., a neighborhood), troubling developments, or turbulent patterns of change. The broad, complex, and differentiated global social context for the operation of governance is really left as unfathomable and unmasterable, and yet it is taken to be governable and sustainable. I have already mentioned the double play of openness and closure inherent in this perspective—of the empty (and open) political signifier of the global, filled with the closure of governance. In order to see what makes that perspective problematic we need to think back to the 'oceanic' metaphor. The global resembles a kind of sea—dark, deep, and so expansive that any single governor or body of governors could never truly hope to survey, much less control, it. Thus Rosenau evokes an image of governance as a matter of steering a ship, a task for the "pilot or helmsman."[32] Foucault also turned to the same image in describing governmentality:

> What does it mean to govern a ship? It means clearly to take charge
> of the sailors, but also of the boat and its cargo; to take care of a ship
> means also to reckon with winds, rocks and storms; and it consists in
> that activity of establishing a relation between the sailors who are to
> be taken care of and the ship which is to be taken care of, and the
> cargo which is to be brought safely to port, and all those eventualities
> like winds, rocks, storms and so on; this is what characterizes the
> government of a ship.[33]

But where is the ship going? Who has appointed the captain? What is
his/her mission? Who sets the course? Which body of water does it
traverse? These are the important metaphorical questions any political
community might want to ask. Foucault has been criticized not only for
not asking them, but also for building an analytical perspective that
does not really allow for them to be asked.[34] The criticism can be
leveled at the global governists. It is therefore no coincidence that the
conservative and far more pessimistic philosopher Michael Oakeshott
should have recourse to the same metaphor of the ship and the sea in
his critique of rationalist attempts to construct a given form of life:

> In political activity, then, men sail a boundless and bottomless sea;
> there is neither harbor for shelter nor floor for anchorage, neither
> starting-place nor appointed destination. The enterprise is to keep afloat
> on an even keel; the sea is both friend and enemy; and the seamanship
> consists in using the resources of a traditional manner of behavior in
> order to make a friend of every hostile occasion.[35]

For Oakeshott, politics is a matter of "attending to the general arrangement of things" based on tradition.[36] While Foucault and the governists,
in contrast, emphasize inventions of and ruptures in forms of governance, all three perspectives share this concern with steerage across a
limited course within the context of a boundless and unknowable sea.
The governists, of course, are not as pessimistic as Foucault (or Oakeshott
for that matter) about the liberating dimensions of governance. The
Commission, in particular, offers lots of suggestions about how to address this or that important problem in the global. But the focus is on
the activity of steering and how to make it work better. Their suggestions "involve reforming and strengthening the existing system of intergovernmental institutions, and improving its means of collaboration
with private independent groups."[37] We would have little basis for identifying structures of domination (most likely inherent in big governance)
and for pointing to, if not informing, strategies and normative bases for

resistance to them. While the Commission may advocate additional forums and congresses, these might become spaces for adjustment to the big governance of international advocates of a free trade, neoliberal structural adjustment regime. Upon what terms could that governance be contested and why? In the unfathomable sea, the broad ocean currents pertinent to such questions disappear from view, to be replaced by the ripples of this or that problem or form of bad global citizenship (e.g., a polluting TNC, a violent ethnic faction, or a corrupt ruling party).

It is, of course, no coincidence that Parsons was accused of not allowing for an analysis of domination. The parallels between governism and structural-functionalism ultimately rest on an overriding concern with the reproduction of an existing social order and what it will take to make it work (even slightly) better, rather than what it will take to contest that order and why. A better starting point would be one that at least evoked both sets of concerns.

NEGATIONS OF GOVERNANCE

The governance approach may not only be lacking a starting point for asking important questions about domination and resistance in global perspective, it actually in some respects may occlude the opportunity to develop such a starting point (except trivially, as a resistance to the approach itself). Global governists are generally so preoccupied with showing which forces of governance can produce order that forces that might challenge governance or undermine order are treated as undesirable disruptions.[38] In one of the rare instances where the Commission deals with such forces regarding the all-important economic realm, it argues that "[w]ithout a representative high-level body developing an international consensus on critical economic issues, the global neighborhood could become a battleground of contending economic forces, and the capacity of humanity to develop a common approach will be jeopardized."[39] But that battleground may be exactly the kind of political challenge and resistance that is necessary for changing policies and political economic structures that are unfair, at least to the worst off on the planet.

This treatment of the forces of disruption is also apparent in the way that Rosenau designates "mechanisms of control" as the central term in the production of governance. Such mechanisms operate on the behalf of controllers "to modify the behavior and/or orientation of other actors." It does not matter if these efforts are resisted or complied with, since with "regularity," "timing," "consensus," "manipulation," and "careful planning," mechanisms can become institutionalized to "sustain governance without government."[40] The implication is not only that resistance is not part of governance, but that it is something to be overcome with effective governance. One may recall the duality Parsons set up between deviance and "mechanisms of social control," the latter of which he defined as "those processes in the social system which tend to counteract the deviant tendencies."[41] Once you begin, like Parsons and the governists, from a starting point that asks the question, "how is order (or governance) possible?" it is quite easy to lapse into viewing those things that appear to disrupt or undermine order/governance as disruptions, if not deviations. While Rosenau and other governists have no pretensions regarding the operation of an equilibrium for the governance system, as Parsons did, there is an explicit commitment in the discourse on governance, as we saw above, to see to it that it all somehow works better; that which undermines this is problematic.

According to Jürgen Habermas, one of the shortfalls in Parsons's paradigm was the inability to "explain the systematic tendencies toward the sort of pathologies that Marx, Durkheim, and Weber had in view."[42] Habermas meant by 'pathologies' the ways modern rationalist administration could create 'iron cages' of alienation, or colonize the lifeworld, as he put it. Not only does governance discourse suffer from this inability (what would bad governance be?), it provides no basis for distinguishing forms of global life that lie outside the grid of functioning governance, that can challenge or resist it. In order to begin to make that distinction, two questions would need to be asked: what works against governance, and what is not subject to governance?

The first question suggests itself based on the structural-functionalist logic of governance discourse. Recall the structural-functionalist concept of 'dysfunction,' which referred to those forces that create "strain, stress, and tension" and therefore threaten to "produce instability" in a given system or order.[43] The hope, of course, is that the system or order can change in response to such forces so that tensions can be abated. In a similar fashion, global governists would need to ask whether there are forces of 'dysgovernance.' If there are, do they want to assume that those forces can be abated through changes in governance mechanisms? For Rosenau, who is by far the most theoretically attuned of the governists, the answer seems to be yes, although the question is never explicitly addressed. Transnational and subnational mechanisms face "challenges," "instabilities," and "disorder" from a whole slew of forces, including material resource pressures (e.g., shortages), violent rivalries, crime, corruption, and alienated populations. Mechanisms can hover on the brink of failure with "severe adaptive problems" as they confront a world sliding between "considerable chaos" and "widening degrees of order."[44] But the hope of a future of governance is filled with the possibilities of inventing and adapting the governance system to these challenges. Rosenau points out that "transnational systems of governance tend on balance to evolve in a context of hope and progress. If there is any resistance around, it is likely to come from "those who have a stake in the status quo."[45]

Notice that in this picture of the world, forces that might work against governance are turned into fuel (however combustible and dangerous) for the evolution of governance. As a result, that which might work against governance in the end can work for it. There is no 'outside' the governance grid, no place beyond governance where political communities could say no. There is a single encompassing logic. Although Rosenau proclaims that the "world is too disaggregated for grand logics" (by which he means a single substantive version of international order, such as that associated with the Free versus the Communist Worlds), it seems it is still susceptible to the operation of a great humming machine that is the system of governance.[46] The system even rolls over the vested interests who might be threatened by change. Unfortunately, the inability to distinguish an 'outside' does not allow an analyst to discern whether in fact such interests might be driven to seek out, rather than avoid, mechanisms of governance to retain their positions of dominance.

But if there is no way to know what works against governance, then can we at least have some sense of what is not subject to governance? This is different from, but related to, the question of what works against governance. Rather than forces associated with dysgovernance, the question is whether there are forces that are ungovernable. Would a collapsed state qualify? Do we need a condition of deep chaos, where interactions are thought to resemble a Hobbesian war of all against all, perhaps in a multilateral civil war where numerous antagonists form, collapse, and reform in a haphazard fashion? Or would a situation, perhaps an economic crisis, qualify, where attempts at steering are useless, and intended outcomes breed unintended ones? What about anarchical revolts where all efforts at steering are resisted, and no meaningful countersteerings are proffered in their place? Within the discourse of global governance there really is no place for ungovernability. This might be how we are to understand Rosenau's claim that anticipating governance in the future means "to search for order in disorder, for coherence in contradiction, and for continuity in change."[47] What might count for some as ungovernability at one point in time would naturally be transformed into dysgovernance, that is, challenges to existing forms of governance. Governors would need to devise new forms of better or good governance, or step aside to make room for new governors who could offer these reforms or inventions.

The problem with this logic is not only that it allows nothing to roam outside the governance grid, since everything moves to dysgovernance. It also assumes that all governance, if it survives, is effective, and that ultimately it is good. This, of course, allows for the analyst or policymaker to insert any set of values s/he may want into the governance grid to produce a sense of good governance. In the 1970s the Trilateral Commission sponsored a Report on the Governability of Democracies, entitled *The Crisis of Democracy*.[48] It argued that Western-style democracies were becoming ungovernable because of increasing demands coupled with decreasing capacities. Rather than giving up on governance, the tentative answer seemed to be to set limits to the demands on democracies, including elements that were profoundly democratic. Ungovernability becomes a condition of dysgovernance, which in turn becomes an opportunity for reorganizing governance mechanisms for the 'better.' Indeed, the Trilateral authors were never really interested in the ungovernable. More generally, in the governance paradigm—Trilateral or globalist—we have no way to gain any theoretical purchase over the terms of transformation from ungovernability to dysgovernance and governance, and no way to begin to ask political questions regarding whose governance we are talking about and what the legitimacy of ungovernable or even dysgovernance forces are (to say nothing of avoiding legitimizing transformations to governability in the first place). Where or what is the political community in which a set of values is embedded? What is their status in relation to other communities? Is such a community unjustly being dominated? Which other communities might be interested in constructing, capturing, or colonizing mechanisms of governance in order to assert their own value system and grid of governance? Are we simply to assume that a global community recognizes the universal validity of a global governing ethic?

Although I have every reason to believe that many of today's governists have profoundly democratic values (see the values advocated in *Our Global Neighborhood*), the global governance conceptualization is open for anybody's business. In general, such openness stems in part from the way, discussed above, that governism, following the basic logic of structural-functionalist analysis, rests on the abstraction of mechanisms from the social context in which they are embedded. Robert Merton showed how structural-functionalist analysis could be employed happily by both radicals and conservatives. For him this suggested "that functional analysis may involve no intrinsic ideological commitment although. . . . it can be infused with any one of a wide range of ideological values."[49] We can imagine the same infusion of values taking place across a grid of governance, shaping institutions and leading to desired policy and practical outputs (notice the Eastonian language). When there is no outside and no boundaries over values and political battles, anyone can define what the inside is, as long as it is effective. For some, that openness may be a good. But to me a kind of global utilitarianism is scary.

LEVELING THE FIELD OF GOVERNANCE

When global governance is conceived as a continuum, it ranges from the kind of micro-steering that is highlighted by Rosenau, to the grand forums of interest aggregation in the halls of a reinvigorated UN stressed by the Commission on Global Governance. It means governance operates across a plurality of spaces, forms of life, and networks of relations, however differentiated these all are in scale and substance. Global governists do not expect or advocate an overarching, hierarchical structure of global governance. But the discourse seems to point to the existence of a kind of seamless fabric of governance in all its multifarious forms. Such a fabric on one level simply reflects the sense that there is a single 'global' within which governance operates. An extreme sense of this fabric is expressed in the call by the Commission for accommodation within the context of a common cooperative management of the problems of global life:

> Governance is the sum of the many ways individuals and institutions, public and private, manage their common affairs. It is a continuing process through which conflicting or diverse interests may be accommodated and co-operative action may be taken. It includes formal. . . . as well as informal arrangements that people and institutions either have agreed to or perceive to be in their interest.[50]

Rosenau is far less sanguine about the formation of any common cooperation or management, and for that matter he may even reject it as a
possibility within the variegated world of governance he describes. But
he still places governance within a single fabric by arguing that the
common element that shapes life in all the diversity of the global is
governance. In Rosenau's cosmology governance can be seen as the glue
of the global fabric.

The possibility of placing or viewing decisions, controls, and efforts at shaping social existence within the same field rests on a commitment to a vision of political life that is *intra-existential*. That is,
there is assumed to be one fabric of global social existence across which
run international, transnational, and supranational relations and interactions. Although individuals, groups, collectives, and publics can form
identifiable and differentiable units, the emphasis is placed on their
permeability and movement within a common social framework. Such
agents are understood to be linked and acting within a common field of
relations, meanings, and cooperation.[51] While conflict, in its broad sense,
is an ever-ready possibility, it unfolds and is resolved within a common
context of mutually legitimated rules and practices. The sense of intra-
existentialism has reached its peak in one recent reflection on the normative concept of 'panarchy' denoting "the rule of all for all" in "an
inclusive, universal system of governance in which all may participate
meaningfully."[52]

By way of contrast, an alternative vision can be labeled *inter-
existential*. In this vision, the emphasis is placed on the discrete and
exclusive nature of the units, whether they are states or, more fundamentally, groups of any kind. Although such units can interact, especially through conflict or the threat of conflict, there is no sense that
they share a common social existence the way individuals in a group or
clan might. Rather than movement, permeability, and cooperation, this
vision stresses defensive positionality, fear of intervention and penetration, and competition.

In international relations the inter-existential view is most closely
associated with realists and the intra-existential view with liberals; they
entail two senses of what politics is about. Politics in the liberal sense
is often understood to involve deliberation within a representative forum, a voicing of interests, voting, competition for office, debate within
a public sphere, or advocacy of a position through the mobilization of
actors (notably citizens). Politics in the realist sense revolves around the
configuration of an environment conducive to one's social existence,

resting on competition over positions of command, balance, survival, or exclusion vis-a-vis 'other' social existences. Perhaps the strongest version of an inter-existential political vision was expressed by Carl Schmitt, who declared, "The political is the most intense and extreme antagonism, and every concrete antagonism becomes that much more political the closer it approaches the most extreme point, that of the friend-enemy grouping."[53]

The governist commitment to an intra-existential vision is obviously consistent with the generally (liberal) democratic values that shape many of the concerns with global governance in the first place. For anyone, including myself, who wants to find ways of allowing for both difference and order, an intra-existentialist vision is eminently tempting. But I believe when we take governance and its norms as the glue of an intra-existential fabric, the distinctive politics we associate with that fabric is displaced. To understand how this happens, we can begin by considering the status of the traditional master site of the political, that is, the state. In the context of a liberal democratic state, deliberation, advocacy, and contest typically occur over the character of policies of supreme authority. Indeed, by the twentieth century, politics was defined, most forcefully by Max Weber, as a matter of configuring the state.[54] The wisdom of this association between politics and the state lies in the way that the state provides an immediate recognition of the stakes of politics, as a relatively effective set of organs for bounding and shaping a particular form of life. Contests and deliberations would be driven by differences over which form of the good life should prevail. (In liberal theory, it is generally hoped that the state itself can be neutral regarding which form prevails.) But in Rosenau's understanding of governance, for instance, these contests become problematic exactly because there is no authoritative center to fight over. The diffusion of governance throughout the global field precludes this. Of course, lots of politics are in operation all across the global in states, local communities, social movements, and NGOs. And Simai's book is filled with concern about the structure and operation of what he calls the international political system.[55] These concerns, such as North-South issues, leadership, multipolarity, and multilaterialism, are the traditional issues of the international relations field. To the extent that they impact and shape international or global order and set agendas and goals, they are relevant to governance (in the way that the field of international relations, in its focus on interstate management and regimes, has always appreciated the existence of governance). However, governance becomes in this case a passive dependent variable, a label for a certain output or outcomes, and something that is achieved in ruling, rather than a robust analytical category. Simai's relatively unproblematic treatment indicates how passive it is. Governance is simply "how people are ruled, and how the affairs of state are administered or regulated."[56] Where is the conceptual or theoretical bridge between governance and political questions about which affairs of state are pursued and how they are arrived at?

The governance concept in itself does not offer us a way to analyze the type of international politics of interest to Simai. Indeed the more we assert that governance is happening, the more the bridge between governance and politics becomes obscured. That is because what the steering and control governists associate with governance happens after governors have selected a direction or course of action. Is it any wonder that the advocates of panarchy as a norm of governance should conclude that "the present arrangement [of governance] falls abysmally short of panarchy"?[57] The concern with democratizing decision- and policy-making across the global, especially acute in the Commission's report misses the point, as my comments above should make clear. If, according to the report, governance is "the sum of the many ways in which individuals and institutions, both private and public, manage their common affairs," then who defines what management is? When whatever is being managed is part of a common affair, what is to be considered public or private, and where lies the boundary between the two. Obviously, the Commission has decided that it can do that defining. Indeed, the report already offers a working vision of what should be done, when, by whom, and why. All that is needed is ratification or some consensus. This, to my mind, is hardly a robust sense of democracy.

The distinct vision for a world governed globally that is offered by the Commission—and Simai—does qualify in its way as an assertion of a global form of life. It is itself a political act. But against whom is it asserted? What contest is it part of? The opponent it defines is the set of global problems—economic, security, and environmental—that are observed to be in need of management. This explains why, despite making arguments for the construction of all sorts of inclusive deliberative forums for making governance policy, the Commission counts on the construction of consensus and the avoidance of creating battlegrounds as essential to the operation of a system of governance. Indeed, the Commission has already designated the type of problems and the form of solutions that should guide governance. Politics, if anything, would be counterproductive. What the Commission implies is necessary are the consent and legitimation of its program. While the Commission's report may itself be a political act, it seems to advocate closing the door behind it on more politics of that or any other form. We have no sense of what kind of political life would form if their blueprint was pursued robustly. What type of power and compulsion would circulate? What would the nature of struggle be? Where would tensions and the political trenches around them form? What about contradictions in governance structures? In fact, the report explicitly claims that contradictions can be solved in a "system of governance" in that the very image of a system implies an order of working interdependent parts.[58] Where would the aporias emerge in the grid of governance? There is no way to ask these questions within the intellectual framework the Commission proffers. Moreover, Rosenau's wish, referred to above, for us to "search for order in disorder, for coherence in contradiction, and for continuity in change" also leaves little room for such inquiries.

One way to understand the relationship between governance and politics is to conceive of governance as essentially postpolitical. Governance is always proximate to politics, but it is something that takes place after goals are set and deliberations, argument, struggle, contest, and competition have played out. Thus governance itself becomes a sort of boundary for the political. (Of course, political process can be governed by rules [of debate for example], but such governance is not necessarily political in itself. It can simply set boundaries to political agency.) In some respects, the relationship between governance and politics resembles the relationship articulated between politics and planning at midcentury. There as well, distinct boundaries were articulated. Karl Mannheim, for instance, explicitly argued that politics needed to be left out of planning.[59] The goals and tasks of planning could be set democratically via state politics, but once planning was embarked upon it should be treated as a matter of a rational administrative, means/ends calculus. The politicization of planning, for Mannheim, would have been disastrous in that the art and logic of planning would be torn by struggle and contest. Even in the postwar era, theorists such as Niklas Luhmann have viewed the construction of a boundary between adminstration and politics as a good thing.[60] Much of what I have argued above suggests that global governance may be becoming the new administration of things for the global, the point being that there is a silence provoked by the concept of global governance on the myriad political questions enumerated above. This leaves those who want to take the concept seriously with a question.

Can the links between governance and politics be developed as a future task of analysis and theory?[61]

RETAKING THE POLITICAL: THE NEXUS OF STATES AND SOCIETIES

I find it odd to have to point to governance as a postpolitical concept. Recall that decades ago David Mitrany's functionalism was criticized for being explicitly apolitical in the way Mannheim would have liked it. Mitrany thought that politics was a phenomenon lodged in states and the state system. He did not want to see his governance structures geared to specific issues or problems confused with top-down international political federation, ideological battles for political domination in the international system, or contests over sovereign authority.[62] Although governance differs from functionalism (it is far more universalistic and does not limit itself to functional agencies), I doubt that any governists would disagree with Mitrany's desire to steer his concept clear of these types of forces. In the end, Mitrany and those governists, unlike Simai, are pursuing a robust normative and analytical concept of governance and want to distinguish their conceptualizations from the business as usual in states and the so-called state system. I believe this desire is what ultimately gets them in trouble regarding the political, especially since the site of politics has historically been the state. Although both Rosenau and the Commission are more than willing to see lots of governance emerging from states, within states, and between states, they are not comfortable with seeing the politics of—or between—states (intra- or inter-existential) as a central term or medium of governance. Of course, they can imagine, along with critical scholars, that we are in the process of a global transformation to the politics of the new—new social movements, new spaces, new communities, new societies, new flows, and even new civilizations. The recourse to this newness, as pointed out above, is problematic in itself, based, above all, on the existing limits of knowable and knowledgeable communities. But it suffers from a far more basic problem, in relation to which the displacement of politics just described is only a symptom. There is no commitment to probe the theoretical and substantive links between governance, states, national civil societies, and the new social forms upon which so much faith for the future rests.[63] I believe there is a great deal at stake in those links, not just for our analysis of the future of global governance, but also for our understanding of political agency in a global context.

Governists are always quick to point out that the state is and will likely remain a central and authoritative actor for some time to come. Yet they do not spell out the nature of this centrality and what its bearing is on governance and political life. The sense I glean from the governance literature is that the state is one form of agency among many in the global realm, however much its power and reach privileges it in that realm. But I do not think governists are willing to recognize just how embedded are governance and the transformation to new political forms within the plurality of states and societies. First, states and the societies they bound are the basic constitutive elements of territorial space, of social and political order, and of international organization. The construction of a post-World War Two international order—based on the norms, regimes, hegemonies, and interstate cooperation that have preoccupied international relations—allows governists essentially to avoid a whole slew of quite thorny problems about crucial issues such as social control, violence, and economic exchange.[64] Moreover, without the provision of order by and in states and national societies that this postwar settlement legitimized, governance that is global would be unfeasible in that the scope and depth of governing from above would far exceed the mechanisms at hand. Relatedly, it would be far harder to point to the myriad forms of governance within the global, as Rosenau does. Instead it would be necessary to invent forms of governance as alternatives to what takes place within states and societies inscribed across the globe. How far we would have to go in this invention is indicated by the relative ignorance in the west about alternative modes of governance in the face of collapsed or collapsing states (the very identity of which rests on the ideal of a robust state).[65]

Second, states and the national civil societies they bound create a social space for the very agencies (such as NGOs and new social movements) that are seen as essential to (if not constitutive of) contemporary global governance and the new forms of the political. It is the political and civil rights and the struggle for them, the public spheres, the information and knowledge exchange, the communications technologies and regulation, the capacities to cross borders with passports, and the visitation privileges that most states and societies allow for, that facilitate the new political agencies.[66] Even a local grassroots organization relies on the capacities for movement, communication, and resistance to state and local power that state and national society formation allows, at a minimum in negative terms (i.e., against the state or against domineering societal actors such as powerful capitalists). While states and societal actors can be powerful oppressors, they also can empower agents—in the least juridically—against local oppressors and borders, including TNCs operating in a given region or village. (Obviously, I am using the term *state* in its wider connotation to mean not just an ensemble of administrative organs or set of rules and laws that govern social relations and practices, but also as a political entity that encodes political practices within a given national territorial and societal space.)

Third, the formation of the plurality of states and societies into an international society (in the more limited Wight/Bullian sense), global in scope, should be seen as requisite for the emergence of the practices, institutions, and even discourse of global governance. The globalization of international society carries with it a profound universalism, based on the reproduction of the state-society form across the globe and the formation of norms and standard practices guiding transboundary relations, interactions, and flows. The dream of allowing this reproduction and formation to usher in a peaceful world order has been reiterated across western modernity in the hopes for workable peace plans (e.g., Rousseau), confederations (e.g., Kant), or world society (e.g., Durkheim). Although governists have not articulated the links, global governance likewise relies on the universalism inherent in international society for its operation. In the least, states have opened the way toward the global and universal by functioning as a brake on fragmentation (e.g., by integrating disparate communities, by resisting minority claims, or by cooperating in supranational institutions such as those of the EU). It is this brake that allows for the discourse of simultaneous fragmentation and integration that so pervades the governist literature.

Finally, the possibility of thinking about the governance both in and of the global rests on the penetration of state power in national societies in the way that Foucault described governmentality. An implicit assumption of governist literature is that governance on a global scale becomes possible only after societies and states have matured to a point where this type of power can operate to guide practices and institution formation; that is, once governance at different spatial levels can aggregate into different steering patterns in various spheres, such as the environment, health care, or trade. This aggregation can be comfortably assumed only because the basic constitution of national and international societies seems secured (minus those troublesome collapsing states).

By indicating how embedded global governance is within states and societies I do not mean to imply that we should simply fall back on the constraining notions of a master state system and interstate order for an understanding of what the political dimensions of governance are. It is far more productive to think of the states and societies that are inscribed across the planet as constituting a nexus that comprises (while not necessarily subsuming) a whole range of social forms, including international society, global civil society, and world capitalism. The nexus can thus include forms of authority and governance, local or regional, that operate in the absence of a workable state. These different forms, together with states and societies themselves, can be thought of as constituting a clustered set of overlapping and intersecting spheres. The nexus of states and societies thus does not imply that states and societies themselves are the ultimate context or system of the global, thereby assigning a fixed ontological core to the global. They are privileged only to the extent that they are central identifying terms in a configuration of associated forms such as international society or a web of cosmopolitan identities. This centrality is based on the deep history of the formation of states and societies as a political site of contest and governance within modernity, as well as the grounding for the kinds of universalism (e.g., of rights and obligations) that circulate across polities, inform struggles and political practices, and thereby make the international and the global, as well as cosmopolitanism, a possibility in the first place.[67] Treating the global as a nexus underscores that moving *across* states and societies is not necessarily moving *beyond* them.

Governists and critical IR scholars should guard against allowing the ahistorical and underdetermining treatment of the state-society nexus by neorealism to set the terms for their own critical analysis, turning away from the politics of states and societies because they are deemed to be associated with a shallow statism. I would argue that realists have not been focused enough on the states, societies, and complex forms of their nexus, and have been far too willing to limit their analysis to the logic of the deployment and use of military power or to the provision of leadership and management at the peak of international society (i.e., hegemonic stability). Analysis based on the simplistic determinism especially inspired by hegemonic stability theory that leads to conclusions that "transnational actors and processes are dependent upon peculiar patterns of interstate relations" should be avoided at all costs.[68] Not only is the nature of the relationship far deeper than that, as argued above. More importantly, hegemonic stability theory covers over the ways that transnational actors and processes can become disembedded from other social contexts and generate logics of operation that appear to be independent rather than dependent. Karl Polanyi saw this happen to the global market economy relative to the international and domestic political and social life of states and societies in the nineteenth century.[69]

Governists and critical IR scholars might want to consider whether they are also participating in a similar act of disembedding in their attempt to see social forms such as global civil society as having "developed alongside but outside" the state-society nexus.[70] It may not be enough to point to the way transnational actors influence or shape the world of states from within their own "not wholly independent" realm.[71]

I raise the possibility of viewing the ontology of the global as a state-society nexus not because of some nostalgia for a golden age of statist politics. Rather, I want to emphasize that contests and struggles over state power will continue to be the main sites of political life on this planet for some time to come. The Chiapas uprising is many things, but the terms of the struggle are directly with the Mexican state, and indirectly with Mexican capital, the US state, and US capital. It is not a struggle against NAFTA per se, but against a state that is shaping its policy around that interstate agreement. I do not want to belittle the value of studying the ways transnational actors, movements, or communities can politically influence and shape policies, practices, and ways of life locally, nationally, and globally that are distinguishable from those of states. Indeed, it will be essential for scholars to remain open to and help think through the empowerment of forms of political life, authority and local governance, especially where states do not take responsibility for the well-being of individuals and collectives. However, to the extent that a focus on these efforts displaces or even silences analyses and theory of struggles over what type of state shall govern what type of society and on whose behalf, it can become problematic. It may be a cruel irony that just when the possibility for popular resistance and contestation within states and societies, especially in the developing world, are potentially at their most robust in modern history, IR scholars interested in global governance elect to legitimize, however unintentionally, a shift of the locus of policy- and decision-making to a politically more elusive plane, and risk becoming increasingly irrelevant to the search for ways of reconfiguring life in states and societies along more just and equitable lines.

CONCLUSION

The arguments I have made about the turn to global governance as a way to think through the character of global life at the end of the twentieth century should not be taken as a proscription against its use as a term of analysis or even advocacy. Rosenau and others have challenged us to think innovatively about phenomena and developments at the end of the twentieth century which we might otherwise miss. Whatever criticism I or any other scholar brings to bear on the concept, it will likely continue to blossom as an approach to configuring relations on a global scale and analyzing that configuration. Thus, the point is to underscore the value of treating the concept in a highly critical manner; to remain always cognizant of its limits, silences, and unwanted legitimations.

A self-consciously critical governance approach can challenge us to keep in view important theoretical and practical issues: 1) about what kind of agency is possible on a global scale (who should do what, how, and on whose behalf); 2) about how we would distinguish governance from, and link it to, other forms of agency (e.g., resistance, command, and contest); 3) about what the political dimensions and implications of projects of global governance are; and 4) about who would win and lose and how such outcomes could be contested regarding particular systems of governance. If one were to take the nexus of states and societies seriously as a starting point of an analysis that places politics in a global perspective, then global governance could be understood to be a part of one project or another for shaping life in, across, and between states and societies. The questions 'whose project?' and 'to what ends?' must be kept close at hand (and not just by neo- or post-Marxist scholars).

Am I asking too much of a seemingly young idea? Is it still too early for a rich constellation of concepts about the character, for instance, of political life, states, societies, and the global, to have formed around the notion of global governance? Perhaps it is, but let us hope, above all, it is not too late.

NOTES

1. Sigmund Freud, *Civilization and Its Discontents* (New York: Norton, 1961), pp. 11 and 19.

2. James N. Rosenau, "Governance in the Twenty-First Century," *Global Governance* 1 (Winter 1995), p. 13 (13–44).

3. Mihaly Simai, *The Future of Global Governance* (Washington, DC: U.S. Institute of Peace, 1994), p. 3.

4. The word is used in The Commission on Global Governance, *Our Global Neighborhood* (New York: Oxford University Press, 1995), p. 183.

5. R.B.J. Walker, "Social Movements/World Politics," *Millennium* 23 (Winter 1994), p. 698, similarly writes of seduction, but regarding global civil society.

6. Michel Foucault, "Governmentality," in *The Foucault Effect: Studies in Governmentality*, Graham Burchell, Colin Gordon, Peter Miller, eds., (Chicago: University of Chicago Press, 1991), pp. 87–104. A detailed reflection on Foucault's governmentality in terms of global order and sovereignty is in Michael Dillon, "Sovereignty and Governmentality: From the Problematics of the New World Order to the Ethical Problematic of the World Order," *Alternatives* 20 (July–September 1995), pp. 323–68. The link between governmentality and global governance is made explicitly by Heikki Patomaki, "Republican Public Sphere and the Governance of Globalizing Political Economy," paper presented at the Annual Meeting of the ISA, Chicago, IL, February 1995. Although Patomaki raises some of the concerns about governance explored below, he does so from a perspective centered on the meaning and analysis of power in international relations, as opposed to politics (although, of course, he is profoundly interested in the relationship between politics and governance). He also focuses mostly on literature from the field of IPE rather than the nascent field of governance.

7. Michael Mann, *The Sources of Social Power*, vol. I (Cambridge: Cambridge University Press, 1986), makes a similar distinction, but is especially concerned to show how the two forms of what he calls "power" coexist in the same state and society.

8. Craig N. Murphy, *International Organization and Industrial Change: Global Governance since 1850* (New York: Oxford University Press, 1994); Stephen Gill, "The Global Panopticon," *Alternatives* 20 (January–March 1995), pp. 1–49; and Martin Hewson, "The Media of Political Globalization," paper presented at the Annual Meeting of the International Studies Association, Washington, D.C., March 1994.

9. See the discussion in Alfredo C. Robles, Jr., "Global Governance and Political Economy: German and French Perspectives," *Global Governance* 1 (Winter 1995), p. 100 (pp. 99–117); and John Gerard Ruggie, "On the Problem of the Global Problematique," *Alternatives* 5 (1979–1980), p. 520.

10. Simai, *Future of Global Governance*, p. xvi.

11. His most thoroughgoing published theoretical exploration of governance is in James N. Rosenau, "Governance, Order, and Change in World Politics," in *Governance without Government: Order and Change in World Politics*, James N. Rosenau and Ernst-Otto Czempiel, eds., (Cambridge: Cambridge University Press, 1992), pp. 1–29.

12. Rosenau, "Governance, Order, and Change in World Politics," p. 12.

13. Hedley Bull, *The Anarchical Society* (New York: Columbia University Press, 1977), p. 20.

14. Barry Buzan, Charles Jones, and Richard Little, *The Logic of Anarchy* (New York: Columbia University Press, 1993), p. 30.

15. Simai, *Future of Global Governance*, p. xviii, calls these spheres "subsystems."

16. Richard Falk, *Explorations at the Edge of Time: The Prospects for World Order* (Philadelphia: Temple University Press, 1992); Yale H. Ferguson and Richard W. Mansbach, *Polities, Authority, Identities, and Change* (New York: Columbia University Press, 1996).

17. See, for instance, Andrew Linklater, *Men and Citizens in International Relations Theory* (London: Macmillan, 1990).

18. The concept of 'knowable community' is developed by Raymond Williams, *The Country and the City* (New York: Oxford University Press, 1973), pp. 165–81. I realize this argument resembles the now classic Marxist duality between a class in itself and a class for itself. But communities are not classes. Indeed if they were, we could also rightfully argue that members of a global civil society do not identify themselves as such because they are suffering from a false consciousness. See also M. J. Peterson, "Transnational Activity, International Society and World Politics," *Millennium* 21 (Winter 1992), p. 377 (pp. 371–88), who writes of the thinness of transnational global loyalty.

19. See, for example, Kathryn Sikkink, "Human Rights, Principled Issue-Networks, and Sovereignty in Latin America," *International Organization* 45 (Summer 1993), pp. 411–41.

20. David Held, *Democracy and the Global Order: From the Modern State to Cosmopolitan Governance* (Cambridge: Polity Press, 1995).

21. Commission, *Our Global Neigborhood*, p. xvi.

22. Edward L. Morse, *Modernization and the Transformation of International Relations* (New York: Free Press, 1976). Morse seemed also to recognize that international relations per se were becoming modernized. However, he mostly viewed this modernization through the lens of the modernization of states and societies.

23. This sense of maturity is neatly conveyed in Hewson, "Media."

24. Rosenau, "Governance," p. 16.

25. See for example, Ralf Dahrendorf, *Essays in the Theory of Society* (Stanford: Stanford University Press, 1968). The debates around these issues are described in Jeffrey Alexander, *Theoretical Logic in Sociology*, vol. I, *Positivism, Presuppositions and Current Controversies* (Berkeley: University of California Press, 1982).

26. Parsons, *The System of Modern Societies* (Englewood Cliffs, N.J: Prentice-Hall, 1971), p. 12.

27. Rosenau, "Governance, Order, and Change," p. 5.

28. Rosenau, "Governance, Order, and Change," pp. 15 and 17.

29. Commission, *Global Neighborhood*, p. xiv. A whole chapter (2) is dedicated to the proper common values.

30. Parsons, *System*, pp. 101–102.

31. Rosenau, "Governance," p. 16.

32. Rosenau, "Governance," p. 14.

33. Foucault, "Governmentality," pp. 93–94.

34. A good review of those criticisms is in Richard J. Bernstein, *The New Constellation: The Ethical-Political Horizons of Modernity/Postmodernity* (Cambridge: MIT Press, 1992), pp. 142–71.

35. Michael Oakeshott, *Rationalism in Politics* (Indianapolis: Liberty Press, 1991), p. 60.

36. Oakeshott, p. 44. See the links between appeals to a formless totality and conservatism drawn out by Theodor Adorno, *Negative Dialectics* (New York: Continuum, 1966), pp. 92–94.

37. Commission, *Neighborhood*, p. 5.

38. While Rosenau, in "Governance, Order, and Change," pp. 22–24, can point to the possibility of systemic change, his discussion of it is limited to global order and not governance.

39. Rosenau, "Governance, Order, and Change," p. 162.

40. Rosenau, "Governance," pp. 14–15.

41. Talcott Parsons, *The Social System* (New York: The Free Press, 1951), p. 297.

42. Jurgen Habermas, *The Theory of Communicative Action*, vol. II, *Lifeworld and System: A Critique of Functionalist Reason*, trans. Thomas McCarthy (Boston: Beacon Press, 1987), pp. 284–85.

43. See Robert K. Merton, *Social Theory and Social Structure* (New York: The Free Press, 1949/68), p. 107.

44. Rosenau, "Governance," p. 20.

45. Rosenau, "Governance," p. 21.

46. Rosenau, "Governance," 16.

47. Rosenau, "Governance," p. 13.

48. Michel J. Crozier, Samuel P. Huntington, and Joji Watanuki, *The Crisis of Democracy* (New York: New York University Press, 1975).

49. Merton, *Social Theory*, p. 93.

50. Commission, *Neighborhood*, p. 2.

51. This concept is further explored in Robert Latham, "Getting Out From Under: Rethinking Security beyond Liberalism and the Level-of-Analysis Problem," *Millenium* 25 (Spring 1996), pp. 77–108.

52. James P. Sewell and Mark B. Salter, "Panarchy and Other Norms for Global Governance: Boutros-Ghali, Rosenau, and Beyond," *Global Governance* 1 (September–December 1995), p. 373 (pp. 373–382).

53. Carl Schmitt, *The Concept of the Political* (New Brunswick: Rutgers University Press, 1976), p. 29.

54. Max Weber, "Politics as a Vocation," in *From Max Weber: Essays in Sociology*, H. H. Gerth and C.Wright Mills, eds. (New York: Oxford University Press, 1946), pp. 77–128.

55. Simai, *Global Governance*, esp. part two.

56. Simai, *Global Governance*, p. 356.

57. Sewell and Salter, "Panarchy," p. 379.

58. Commission, *Neighborhood*, p. 9.

59. Karl Mannheim, *Man and Society in an Age of Reconstruction* (New York: Harcourt, Brace & World, 1940), pp. 360–66.

60. Niklas Luhmann, *Politische Planung* (Opladen: Westdeutscher Verlag, 1971).

61. I believe the most advanced thinking along these lines is in Patomaki, "Republican Public Sphere," which stands out more as an exception than an example. As the next section should make clear, however, I think Patomaki falls into the same trap as other governance approaches in his desire to think beyond state politics.

62. See for example, David Mitrany, *A Working Peace System* (London: National Peace Council, 1946), chap. 1.

63. The signal exception to this observation from a normative perspective is Held, *Democracy and Global Order*.

64. I have described some of the dimensions of this order in Robert Latham, *The Liberal Moment: Modernity, Security, and the Making of Postwar International Order* (New York: Columbia University Press, 1997).

65. What is needed is far more fieldwork on governance forms that are alternative or complementary to the state. In a sense, our abstract notions of governance in international relations have far exceeded what we can identify in the practices of knowable communities. I owe this observation to a conversation with Ron Kassimir at Social Science Research Council.

66. Cf. Peterson, "Transnational Activity," p. 379.

67. This point is further developed in Latham, "Getting Out From Under."

68. Robert Gilpin, "The Politics of Transnational Economic Relations," in *Transnational Relations and World Politics*, Robert Keohane and Joseph S. Nye, Jr., eds. (Cambridge: Harvard University Press, 1972), pp. 53–54.

69. Karl Polanyi, *The Great Transformation* (Boston: Beacon Press, 1944).

70. The words are Samuel Huntington's, "Transnational Organizations in World Politics," *World Politics* 25 (April 1973), p. 368, expressing his understanding of the status of transnational organizations in relation to the nation-state system.

71. Paul Wapner, "Politics beyond the State: Environmental Activism and World Civic Politics," *World Politics* 47 (April 1995), p. 339.

CHAPTER 3

Global Governance
and Social Closure

---

or Who Is to Be Governed in the
Era of Global Governance?

RONEN PALAN

Taking piano lessons as a child,[1] my teacher suggested that to completely appreciate music, and therefore to be able to play it properly, I should listen carefully to hidden, intermediate notes and tones that resonate within the formal notation. "Only by listening attentively to those echoes that lie buried deep in the tones," he said, "will you begin to understand the true nature of harmony." Attention to those hidden notes, " . . . the murmurs and the games of these other languages . . . forgotten in the name of pragmatic and ideological interests," characterizes the structuralist and post-structuralist research agenda.[2] This chapter seeks to identify some of the other messages that are broadcast and possibly give credence to the current debate on global governance.

The literature on global governance concerns itself with some of the pressing issues of our time. It derives inspiration, it seems to me, from one common interpretation of globalization. According to this interpretation, until fairly recently the dominant mode of social organization, or the locus of governance, was the nation-state. The nation-state provided the conditions for an orderly conduct of social activity ensuring that contracts are fulfilled, and so on. The state proved, in addition, fairly adept at confronting change. The dispersion of the modern state throughout the world disseminated the infrastructural preconditions which aided the growth of international trade and production. But as the nineteenth century was drawing to a close and production facilities began to spill beyond national boundaries, the question of a transitional political and economic order was placed firmly on the agenda. This period ended, however, in disaster. For some the disaster was largely due to the absence of a hegemonic state. The ensuing world war and the victory of the Allies ushered what was called at the time a new world order. Like its latest version, called for by Gorbachev and Bush, the older new world order was grounded in the principles of free trade.

However, the conventional interpretation continues, the present phase in the internationalization of production is characterized by a contradiction. On the one hand, the traditional locus of order and governance, the nation-state, is proving incapable of discharging its role. On the other, the need for an ever tighter framework of global governance is rising. A perilous deficit in national and international governance is emerging.[3] In particular it is felt that the integration of global markets and the exponential rise in offshore activities are not matched by an effective and premeditated transnational regulatory framework.

These are important questions no doubt. The thesis I wish to put forward in this paper is that global governance is not, nor can it ever be, simply about the technical aspects of good governance. Policy-oriented research is a conduit for social values and norms. I would liken it to a radio FM signal: on the face of it appearing simple and straightforward, but once deciphered showing itself as a carrier of additional information. I shall argue that the global governance debate serves as a comment about the entity that is to be governed, that is, society. Since it is essentially an argument about the failure of such an entity, correspondingly and implicitly it is an argument which falls within the ambit of the current and more generalized critique of state and politics.

This helps to answer the question, who is to be governed by global governance? If modern society is an historical construct, then it follows that a critique of such a construction must, among other things, create an alternative construction. Such alternative construction is predicated upon a new form of collective identity—its own imaginary closure. For an imaginary closure to be effective, a community must be presupposed: presenting itself in discourse as naturally given, unthinkingly already-in-existence. The construction of such presupposed communities takes place when someone or somebody begins to talk in its name. One suspects that global governance is written in the name of and for someone; there is a hidden voice that struggles to express its grievances. This chapter is concerned therefore with social closure, because the processes of construction of such new imaginary identities are ultimately about the signing off of who lies within and who is without; who is a full member of the constructed community and who is not. These are the hidden identities that lie buried in the debate of global governance.

The chapter is organized as follows. In Section 1, I shall briefly defend the interpretive or hermeneutical research agenda of emphasizing the importance of discourses in historical change. In Section 2, I revisit discourses of governance that arose with the nation-state in Europe. These involved an imaginary closure formed upon the identity of national subjects inhabiting closed entities. The main part of the chapter inquires into the relation between imaginary closure and contemporary discourses of society (Section 3), the state (Section 4), and global governance (Section 5). Ostensibly they each challenge the former imaginary closed entities. Yet I argue that they too convey an imaginary closure formed upon the identity—a global public of consumers—that is to be governed by global governance.

1. IN DEFENSE OF INTERPRETIVE RESEARCH

The thesis I am advancing is by its very nature interpretive. This section briefly advances the theoretical argument in support of such a research agenda. In conventional approaches, or what is commonly described as positivism, concepts and ideas are treated as approximations of identifiable and definable social phenomena.[4] Concepts are deemed unhelpful if they fail to correspond to identifiable phenomena, or if they are indistinct and allow for the description of a variety of phenomena. Easton argues, for instance, that due to the multiplication of the definitions of the state, "neither state nor power are good concepts."[5]

Alternative approaches, broadly described as nonpositivist or constructivist, maintain that concepts are intrinsically interrelated. Against Easton, our understanding of the state cannot be disentangled from some underlying notion of society, people, and politics. The problem is that under close examination, ancillary concepts such as 'society' or 'politics' are intrinsically related to other concepts, containing as it were, within them already a kernel or an echo of a specific conception

of the state. In this view there is not, nor can there be, a stable meaning
to any of our categories. So the quest for essential meaning is mis-
guided.

Interpretative methodologies therefore seek to examine the structural properties of discourse. They seek to subject common sense or
the language of everydayness to critical evaluation by interpreting
what is taken for granted. They seek to identify the hermeneutical
dimension by stepping outside the commonsense attitude and adopting a self-consciously reflective attitude to theory. Following in this line
of thought, I would argue that the very concept of global governance
is both an implied critique of the nineteenth century (imaginary) conception of society as well as constructor of modern imaginary identities.

2. CLOSURE AND THE NATION-STATE

In globalist literature the tendency had been to represent the nation-
state as an institutional mechanism that can be tinkered with, adjusted,
and dispensed with at will. Such a critique misjudges the complex
mechanisms and deeply rooted preconditions without which the machinery of the state would be uprooted.[6] Just as a car cannot be rede-
signed simply by pulling and cutting it this way or that, because of the
harmful effect this might have on the chassis, engine, balance, and so
on, so the state cannot be reduced to the machinery of governance. I
view the nation-state as a specific type of social organization which
emerged in the beginning of the nineteenth century and which should
be understood in its totality. In this section, I discuss some of those less
obvious dimensions of the nation-state as a totalizing experience.

The early nineteenth century witnessed three sets of interrelated
changes defined usually by the terms the *industrial revolution, modernism*, and the advent of the *infrastructural state*. These developments
expressed themselves in what I call the increasing discretization of the
European scene. By this I mean that unity and difference were increasingly discerned.

The cognitive process by which a unity is recognized is of political significance. How we discern a unity (society, state) is as pertinent
to social investigation as the traditional question, what does the unity
consists of? I would suggest that in the nineteenth century there was
a process of discretization. The etymological origin of the concept
'discrete' is 'to discern'.[7] It entails an act of visualization which is simultaneously an epistemological statement about a relationship between an

observer and an observed. One discerns a unity, a difference. It is always useful to remind ourselves that an inanimate unity is discerned in a process that links an observer and the observed. For example, the images I see on the television screen are agglomerations of dots, which take shape by a process that happens in my brain. In other words, visualization can be manipulated. The relationship between the observer and an observed is significant therefore with regard to inanimate matter, doubly so when it comes to social entities.

One of the defining attributes of social collectivities is closure. Although 'society' is a contested concept, at minimum it is agreed that the concept implies some notion of a boundary separating certain aspects of social life.[8] In that sense the concept of society belongs to the category of concepts sociologists call social boundary systems. I would distinguish between physical closure, which implies physical restrictions on the movement of people, goods, capital, and ideas, and imaginary closure, or the processes that lead subjects to believe they inhabit a closed entity. The imaginary closed social entity is in fact a discrete social entity.

How did such presupposed imaginary entities come into being? The rising fortune of the modern concept of society, which is the modern conception of social closure, has been pinpointed with some accuracy.[9] 'Society' came about when the concept of the 'the nation' became more inclusive in the early nineteenth century to cover all those who inhabit the territory.[10] This inclusive conception of the nation denoted a reordering of the national space. It implied, as Poulantzas points out, a rereading of the relationship between individuals and the social whole; state and society coalesce so that the two categories are perceived as two sides of the same coin.[11] Such coalescence opened the door for, as much it coincided with, a change in the political agenda. The state, previously viewed as an outgrowth of the royal household, was now seen as an integral part of the social context, subordinated to the "common good."[12] The political economy of the subordination of the state, or the system of governance, took the paradoxical form of an increasing penetration of society by the state. This was the emergence of what Mann calls the infrastructural state. But the very process of penetration was concomitantly a process by which the penetrated subject, society, took shape; it was a process by which a presupposed ontological unity was discovered.[13]

Here we are concerned primarily with some of the practical implications of the discovery of the new presupposed unity. While the normative foundations of the nation-state were originally expressed by two different traditions, the liberal and the nationalist-romantic, both may be read as reflecting divergent experiences. The liberal tradition reflects the experience of early discretizers like England and France, while the nationalist-romantic tradition reflects the experience of late discretizers such as Germany and Italy. Nonetheless, despite the difference in language and conceptual kit, certain commonality of experience also existed. I would emphasize four major common features of the discretization movement:

(i) To begin with, there was the presumption of spiritual unity. Since nationalism is often studied as an ideology, the practice of nationalism is often reduced to mere ideological or rhetorical devices. But the concept of the 'nation' as understood in the nineteenth century was predicated upon the presupposition that members of the nation share in some epic spiritual journey.[14] The agglomeration of people who happen to reside within a given political boundary or share linguistic or other attributes are viewed as having a common destiny. Nationalism attributes meaning to the collectivity and to the role of the individual within it, which in turn entails a modification of behavior that attends a concept of a shared destiny.[15]

The presumption of spiritual unity begets an assumption of responsibility: individuals now have a responsibility towards their forefathers, towards their descendants, and by implication, towards each other. The nation became a constitutive absence. The location of the primacy of the social whole at the very ontological level implied a necessity by individuals, legally and morally constituted as members, to subordinate themselves to the common good. "The worth of individuals is measured by the extent to which they reflect and represent the national spirit, and have adopted a particular station within the affairs of the state as a whole . . . the individual's morality will then consist in fulfilling the duties imposed upon him by his social station."[16] Shunning such pathos, the liberal or Hobbesian tradition comes up, nonetheless, with similar prescriptions.

(ii) In addition to presumed spiritual unity, there was the duty of collective organization. The pursuit of the common good is a matter of choice. Yet, the imaginary absence, the nation, was, unlike an externality such as God, immanent to itself. The implication was that it must take control over its shared destiny. God-fearing people are likely to entrust their destiny to God and to His emissaries on earth because choice entails following His injunctions. A community must, however, make choices as a community. Choice has to be organized collectively. Consequently the nation has to organize itself so that its spiritual aims are fulfilled. It is incumbent upon the nation, for instance, to educate its people "to substitute from the egotism and self-love another love, a love for the common good, for the nation."[17]

The argument I am advancing here is that a certain logical imperative is embedded in the new concept of the nation. The notion of an immanent and discrete collectivity represents the nation as a self-organizing historical entity, which in turn raises the question of collective goals. The matter of collective goals is simultaneously a question about ethics, that is, which of these goals are honourable, and a question about technique: how a self-organizing community is to go about self-organizing itself to achieve such goals. Modern political science and sociology, both of which are studies in the mechanisms of self-organization, are therefore modern not only because they happened to emerge in the modern period but because they are predicated in a profound way on the presumption of the ontological unity of the people as an immanent unity.

(iii) The presumption of collective organization implied the state. Since members of the nation share a destiny, states are viewed as the mechanisms for the organization of these mutual-care societies. The state emerged from the French revolution as an organization which is supposed to respond to the needs of the people who inhabit the territorial space. The state is given the task of maintaining peace and harmony at home and defending the territorial integrity of the nation. There are naturally diverging interpretations as to the mechanisms that will ensure such beneficial outcomes. Conservatives are happy to leave such practical matters to the government; liberals place their hopes in the democratic process which requires constant communication between rulers and ruled.

I would argue therefore that social discreteness, the subjective belief in the closure of the national entity, is a necessary precondition for the democratic process. Unless the social scene is legally and functionally discrete, potentially anybody can lay claim to resource allocation. By closing down the membership of the nation, and hence by presenting it as a contractual relationship, or membership, the possibility is open in principle for the members to be given a measure of voice in determining how they wish to conduct their common responsibility. While discreteness does not guarantee democracy, democracy requires social discreteness.

(iv) Finally, a fourth implication of imagined closure in the nation-state quickly emerged; it does not take long to figure out that the unity of people does not carry with it any guarantees about uniform experiences. On the contrary, the people can have divergent opportunities which may classify them as belonging to different social classes. Indeed, the advance of one class implies the retreat of another. It is not therefore by accident that Marx represents a Left Hegelian trend. The point is quite simple: a unity must be presupposed for class struggle to be discovered.

These, then, were the implications of discerning an imaginary closure or the formation of discrete social entities which we call the nation-state: it is a contradictory unity, an imaginary shared space internally dissected by class and groups, a unity of the common good defined by parochial interests. In the following sections I argue that the normative and political implications of the coalescence of the imaginary state and society are those that find themselves criticized implicitly by contemporary literature of social theory, the state, and global governance.

3. CLOSURE AND 'SOCIETY'

The experience of an imaginary discretization of the European scene became the point of departure for a sociological debate between holists and nominalists over the concept of 'society.' The problem developed in nineteenth-century sociology as follows. Holist social theory mistook imaginary closure for a physical (real) closure; then the implied physical closure of society served as the basis for a deductive interpretation of social life. Against this, nominalist social theory reached the conclusion that holism is empirically incorrect. But in doing so, nominalist sociology failed to appreciate that it was producing alternative forms of imaginary closure all in the name of more accurate (real) sociological theories.

Let us first consider holism. Physical and organic images were widespread in understandings of society. One of the trenchant critiques of the concept of society is that it evokes false images of tangible bodies inhabiting a territorial space.[18] In classical as well as modern speculative philosophy, society is frequently envisioned with the aid of an object, an entity. From early Greek thought, reflections on social experience found moorings in familiar metaphors drawn from voluminous objects such as the 'body politic,' the 'Leviathan,' 'Behemoth' (respectively, "whale" and "hippopotamus" in Hebrew), the 'machine' and lately, the 'system.'

Such images served as the basis for many interpretations of the social experience of closure. The image of social closure, whereby society is understood to constitute something akin to an organic social body, is pervasive. Such images and analogies drawn from the physical world are probably inevitable. As Quine notes, "[b]odies are our paradigmatic objects . . . [therefore] Beyond them there is a succession of dwindling analogies."[19] Since social entities belong to this realm of dwindling analogies there is no escape but to represent them in metaphors and analogies. And yet, this metaphorical language is not neutral; it appears to project onto the object "out there" certain spatial qualities which it may not possess.

The perception of physical closure ran into trouble, however, in the second half of the nineteenth century. As sociology as a discipline was contemplated, the centrality of social bounding in the organization of the social underwent an extended review. Under the impact of the spectacular improvements in the technologies of transportation and communications, doubts were creeping in. By the end of the nineteenth century, sociology bifurcated into two camps ostensible holding to opposing images of society. The first image, associated with the works of Durkheim and subsequently with the functionalists and the structural functionalists, represented society as a cohesive community which acts and behaves as a unit.[20]

But nominalists argued that this image of closure cannot be empirically validated. Alternative nominalist conceptualizations of society took a variety of forms. According to one tradition of thought, the state is dependent on other civil organizations for support. A second and related tradition maintains that the dominant view fails to recognize the different social and cultural systems that inhabit a social formation. The problem, argues Mann, is that society is "not a system" but "multiples of overlapping and intersecting power networks."[21] This tradition postulates no a priori or special relationships among social practices and the social whole but recommends instead concentrating upon the "real interactions between individuals."[22] In this view, our concept of society is historically specific attendant to the rise of the state; it was constructed and produced as a form of power relationship. A third variant takes the view that under modern conditions order must emerge from individual choice.

The nominalist critique of holism rarely takes onboard, however, that the critique itself works on a number of concomitant levels: the Real, the Imaginary and the Symbolic.[23] The crux of the matter are those normative connotations that have attached themselves to the conventional concept of society so that the bounded community has become associated, historically as well as concurrently, with the rational, if not the natural, order of things. The conventional picture of society connotes, in Fortes's words, a "self-balancing, internally coherent, and harmonious arrangement of recognized relationships based upon fundamental conceptions common to all humanity."[24] While the ultimate source of such allegedly beneficial outcomes (harmony, etc.) has often been attributed directly to God, concretely the implications of such arguments—and these implications seem to hold to the vast majority of social theories of today—are twofold. The first implication is that society or a collectivity is a necessary precondition for human beings to live harmoniously, productively, and hence ethically. The second implication is that this precondition can only be met within some form of a bounded collectivity.

The conclusion to be drawn from this episode of intellectual history is this: implicit in the quest for political order, regional, national, international, or global, there is always therefore an attended, if little explored, quest for boundedness and closure. And if current forms of collective identities (closure) have failed us, then new ones are being explored. This is the basis for my contention that current explorations, to which the literature of global governance belongs, take the form of a search for new closure. Some conceptions of closure are becoming explicit. Hayek, for instance, still works with the idea of an harmonious, bounded collectivity. The best way for achieving harmony and balance, he argues, is to let the market act on its own. It may be argued that neoconservatism's great success lies in its ability to fuse utilitarianism with ethical and spiritual philosophy. It challenges the traditional perception of social closure and the need for collective action, maintaining that the very traditional goals of harmony and spirituality cannot be accomplished through the collectivity. Left-liberal nominalists like Mann or Skocpol (the left neo-Weberians), however, refuse to draw upon Weber's (and others) deeply conservative politics; they have ended up therefore simply abandoning the problematic of order and ethics, proposing to settle the issue by observation, as if theirs is the correct perception of the real, confronting a biased and ideologically laden perception of the social whole.

4. CLOSURE AND 'THE STATE'

In addition to debates on the meaning of society, imaginary closure has become the point of departure for today's debates on the idea of 'the state.' The challenge to the conventional concepts of society can develop as a challenge to the pre-existing community (the nation) which is now believed to be a purely imaginary construction. Seen in this light, modern debates, of which global governance plays a supporting role, gain different meaning. In this view, the tilting balance towards nominalism is not merely an academic issue; it impacts on our traditional perception of the role of individual and society in very specific ways. Once the whole is discovered to represent nothing but an imaginary closure, then by implication the state is seen no longer as the political expression of some prior unity called the people or the nation. The state is viewed rather as a set of formal relationships which, "when it appeared . . . distorted or shattered all previous formations and institutions."[25] The state, now supposedly evacuated of its metaphysical meanings, becomes therefore merely a social organization for control.

It is interesting to note, in this context, how recent state theory strives to debunk old statist assumptions. Auster and Silver were pioneers in this new "hard-edged" no-nonsense state theory. The state, they argue "is usually surrounded by a powerful mystique. It is not viewed as simply another of the myriad institutions contained in any society, owned of necessity by certain individuals and not by others. The state is seen in other ways; often it is viewed as the expression of some transcendental force: the 'leader,' the 'nation,' the 'workers,' the 'general will,' or divine will." But these metaphysical notions are nonsense. In fact, "The state provides the service 'protection' and punishment, and through these it manipulates the level of order."[26] The implications are, of course, that if the state fails to provide adequate protection or perhaps overcharges for its services, then one may legitimately seek to avoid paying tax.

This is essentially the metalanguage message of contemporary neo-Weberian state theory: it is the message of a "new contract" between rulers and ruled. But who then are the ruled? Who belongs to this new community? The nation, that is, all those who reside in a territorial forum, clearly does not define anymore the new community, because national unity is debunked as well. Once the mythical shared destiny of a people is withdrawn, then the correlate notion of mutual responsibility between individuals and classes is difficult to uphold. In the new nationalism, national unity is represented as a class compromise: the unity of purpose and choice in which employees and employers come together in order to compete with other similar national alliances. This is the space into which Porter could interject his notion of the 'competitive advantage of nations.'[27] This is no longer the horizontal transnational alliance of classes but vertical alliances of classes facing one another over a loosely defined territorial fence.

This imagined unity of capital and workers facing an alliance of capital and workers of other nations demystifies the concept of the territory. It offers however a new concept of closure redefining who is within and who is without. The nation is increasingly defined as the portion of the people who are involved in the competitive game, that is, those who are employed. Hence Clinton's emphasis on the "middle classes" is of importance. The modern language of politics has shifted attention imperceptibly from the 'people' to the 'public'—the public being a portion of what we used to think are the people. Now, however, there is even evidence that the 'public' is still too broad and imprecise. The nation has been narrowed down again and replaced by 'the consumer,' pure and simple.

The next stage in the emergence of the new hidden unity is a frontal attack on the very institutional arrangement of democracy—the institutions that give voice to the imagined national unity. This is accomplished through the proposition that since the voters are a group of no-hope fools, we can rely only on their immediate desires as consumers. In an aptly titled book *Power, Inc.*, Mintz and Cohen demonstrate the utter degradation of the institutions of democracy.[28] And since democracy "does not work," one has to rely on consumers "voting with their purse" to know what the public really wants. The forms of Imaginary social closures that are now being experimented are therefore increasingly and undemocratically utilitarian; they are born out of the conviction that the democratic process does not offer the best method of promoting the public's common good. Since public good is demystified and proved to be an unworkable proposition, the only credible expression of the public interest is consumption.

Public policy and sociology are at the forefront here, speaking in the name of this aggrieved consumer. They do so increasingly by debunking the myth of democratic institutions and social cohesion. They do so in the name of some hyper-real (not in Baudrillard's terms), hyper-cynical reality. The entire democratic process is perceived as largely a public relations exercise in which everyone pretends to be politically involved. Those who do not understand the nature of this theater, those who fail to take advantage of the media, those who actually believe, or seem to be genuine truth-seekers, are cast aside. Thus, for the new imaginary closure, it is quite important that we all know that the president is a media personality; his own real personality is an enigma. It is absolutely essential that we all know that interests are best represented by people who do not take a direct interest in the interests they pursue: lawyers, accountants, and the professional lobbyists are the paradigm of the new politics. We are scandalized and reassured at the same time. An introverted hall of mirrors has been forged, a consuming and intricate game of politics takes place replacing our traditional notion of the political process.

5. CLOSURE AND 'GLOBAL GOVERNANCE'

Just as debates on society and the state challenge national closure while creating new imagined closures, so too do debates on global governance. The implicit assumption in this essay was that the language of global governance, with its attendant rather unflattering insinuations about the functions, legitimacy, and aptitude of the state (and society), draws on a Batesonian metalanguage. It makes sense only once an agreement is reached about some prior, if normally undeclared, common human goals, political functions, and so on. The social sciences are sites as well as creators of new imagery of social closure based on utilitarian principles pursued in the name of some abstracted consumers.

This is not to say that the global regulation is not necessary or important. Clearly it is. The issues in global governance certainly represent attempts to solve a series of functional problems. But the discussion, the solutions, and the analysis of the problems set out a separate metalingual perspective which contributes to the changing nature of politics and society. I have advanced the proposition that the concept of society cannot be theoretically and historically delinked from either the concept of the state or the concept of social closure. In the same way, the changing fortune of the state cannot be delinked from the changing fortune of society and closure. The alleged dysfunctionality of the state has to be seen in the context of the criticism of the dysfunctionality of society. And since society is a form of an imaginary closure, the globalist critique of the state is by implication an attempted construction of new closures. The argument I am advancing here is meant not as a nostalgic yearning for the good old days of collective spirituality, but as a study in the emergence of new closures.

The idea of the public, or of the consumer, serve as focal points of the organizing principle of closure in the modern world. The public, the middle classes, are clearly not joined together by some sort of spiritual bond, and the link to the land and the territory is tenuous, perhaps nonexistent. The public is joined together insofar as the unity in which it chooses to join serves provisionally better the consumptive desires of the isolated individuals that make it up. The public is a realm in which the individual expresses his or her individual needs in a collective fashion.

In that sense, the public can belong concomitantly to different units, one of which represents itself as global. A more diffused type of governance comes to seem appropriate, some of which can be provided by the state, some by private agencies, some by multilateral agencies. The notion of 'global,' however, can be misleading. Contrary to common assumptions, it is global only in scope, not in aspiration. Globalism is about the claim to be able to run things better for the consumer on a global basis. 'Global' is perceived therefore as a challenge to a still very much international situation. Only the national itself is a different unity; the national is not an intrinsically spiritual unity but a consumerist association which may wish to coordinate its efforts internationally. Global governance is about the coordination of such efforts, coordination that can take both public and private forms.

CONCLUSIONS

This chapter offers a critical scrutiny of the debate on global governance by situating it within a broader discourse. Calls for global governance are implicitly about the failure of the entities we have hitherto called society and the state. Such calls share much, I have argued, with the critiques of society and state within contemporary social and political thought. This is the context within which global governance theory gains its meaning and purchase.

Once we situate the debate on global governance in this discourse, a very significant implication begins to emerge. The hidden, intermediate notes within this music play a tune that is not so new as may be supposed. The search for new kinds of imaginary closure proceeds apace. Beliefs that we inhabit closed entities accompanied the rise of the nation-state in nineteenth-century Europe. Such beliefs have not disappeared. Instead they are being refocused, in part by global governance thinking, upon the imaginary of the consumer. What is missing is the argument that social harmony does not necessitate boundaries. But this may be an argument too revolutionary to be taken seriously at the present time.

NOTES

1. Thanks to Angus Cameron, Timothy Sinclair, and especially Martin Hewson.

2. Michel de Certeau, *Heterologies: Discourse on the Other* (Manchester: Manchester University Press, 1986), p. 53.

3. Susan Strange, "The Defective State," *Daedalus* (1995) 124, 2: 55–74.

4. General sociology, argued Weber, "seeks to formulate type concepts and generalized uniformities of empirical process." Max Weber, *Economy and Society*, vol. II, Guenther Roth and Claus Wittich, eds. (Berkeley: University of California Press, 1978), p. 19.

5. David Easton, *The Political System* (Chicago and London: The University of Chicago Press, 1953), p. 106.

6. See, for instance, the studies on neopatrimonialism by Jean Francois Bayart, *The State in Africa: The Politics of the Belly* (London: Longman, 1993) and Ronen Palan and Jason Abbott, *State Strategies in the Global Political Economy* (London: Cassel, 1996), ch. 9.

7. Ernest Klein, *A Comprehensive Etymological Dictionary of the English Language* (Amsterdam: Elseivier Publishing, 1966).

8. "A society is a network of social interaction at the boundaries of which is a certain level of interaction cleavage between it and its environment," Michael Mann, *The Sources of Social Power, Vol. I: A history of power from the beginning to A.D. 1760* (Cambridge: Cambridge University Press, 1986), p. 3. One may recall Talcott Parsons, who warned that "however important logical closure may be as a theoretical ideal, empirically social systems are open systems," Talcott Parsons, et al, *Theories of Society Foundations of Modern Sociological Theory* (The Free Press of Glencoe, 1961), p. 36.

9. Michel Foucault, *Les mots et les choses* (Paris: Gallimard, 1966); Karl Polanyi, *The Great Transformation* (Boston: Beacon Press, 1957), p. 115.

10. J.C. Herder, *Herder on Social and Political Culture*, ed. F. M. Barnard (Cambridge: Cambridge University Press, 1969 [1774]).

11. Nicos Poulantzas, *State, Power, Socialism* (London: New Left Books, 1978).

12. Ronen Palan, "Ontological Consternation and the Future of International Political Economy," *Economié et Societé* (1997).

13. Michael Mann, "The Autonomous Power of the State: Its Origins, Mechanisms and Results," *Archives europeennes de sociologie*, vol. 25 (1984). Ronen Palan, "Technological Metaphors and Theories of International Relations" Chris Farrands, MikeTalalay and Roger Tooze (eds.), *Technology, Change, and Competitiveness* (London: Routledge, 1997).

14. "The nations are the concepts which the spirit has formed itself," Georg Wilhelm Friedrich Hegel, *Lectures on the Philosophy of World History:*

Introduction (1975), p. 51. The concept of the 'people,' the 'volk,' discovers en route great historical experiences in the misty days of the destruction of Troy (for the French) or the medieval Teutonic past (for the Germans). J. G. Fichte, *Discours a la Nation Allemande*, trad. S. Jankelevitch (Paris: Aubier, 1981).

15. An inclusive theory of the state that united state with society was rooted in Roman law: "Etat et peuple sont des équivalent" was the common slogan. Nationalism is only the latest version of this theory of equivalence. Blandine Barret-Kriegel, *Les Chemins de L'état* (Paris: Calman-lévy, 1986).

16. Hegel, p. 80.

17. Fichte, p. 80 (my translation).

18. Herman Strasser and Susan C. Randall, "The Use of the Organismic Model and Its Consequences," in Strasser and Randall (eds.), *An Introduction to Theories of Social Change* (London: Routledge & Keegan Paul, 1981).

19. W.V. Quine, *Theories and Things* (Cambridge, MA: The Belknap Press of Harvard University Press, 1981), p. 9.

20. Emile Durkheim, *Les Regles de la Methode Sociologique* (Paris: PUF, 1937).

21. Michael Mann, *The Sources of Social Power, Vol. I: A history of power from the beginning to A.D. 1760* (Cambridge: Cambridge University Press, 1986), pp. 1–2.

22. Randall Collins, "A Comparative Approach to Political Sociology," in Reinhard Bendix ed., *State and Society: A Reader in Comparative Political Sociology* (Boston: Little, Brown and Company, 1968).

23. On Jacques Lacan's concepts of the Real, the Imagined, and the Symbolic, see Gerald Hall, "The Logical Typing of the Symbolic, the Imaginary, and the Real," in Anthony Wilden, *System and Structure: Essays in Communication and Exchange* (London: Tavistock, 1972) and Ronen Palan, "Recasting Political Authority: State and Globalization," in Randall Germain ed., *Globalization and Its Critiques* (London: Routledge, 1997).

24. Meyer Fortes, *Kinship and the Social Order: The Legacy of Lewis Henry Morgan* (London: Routledge & Keegan Paul, [1936] 1969).

25. Fernand Braudel, *Civilisation and Capitalism, 15th–18th Century* (New York: Harper & Row, 1979) II, p. 515.

26. Richard D. Auster and Morris Silver, *The State as a Firm: Economic Forces in Political Development* (Boston: Martin Nijhoff, 1979), pp. 7, 21.

27. Michael E. Porter, *The Competitive Advantage of Nations* (London: Macmillan, 1990).

28. Morton Mintz and Jerry S. Cohen, *Power, Inc.: Public and Private Rulers and How To Make Them Accountable* (New York: Viking, 1976).

PART TWO

TECHNOLOGY, DISCOURSE, AND
GLOBAL GOVERNANCE

CHAPTER 4

Environmental Remote Sensing, Global Governance, and the Territorial State

KAREN T. LITFIN

Global ecological interdependence is not just a physical phenomenon, but is socially constructed through multiple struggles over contested knowledge claims. Epistemic authority, or the ability to make knowledge claims that are perceived to be legitimate, is therefore a crucial element in emerging patterns of global governance with respect to environmental problems. Moreover, the gathering of environmental data and its translation into useable knowledge are mediated by technologies of varying scale, scope, and sophistication, and these technologies are never neutral tools. Rather, they should be seen as power/knowledge complexes which embody political cultures and are closely tied to concrete material and ideological interests. Technologies of knowledge production are therefore not only key political assets in agenda setting and policy formulation, but they also promote certain actors and discourses as authoritative in the evolution of global governance.

Increasingly, the information that guides environmental decision making—locally, nationally, and globally—is being obtained through space-based instruments orbiting Earth on satellites. Earth remote sensing (ERS) can generate data on an enormous range of issues, including forest cover, the health of crops, atmospheric concentrations of many pollutants, drought conditions, crisis monitoring, resettlement of refugees, storm warnings, and the locations of many resources, from drinking water to petroleum and mineral deposits, to endangered species.[1] During the 1990s, approximately fifty Earth observation satellites will be launched by the spacefaring nations of the world. NASA's Earth Observing System (EOS), with a pricetag of roughly $40 billion, will be by far the largest of these ERS projects.[2] These satellites will generate unprecedented quantities of data, which will be incorporated into databases and computer-based image manipulation and analysis. This marriage of satellite and computer technology, sometimes referred to as "geomatics," will "make possible quantum leaps in the ability to observe and understand Earth."[3] Computer-driven cartography, it has been said, is leading to "the greatest explosion in mapping and perhaps the greatest consideration of space" since the times of Babylon.[4] Mapping and surveillance have been central to the production of political order and authority throughout the ages, and this is no less so under current patterns of globalization. While ERS technologies are substantially controlled by states, the information generated by them is empowering nonstate actors in some surprising ways, thereby creating new patterns of epistemic authority.

Earth remote sensing and its derivative geomatics are not only useful tools, they are also power/knowledge complexes whose political and social implications have gone largely unexamined. The apparently ubiquitous applicability of ERS technologies, which lends them the guise of the ultimate all-purpose neutral tools, may also impede serious analysis of them as power/knowledge constructs. This chapter examines three attributes of these technologies—their transparency, their globality, and their high-tech nature—in order to begin to map out an understanding of their role in global governance. In particular, it asks whether ERS technology poses any significant challenge to the epistemic authority of the state.

The implications of ERS for the territorial state are not altogether obvious, although the balance of the evidence suggests that these technologies serve to undercut the state's quasi monopoly on epistemic authority for global environmental governance. On the one hand, as a manifestation of Big Science and a supplier of information as a public good, ERS simultaneously relies upon and supports the role of the state. As both Anthony Giddens and Michel Foucault have argued, surveillance technologies have been the basis for the state's administrative power throughout the modern era.[5] Indeed, *statistics* and *state* even come from the same root (Latin, "to stand") and, not coincidentally, the large-scale collection of statistics began with the emergence of the modern state.[6] Not surprisingly, satellite technologies were first employed by the militaries of the two superpowers in the name of national security, and the state remains the primary producer of satellite-based information.

On the other hand, as the range of applications and the number of users have grown exponentially in the past two decades, satellite technology increasingly lends itself to forms of global governance which exceed traditional state-based forms of politics. Today's users include multinational corporations, scientists, policy makers, grassroots environmental groups, and indigenous peoples. The multibillion dollar industries of satellite communications and geographical information services (GIS) now dwarf the military uses of satellites.[7] The loosely coordinated international global change research program, which relies primarily on satellite observations for its data, is likely to become the largest research project in human history, despite the prevailing budget-cutting mood of many governments.[8] Information gathered through ERS will be a key source of epistemic authority applied by diverse sets of actors to highly politicized purposes, including assigning responsibility for environmental degradation and other dimensions of global governance.

In this chapter, I first describe the technologies in question, after which I examine the relationship of ERS to the state's claim to territorial exclusivity, and then turn my attention to the impact of ERS technologies on the global power/knowledge nexus. While I do not draw any grandiose conclusions about the ability of satellite technology, in and of itself, to fundamentally challenge the nation-state system, I do find evidence to support the claim that ERS technologies are facilitating the emergence of alternative patterns of global governance. Whether those patterns of governance fostered by ERS technologies tend to move in the direction of participatory politics or towards the greater monopolization of power and wealth cannot be discerned at this point, although there is evidence to support either claim.

ERS AND RELATED TECHNOLOGIES

Geomatics is the new term for the enhancement of traditional mapping methodologies by advanced information technologies for the recording, storage, and manipulation of geographical imagery.[9] Geomatics is comprised of three sets of technologies: remote sensing data delivery systems, the global positioning system (GPS), and geographic information systems (GIS). While aerial imaging, especially conventional aerial photography, can be an important source of data for some local applications, satellite-based remote sensing systems are the primary source of geographical data on a global scale. Thus geomatics, fundamentally based upon satellite technologies and inherently global in scope, is becoming a key source of epistemic authority for global governance on environmental issues.

The GPS is a web of twenty-four navigation satellites originally deployed by the US Navy as a navigational tool to help submarines to locate themselves and travel between points. A GPS receiver, which operates like a transistor radio, receives signals from three or four satellites, computes its triangulated position, and displays it as longitudinal, latitudinal, and possibly altitudinal coordinates. While GPS receivers are supposed to be accurate to thirty meters, the Pentagon may degrade signals substantially for national security purposes.[10] Their accuracy can be improved by using multiple systems or by coupling GPS with other technologies which are becoming less expensive.

GIS technologies range from relatively cheap and unsophisticated PC-based software packages for image manipulation and map production to advanced analytical technologies capable of correlating and manipulating many layers of geographical information. The diverse and rapidly proliferating users of GIS include researchers in government and university as well as local communities and indigenous peoples. But it is geodemographics, a powerful marketing tool which helps businesses to "know everything about their consumers," which is the fastest-growing segment of the GIS industry.[11] Most important from an environmental perspective, GIS technologies will be key to making the vast quantities of data generated by Earth-observing satellites in the coming years useable.

The US led the way in deploying Earth-observing satellites for civilian purposes, launching the moderate-resolution satellite which became known as Landsat in 1972. Landsat generates images in four spectral bands which cover a wide area (160 km × 160 km) at a ground resolution of thirty meters. The resolution of an image is the size at which objects become recognizable; images from military reconnaissance satellites generally have resolutions of less than ten meters. The French SPOT (Systeme Probatoire d'Observation de la Terre), launched in 1985, returns 36 km × 36 km images to Earth with ground resolutions of twenty meters in color and ten meters in black and white. While both SPOT and Landsat images are retrievable in real time, a Russian system uses conventional camera film which must be transported to Earth for processing. In the late 1980s, a Russian consortium, Soyuzkarta, began marketing that system's images, whose resolution is even higher (between two and five meters). Within the last year, Canada launched its RADARSAT, whose images are similar to those generated by SPOT, but which has the ability to "see" below cloud cover. Even at a cost of $2,000 to $6,000, the price of satellite-generated images does not come close to covering the capital investment in the systems. By themselves, ERS images are not particularly useful. Thus a burgeoning value-added industry has sprung up around the interpretation of satellite data.[12]

Because ERS and its related geomatic technologies are new and perhaps revolutionary, their long-term implications for science and the global control and distribution of information cannot be predicted with any degree of accuracy. Nonetheless, certain motifs are already visible. The global view and the transparency furnished by ERS technologies pose a serious challenge to the state's control over information about events and processes within its own borders. Although the sophisticated nature of ERS and associated technologies may render them useable primarily by the technical elite, the club of users turns out to be surprisingly diverse.

THE TERRITORIAL STATE

There is perhaps no form of technology better suited to exemplify the "unbundling of territoriality" than ERS, which inherently erases territorial boundaries by virtue of the global scope of both its observations and its diffusion of information through value-added technologies.[13] Yet while the transparency rendered by ERS no doubt undercuts the principle of territorial exclusivity (and this may indeed be its primary effect), ERS technology also may reinforce state control and authority in some surprising ways. In this section, I explore the impact of the diffusion of ERS technologies on the territorial state. I first examine the intersection of traditional national security and the new environmental applications of military photo reconnaissance. I then look at the specific concerns of developing countries, after which I turn to the very different concerns of the US with respect to the globalization of ERS technologies.

FROM SPY SATELLITES TO ECOLOGICAL MONITORING

The early space age, which gave birth to ERS technologies, was characterized by fierce national competition. For the superpowers, and to a lesser extent for the latecomers to space technology, large-scale space programs were potent symbols of national prestige and crucial guarantors of national security.[14] Military reconnaissance came to be viewed as a staple in the superpowers' exercise of territorial sovereignty; knowing the adversary's military and industrial capabilities was seen as essential to preventing foreign intervention. Paradoxically, just as the mutual acquisition of nuclear weapons by the superpowers rendered those weapons effectively unuseable, the mutual acquisition of satellite reconnaissance technology rendered the state's territorial space utterly transparent. While satellites may have offered some protection against military intervention, they opened the door to visual intervention even as they bolstered the epistemic authority of the state.

Even today, with international cooperation and the proliferation of commercial and scientific satellite data, the technology's military roots are continually evident. Military agencies still control the lion's share of high-resolution satellite imagery and are reluctant to share it. Under pressure to redefine their post-Cold War mission, the superpower militaries have become involved in environmental research.[15] For decades, the security forces of both superpowers did a good deal of inadvertent environmental research, which scientists now are slowly beginning to acquire.[16] Yet, in a profound clash of cultures, the highly secretive nature of the military is notably at odds with the expectations and conventions of both commercial and research partners.[17] At stake is the principle of territorial exclusivity in a world rendered transparent by satellite technology. The most recent example of the greening of military reconnaissance is the US MEDEA project (Measurements of Earth Data for Environmental Analysis), spearheaded by Vice President Al Gore and coordinated by the Central Intelligence Agency. This project will use high-resolution spy satellites to monitor about five hundred ecologically sensitive sites around the world over a period of decades. The data, however, will only be accessible to scientists in future generations and will remain secret for now in order to conceal the technical abilities of US reconnaissance systems.[18]

This tension between conventional national security and scientific interests reflects the incongruity of the nonterritorial nature of outer space in a world of sovereign states. While the air space above a state's territory lies under that state's jurisdiction, the space above the earth's atmosphere (outer space) was declared in the 1966 Outer Space Treaty to be a res communis, or the common province of humanity.[19] The prohibition of territorial claims in outer space stands in a tense relationship with the efforts of states to enhance their own security through the use of satellites stationed in nonterritorial space. Given the military's leadership role and the resources required to conduct space activities, space issues would seem to reinforce the nation-state model of international relations. Yet the nonterritorial nature of the arena of space activities may serve as a harbinger for challenging traditional notions of territorial exclusivity and the state's privileged claims to epistemic authority.[20]

Questions of epistemic authority, framed in terms of territorial sovereignty, were hotly debated during the negotiations on both the use of geosynchronous orbits and the principles governing the use of satellites in television broadcasting. In both cases, the principle of nonterritoriality prevailed, with implications for environmental remote sensing. In the 1976 Bogota Declaration, the equatorial nations argued that their sovereignty extended 22,300 miles up to the prized geosynchronous orbits over their territories. They argued that the existence of the orbit depended upon the Earth's gravity, was therefore a "physical fact linked" to the planet, and was thus subject to national sovereignty.[21] A majority of the UN General Assembly, however, rejected this interpretation, and the coveted geostationary orbits became part of outer space.

In a similar debate over the territorial status of outer space, the former Soviet bloc and most developing countries held that lack of control over direct broadcasting within their territories would amount to cultural imperialism. The US freedom-of-information perspective, however, premised upon the "global commons" status of outer space, ultimately prevailed.[22] These two outcomes, upholding the nonterritorial character of outer space, have some important implications for ERS. If states may not claim territorial jurisdiction over the orbits overhead, then their claims regarding the right to control images and data gathered from the satellites stationed in those orbits are substantially weakened. The availability of satellite data to nonstate actors thereby challenges that state's epistemic authority.

THE AMBIGUOUS STATUS OF DEVELOPING COUNTRIES' EPISTEMIC AUTHORITY

Beginning in the 1970s, countries without access to satellite technology suspected that an open skies policy with respect to ERS might violate their territorial integrity. Although they may have harbored such fears earlier with respect to spy satellites, the fact that superpower images were not available on the commercial market was a source of comfort. Consequently, when NASA espoused an open skies policy with its first launch of the Earth Resources Technology Satellite (later renamed Landsat), some Latin American countries countered that their sovereignty over natural resources extended to the dissemination of information about them. Mexico, for instance, declared that "no data would be collected over Mexican territory from air or space without prior permission."[23] NASA's response was threefold. First, it argued from international law that there were no legal restrictions on the use of ERS for peaceful purposes. Second, it labeled Landsat an "experimental," rather than an "operational," project until the 1980s. Third, and most effectively, it held out the enticing promise to developing countries that the open dissemination of satellite data would extend, not reduce, their ability to control the development of their resources. To add credence to that promise, NASA established an educational program to train scientists from developing countries to use ERS data.[24]

Indeed, some countries concluded that transparency and the global diffusion of data could actually reinforce their ability to make legitimate knowledge claims, with the practical effect of enhancing their territorial sovereignty. By 1980, ten countries had built ground stations and were committed to paying NASA an annual fee of $200,000 for data transmission; dozens more were purchasing Landsat images and data tapes. For example, Brazil reported that the first Landsat images resulted in the discovery of several large islands within its territory and a major rectification of Amazon tributaries on its maps. The US Embassy in Mali reported that "the U.S. government has gained a million dollars worth of Malian political mileage" from Landsat.[25]

Satellite data, then, may help to prepare a given territory for the exercise of sovereignty and thereby enhance the state's epistemic authority. Nature is not inherently constituted as an object of state sovereignty, but is rather socially constructed as "territory."[26] Mapping is a crucial element in this social construction. There are no lines of latitude and longitude in nature; overlying the globe with this symbolic organization imposes an artificial order and serves specific political and economic purposes. Thus cartography has been labeled "the science of princes." As geographer J. B. Harley notes, there is plenty of evidence that " 'explorers', terrestrial and intellectual, must align their professional and personal ambitions with wealthy and powerful nations, which can afford the expeditions (or 'experiments') that chart and stake a claim to new territories."[27] The burgeoning application of GIS technologies, which use space as a common key between sets of satellite data, can strengthen territorial claims in countries with isolated areas. Thus, the utility of ERS data for mapping and locating resources suggests that the logic of satellites does not always run contrary to the principle of territorial exclusivity, and may in fact fortify the state's control over its territory.

Despite these benefits, developing countries have not always been satisfied with their role in the emerging ERS regime. By the early 1980s, developing countries were concerned with preserving open and nondiscriminatory distribution of Landsat data, which was threatened by the Reagan administration's move to privatize Landsat.[28] Many observers believed that Landsat data should remain a public service, analogous to census, cartographic, and meteorological data; several studies concluded that Landsat could not be successfully commercialized. Despite the objections, control over Landsat's data was given to EOSAT, a joint venture of Hughes Aircraft and General Electric, under the Land Remote Sensing Commercialization Act of 1984.[29] One of EOSAT's first acts, which was greatly resented by scientists as well as developing countries, was to quadruple the price of each Landsat image.[30]

Cost is just one of the factors limiting the utility of ERS data, both from Landsat and SPOT, in developing countries. Because ERS is fundamentally a high-tech endeavor based in the industrialized countries, its use elsewhere entails a host of complex technology transfer issues. The use of ERS data requires skills in photogrammetry and computing which are scarce in most developing countries. As a first step in overcoming this problem, the United Nations has initiated Centres for Space Science and Technology Education on a regional basis in developing countries.[31] Yet since commercial ERS programs tend to be designed with the needs of paying customers—primarily multinational agricultural, mining, and oil exploration companies—in mind, ERS data continue to remain inaccessible to potential beneficiaries.[32] For instance, the public health sector, which could employ this technology to combat many diseases, has enjoyed little access to ERS data.[33] Nor do the large global change research programs that rely upon ERS data emphasize the kinds of information on land use and ecological change that are most urgently needed in developing countries.[34] The tensions in US-Brazilian climate research, for instance, have motivated Brazil to expand its own space capabilities and to broaden its international sources of data.[35]

With the exception of India, China, and Brazil, which have built their own ERS systems, all other developing countries have depended on imagery from Landsat, NOAA, or SPOT satellites.[36] Because of dissatisfaction among developing countries with existing arrangements, the United Nations Committee on the Peaceful Uses of Outer Space (COPUOS) has emerged as a champion for their interests. In 1991, several developing countries submitted a working paper to the Legal Subcommittee of

COPUOS arguing for a kind of affirmative action program, expressed in a new treaty, for developing countries with respect to space technology.[37] They based their position on Article I of the 1966 Outer Space Treaty, which states that the use of outer space "shall be carried out for the benefit and in the interest of all countries, irrespective of their degree of economic or scientific development, and shall be the province of all mankind." In order for all countries to share equitably in the benefits of space technology, including ERS programs, developing countries insisted that international cooperation must be based on a system of preferential treatment for developing countries. They also referred to the Principles on Remote Sensing of the Earth from Outer Space, adopted by the UN in 1986, which call for international cooperation in the use of ERS technologies.[38] Thus, taking a notably different tack than they had in the 1970s debate over the territoriality of satellite orbits, the developing countries attempted to use the common property argument on their own behalf.

The US and the UK, however, used a traditional sovereignty argument to counter the developing countries and thereby bolster their epistemic authority. Attempting to appease them, on the one hand, they cited many examples of bilateral and multilateral programs in space technology. On the other hand, however, they claimed that any attempt to impose legal obligations for cooperation would weaken states' abilities to exercise sovereignty when deciding which cooperative programs to enter into. The developing countries split ranks when Brazil and Nigeria concurred with this line of argument, scuttling efforts to negotiate a new treaty. The effort may have been successful, though, in serving notice to the space powers that they should work harder to ensure that ERS and other forms of space technology benefit the developing countries.

Developing countries have apparently embraced ERS, but not without some reservations about the technology's impact on their epistemic authority and territorial sovereignty. One feature of ERS is its dual role in providing an information base and as a technology for monitoring. Sovereignty has traditionally been invoked to shield states from external intrusion, yet satellites render territory effectively naked.[39] Compliance with international environmental agreements has tended to be voluntary, with nongovernmental organizations frequently functioning in a watchdog capacity. When mandated, verification of compliance has generally proceeded through self-reporting. Thus, certain developing countries have expressed the concern that ERS could foster "green conditionality" and other types of "eco-imperialism." Just as satellites can be used to monitor treaty compliance, so too can they be used for industrial espionage. Some observers believe that "in the future, commercial remote sensors will not only be able to detect pollutants leaving a factory, but determine what a factory is producing."[40] Consequently, developing countries have insisted that recent announcements contain no references to the use of ERS for "monitoring," but only for "observation."

INDUSTRIAL COMPETITIVENESS AND THE EROSION OF U.S. EPISTEMIC AUTHORITY

Yet it has been primarily the US, not the developing countries, which has sought to place restrictions on ERS data and technology in the name of territorial sovereignty. The US restrictions harken back to ERS's roots in military reconnaissance. In 1978, President Carter upheld the Pentagon's interests over NASA's by signing a directive that set ten meters as the resolution limit for nonmilitary remote sensing.[41] But the entry of SPOT, with a resolution of ten meters, and the Soviet satellite photographs of roughly five meters, soon made this rule essentially obsolete. The Reagan administration deleted the rule in 1988 after being persuaded that it put American satellite operators, especially the now-privatized Landsat data marketing firm, at a disadvantage. In an effort to uphold traditional national security interests, the new directive granted veto power to the secretaries of Defense and State over the licensing of US commercial remote sensing satellites.[42] But US officials were at a loss to describe how they would enforce a ban on the dissemination of pictures from space, since the US no longer enjoyed a monopoly on Earth-scanning satellites even in the west. And, of course, the most likely beneficiaries of tight American regulations would be foreign satellite operators. As a SPOT spokesperson observed, "Open skies, open access is a precondition of commercial success in the remote-sensing industry."[43] The Clinton administration has essentially upheld the Reagan rule, with the important amendment that licensing applications for ERS systems whose capabilities are already available or are in the planning stages would be favorably considered.[44]

The emergence of high resolution satellite imagery on the world market provides an interesting example of how state practices can be driven by technological developments and globalization. It makes little sense to place domestic restrictions on high-resolution data which are easily accessible from foreign suppliers. A technology that cannot be controlled by a single government is impossible to contain; satellite images can only be suppressed if the data are sent to a ground station under control of the censoring government. Consequently, in the case of the US, the state has been compelled to acquiesce in the erosion of its

own epistemic authority and to revise its conceptions of national security in the name of industrial competitiveness.

It might be an overstatement to declare, as some have, that satellites have "abolished the concept of distance," but it is certainly the case
that the practices associated with territorial exclusivity are being re-
vised.[45] There is no single, straightforward logic to ERS technology.
Certainly, it still bears the imprint of its origins in military reconnaissance and the protection of the superpowers' territorial integrity. Moreover, ERS is being used by some developing countries to expand and
reinforce their territorial claims. Yet, the emergence of ERS data on the
world market has dramatically eroded the ability of states to control
information about the resources within their borders. The almost universal availability of ERS data has rendered much of the world transparent, and its global nature may be undercutting the characteristically
modern conceptualization of Earth as territorially demarcated.

In the following section, I address the question of whether there is a
distinctive logic of ERS as a power/knowledge nexus which tends to legitimate certain knowledge claims and certain political actors over others.

THE POWER/KNOWLEDGE NEXUS

Because of its central role in the dissemination of knowledge about
Earth, the most interesting political questions involving ERS technology
are about epistemic authority, or the ability to make legitimate knowledge claims. The control of knowledge and the purposes to which
knowledge is applied are therefore paramount political issues in the
globalization of environmental governance. Information has inherent
public-goods attributes, so that governments are likely to continue to
play a significant role in ERS funding and application.[46] While information is "slippery" by nature, its close relationship to power kindles
many conflicts over the control of ERS data.

Conflicts over the control of ERS data abound. Developing countries' lack of confidence in an uninterrupted supply of ERS data from
the US, particularly after the privatization of Landsat, has led the largest of them to build their own remote-sensing satellites.[47] Researchers
have harbored similar sentiments, but they lack the option of building
their own satellites. According to one scientist, the tenfold increase in
the cost of Landsat data after privatization over the 1970s price effectively impeded a good deal of scientific research.[48] Both government

agencies and scientific researchers feel that commercialization threatens their access to data. SPOT, for instance, implemented a policy in 1989 of giving preferential service to its largest customers, the oil and mining industries, potentially placing certain government agencies at a disadvantage in obtaining urgently needed data.[49] More recently, European governments have threatened to launch a "data war" by attempting to restrict commercial access to ERS data from weather satellites. Their moves have inflamed researchers, who claim that scientific and commercially data are not easily distinguishable.[50] All of these conflicts are essentially about epistemic authority in a global information age.

New technologies do not emerge as neutral tools; rather, they arise in a context of ongoing struggles for control and authority, amplifying certain voices and inhibiting others. Any technology as useful as ERS is inevitably contentious. Is there, then, a distinctive logic to ERS as a power/knowledge complex that tends to legitimize or empower certain voices over others? If knowledge is a preeminent source of power in late modernity, then what do the globality, the transparency, and the high-tech nature of ERS entail for the distribution of social and political power? These questions can be asked in the context of two fundamental tensions implicit in ERS as a power/knowledge complex: expert/nonexpert and local/global.

At first glance, the logic underlying ERS appears to be profoundly technocratic. The skills required to operate satellites and sensors, and to decipher ERS data and imagery, are concentrated in the hands of "high priests" who are generally white, male citizens of industrialized countries.[51] At times, ERS experts sound very much like technocratic zealots. Space technology is said to offer "unlimited perspectives on ourselves, the world, and the cosmos around us."[52] One champion of ERS technology even suggests that human survival depends upon Earth Science, which relies primarily upon satellite imagery:

> The great opportunity for progress in the world in the 20th century was physics, which built the world we live in. The great opportunity for creative progress in the next century will be Earth Science. It will determine if humankind is in the universe to stay.[53]

As ERS capabilities expand, such sentiments may become even more prevalent. New ERS systems, for instance, can incorporate "cloud editing," the capability to detect clouds, remember where they are and replace them with clear data later.[54]

While the technocratic potential of ERS may be evident, other forces could compel the architects of ERS technology to become more accountable to the users. Even if many users appear to be "high priests," the very multiplicity of their voices suggests the potential for a diffusion of power along multiple channels. The state may be an important channel, but it is neither the only one nor a univocal one. As Big Science projects lose their appeal in a time of budgetary conservatism, and as their prestige value is diminished with the end of the Cold War, space agencies must increasingly justify ERS programs in terms of their users' requirements. One space scientist calls this a "thoroughly post-modern approach," stating that "No longer will the development of new technology be driven by an elite of scientists and engineers, but a broader base of consultation will be required with the many user constituencies."[55]

As a multifaceted power/knowledge complex, ERS incorporates sometimes contradictory tendencies. On the one hand, the global view afforded from the vantage point of space seems especially conducive to notions of "planetary management" and the centralization of power. Indeed, in the discourse surrounding ERS, terms like "managing the planet" and "global management" abound.[56] Yet global science is inherently decentralized, depending upon "countless loosely knit and continually shifting networks of individual researchers—most of whom resist outside intervention—in communication that crisscrosses the borders of well over a hundred sovereign nations."[57] The decentralized nature of global science is likely to have important social and political implications for efforts to cope with global ecological interdependence.

While the global science based upon ERS data has many of the earmarks of a mammoth technocratic enterprise, it is not immune to public opinion; nor are its fruits available only to the elite. For instance, NASA's Mission to Planet Earth program was conceived as a vehicle for restoring the confidence of the American public, newly concerned about the environment, in the space agency after the Challenger disaster.[58] Even in Japan, popular environmental concern shifted the emphasis of its Earth resources spacecraft, ADEOS, away from pure research objectives.[59] In the future, ERS satellite systems could provide citizen groups with the means to verify compliance not only with environmental treaties, but with arms control treaties as well, with potentially interesting ramifications for the globalization of participatory democracy. Thus, ERS may contribute to the decentralization of epistemic authority on a global scale, indicating that global governance may not be as monolithic an enterprise as it sounds.

Moreover, ERS data can facilitate the localization of control in some surprising ways. Perhaps most interesting is the use of satellite data by indigenous peoples for mapping their customary land rights and documenting the role of the state and multinational corporations in environmental destruction. Environmental advocacy groups and indigenous rights groups in Indonesia, Nepal, Thailand, and the Pacific Northwest are using satellite-generated data to reterritorialize their political practices to an extent previously inconceivable.[60] Although ERS data may deterritorialize political practice at the level of the nation-state, when used for "counter mapping" by indigenous peoples it seems to be have exactly the opposite effect.[61] We should note, however, that while spatial information technologies may facilitate claims of local people against the state, that power "comes with a price—it destroys the fluid and flexible nature of their traditional perimeters."[62] The democratization of epistemic authority through the use of ERS data validates a particular technologically mediated perspective on the natural world.

The use of ERS data in developing countries raises complex cultural, political, and ethical issues, and the technology is not without its critics. For instance, Masahide Kato criticizes nonprofit groups based in industrialized countries who supply satellite-generated information to remote areas of developing countries. He believes they represent a new form of imperialism rooted in a "globalist technosubjectivity" which renders the indigenous peoples' territory as resources.[63] Indeed, satellites seem to offer the tantalizing prospect of a totalizing knowledge; as one early enthusiast proclaimed, they "show vast terrains in correct perspective, from one viewpoint, and at one moment in time."[64] Not surprisingly, that "one viewpoint" is generally located in the North. Moreover, that "one moment in time" cannot capture centuries of past environmental abuse, a fact which may prove profoundly disadvantageous for developing countries when ERS data are used to assign responsibility for ecological degradation.[65]

While Kato perhaps too quickly condemns ERS technology, which we have seen can also be used to promote the interests of local communities and indigenous groups, his critique reveals two interrelated questions regarding the political culture of epistemic authority implicit in ERS technologies: the control of knowledge (who controls it and for what purposes) and the constitution of knowledge (what counts as knowledge). One point seems unassailable: by employing ERS data, environmental and indigenous rights groups legitimize it as a source of credible knowledge. This is the price paid when local communities gain the mantle of scientific objectivity by transposing their traditional practices into the language of GIS. The kind of knowledge supplied by ERS technologies, it may be argued, promotes precisely the impersonality and technological rationalism which are the defining traits of modernity and which have been a primary source of environmental destruction.

Moreover, the voyeuristic nature of photography, including satellite imagery, may promote a view of nature that is antithetical to the ecological goals of grassroots groups. In her famous essay, *On Photography*, Susan Sontag has argued that "cameras implement the instrumental view of reality. [They] arm vision in the service of power—of the state, of industry, of science."[66] Space-based Earth observation represents the ultimate Panopticon, whereby the gaze of disciplinary power is globalized and internalized in people's consciousness everywhere.[67] Yet some grassroots groups are wagering that ERS can also "arm vision in the service of power" at the local level. Their efforts are perhaps too recent for us to draw any decisive conclusions.

Users of satellite-generated Earth data have powerful cultural and rhetorical tools on their side—specifically Enlightenment ideals about the liberating power of knowledge. According to one commentator, programs employing ERS information should be based on the premise that "greater knowledge leads to greater wisdom," a premise that is at least debatable.[68] But if the link between knowledge and wisdom is weak, the link between knowledge and power may be more tenable. Indeed a core assumption of the architects of ERS systems is that they offer "a whole new tool with which to understand our own world, and once we understand it, we can manage it."[69] Such statements seem to presuppose a specifically modern conception of agency and responsibility, with a rational, autonomous self capable of knowing (and thereby controlling) the Other embodied in the natural "environment." Nonetheless, if this hallmark of modernity is actually at the root of the global environmental crisis, then the faith in ERS technology may be fundamentally misplaced.

Given the deep entrenchment of the knowledge/power nexus as a cultural cornerstone of modernity, to question the need for information approaches heresy. Yet, given the stakes, one must wonder just what practical results the information generated by ERS will yield. NASA's Earth Observing System (EOS) will produce an unprecedented quantity of data, at a cost of perhaps $20 billion; its data information system (EOSDIS) will be the largest data handling system ever constructed, with a capacity of fourteen petabytes (a petabyte is 10^{15} bytes, or one billion megabytes).[70] The primary purpose of this information is to guide policy makers in addressing global climate change. Given that less than five percent of Landsat's data has ever been used, one might anticipate that ERS will generate more information overload than wisdom.[71] According to the World Meteorological Organization, a satellite-based Global Climate Observing System, with EOS as its core, "will require substantial resources, but the costs to society from continuing the present level of uncertainty about climate change are very much larger."[72] What those costs are, who bears them, and how ERS data will decrease them, are not discussed.

The assumption has been that ERS data, augmented by better computer models, will reduce the uncertainties surrounding climate change and serve as a guide to rational action. Yet the recent IPCC (Intergovernmental Panel on Climate Change) scientific assessment has substantially undermined the claim that there is too much uncertainty to take decisive action. While the 1990 IPCC assessment concluded that it was too early to say whether climate change was underway, the 1995 report concludes that "the balance of evidence suggests a discernible human influence on global climate."[73] That assessment, which took two years to complete and involved more than two thousand scientists worldwide, provides the scientific grounds for a major shift in the policy discourse towards the serious consideration of fossil fuel alternatives and other mitigation strategies. The contribution of ERS data to that discourse is far from clear, but to the extent that its link to the policy discourse goes unexamined, ERS runs the risk of falling prey to the "technological imperative" of innovation for its own sake.[74]

A global ERS system is expected to provide "the long-term measurements to determine the habitability of the Earth."[75] Yet if our planet's habitability is truly at risk, then the more fundamental questions should be how to act under uncertainty, not how to "build a comprehensive predictive model of the Earth's physical, chemical, and biological processes."[76] Will the knowledge gained through ERS technology tell us how to live sustainably? The answer to the question will depend not only upon who uses the information and to what purposes it is applied, but also upon a willingness to uncover the hidden assumptions in the celebratory discourse surrounding ERS. In others words, the patterns of epistemic authority which ERS promotes must be uncovered and interrogated.

CONCLUSION

The transparency, globality, and technological sophistication associated with ERS technologies entail multiple and sometimes contradictory implications for epistemic authority in the emerging global knowledge structure. There is no single political logic for ERS as a power/knowledge complex, partly because technologies tend not to be monolithic cultural constructs. In many ways, ERS stands at the intersection between modernity and postmodernity. First, ERS is fundamentally an information-age technology, with all the concomitant implications for the power/knowledge nexus that arise when data, along with their interpretation and control, become the currency of power. The world of ERS is a world of representation, where manipulable signs and images constitute nature as object.

Second, ERS contributes to the unbundling, but not the abolition, of territoriality. While the transparency and globality associated with ERS technologies very often deterritorialize state practices, they are also capable of bolstering the state's territorial control, even for developing countries. Most ERS technologies and data remain under the control of the state, not nonstate actors. Yet information is slippery, and ERS data appears to be helping local environmental and indigenous groups to reterritorialize their political practices in ways that challenge the state, thereby reconfiguring epistemic authority.

If modernity is interpreted as the enclosure of the globe via the twin institutions of private property and the territorial exclusivity of the state, then ERS technologies at once epitomize and challenge that trend. On the one hand, by making visible the invisible, satellite imagery renders nature subject to claims of ownership and control, thus reinforcing the patterns of epistemic authority associated with modernity. On the other hand, in light of the globality and transparency inherent in ERS technologies and the diffusion of geomatics to nonstate actors, ERS has the potential to become a tool in the revisioning of nature as a global commons and the repatterning of epistemic authority beyond the territorial state. In either case, ERS technologies will be a key factor in the unfolding structures and institutions of global environmental governance in the coming decades.

NOTES

I am grateful to Raymond Duvall, Martin Hewson, Judith Mayer, and James Rosenau for their helpful comments on earlier drafts of this chapter. Some of the material from this chapter is included in my article, "The Status of the Statistical State: Satellites and the Diffusion of Epistemic Sovereignty," *Global Society* 12, 2 (May 1998).

1. Committee on Earth Observation Satellites (CEOS), "The Relevance of Satellite Missions to the Study of the Global Environment," produced for the

UNCED conference at Rio de Janeiro (Washington, DC: CEOS, 1992). On the multitude of uses for ERS, see Doug Stewart, "Eyes in Orbit Keep Tabs on the World in Unexpected Ways," *Smithsonian* 19 (December 1988), pp. 70–76.

2. "A Survey of Space: The Uses of Heaven," *The Economist* (June 15, 1991), p. 17.

3. Branislav Gosovic, *The Quest for World Environmental Cooperation: The Case of the UN Global Environmental Monitoring System* (London: Routledge, 1992), p. 119.

4. Stephen S. Hall, *Mapping the Next Millennium: How Computer-Driven Cartography Is Revolutionizing the Face of Science* (New York: Vintage, 1993), p. 8.

5. Anthony Giddens, *The Nation-State and Violence* (Berkeley and Los Angeles: University of California Press, 1987), pp. 52, 309; Michel Foucault, *Discipline and Punish: The Birth of the Prison* (New York: Vintage, 1979).

6. Peter J. Taylor and Ronald J. Johnston, "Geographical Information Systems and Geography," in John Pickles, ed., *Ground Truth: The Social Implications of Geographical Information Systems* (New York: The Guilford Press, 1995).

7. Joseph N. Pelton, "Organizing Large Scale Space Activities: Why the Private Sector Model Usually Wins," *Space Policy* 8, 3 (August 1992), p. 234.

8. "A Problem as Big as a Planet," *The Economist* (5 November 1994), pp. 83–85.

9. The information in this section is drawn primarily from Peter Poole, "Guide to the Technology," in *Geomatics: Who Needs It?*, a special issue of *Cultural Survival Quarterly* (Winter 1995), pp. 16–18.

10. Irving Lachow, "The GPS Dilemma: Balancing Military Risks and Economic Benefits," *International Security* 20, 1 (Summer 1995): 126–48.

11. Jon Goss, "Marketing the New Marketing: The Strategic Discourse of Geodemographic Systems," in John Pickles, ed., *Ground Truth: The Social Implications of Geographic Information Systems* (New York: The Guilford Press, 1995), pp. 130, 132.

12. Vipin Gupta, "New Satellite Images for Sale," *International Security* 20, 1 (Summer 1995): 94–125.

13. John Gerard Ruggie, "Territoriality and Beyond: Problematizing Modernity in International Relations," *International Organization* 47, 1 (Winter 1993), p. 171.

14. Pelton, p. 242.

15. Ironically, the Russian consortium, Soyuzkarta, has made formerly top-secret high resolution imagery from Soviet military satellites available on the mass market while Americans debate the terms of US security. The end of the Cold War, however, does not spell the obsolescence of military reconnaissance. See Jeffrey T. Richelson, "The Future of Space Reconnaissance," *Scientific*

American vol. 264, no. 1 (January 1991), pp. 38–44, and John Trux, "Desert Storm: A Space Age War," *New Scientist* 27 (July 1991), pp. 30–34. On NASA's Mission to Planet Earth program and the conversion of missiles to environmental purposes, see Ann Florini and William Potter, "Goodwill Missions for Cast-off Missiles," *Bulletin of the Atomic Scientists* (November 1990), pp. 25–31.

16. Robert Dreyfuss, Spying on the Environment," *Earth Action* 6, 1 (February 1995): 28–36.

17. On the potential pitfalls of involving the military in ERS, see Ronald Diebert, "Out of Focus: U.S. Military Satellites to the Environmental Rescue," in Daniel Deudney and Richard Matthews, eds., *Contested Grounds: Security and Conflict in the New Environmental Politics* (Albany: SUNY Press, 1997).

18. William J. Broad, "U.S. Will Deploy Its Spy Satellites on Nature Mission," *New York Times* (November 27, 1995), p. A–14.

19. "Legislating the 'Last Frontier,'" *UN Chronicle* 29 (December 1992), p. 54.

20. David Green, "The Reassertion of Social Aspects of Science and Technology," *Space Policy* 10, 3 (August 1994), p. 242.

21. Carl Q. Christol, *The Modern International Law of Outer Space* (Oxford: Pergamon, 1982), p. 468, quoted in Joanne Irene Gabrynowicz, "Bringing Space Policy into the Information Age," *Space Policy* 8, 2 (May 1992), p. 168.

22. See "Legislating the 'Last Frontier,' " p. 55.

23. Pamela Mack, *Viewing the Earth: The Social Construction of the Landsat Satellite System* (Cambridge, MA: The MIT Press, 1990), p. 187.

24. David T. Lindgren, "Commercial Satellites Open Skies," *Bulletin of the Atomic Scientists* (April 1988), p. 34.

25. Mack, pp. 189–192.

26. Thom Kuehls, "The Nature of the State: An Ecological (Re)Reading of Sovereignty and Territory," in M. Ringrose and A. Lerner, eds., *Reimagining the Nation* (Buckingham: Open University Press, 1994), pp. 141–55.

27. J. B. Harley, "Maps, Knowledge, and Power," in D. Cosgrove and P. Daniels, eds., *The Iconography of the Landscape* (Cambridge: Cambridge University Press, 1988), pp. 227–312; quoted in John Pickles, "Representations in an Electronic Age: Geography, GIS, and Democracy," in Pickles, ed., *Ground Truth*, p. 21.

28. Pamela Mack, p. 188.

29. "Report Criticizes Landsat Commercialization," *Aviation Week and Space Technology* 118 (May 9, 1983), p. 18; Mack, p. 206.

30. Eliot Marshall, "Landsat: Drifting toward Oblivion?" *Science* 243 (February 24, 1989), p. 24.

31. Adgun Ade Abiodun, "An International Remote Sensing System," *Space Policy* 9, 3 (August 1993), p. 183.

32. Rheem, March 4, 1987. In 1991, British Petroleum's in-house remote sensing department maintained the largest satellite data archive in Europe; Texaco has its own remote sensing program as well. See Morgan, August 1994; BNA, June 21, 1993.

33. Peter Jovanovic, "Satellite Medicine: Space Technology in Primary Health Care," *World Health* (January 1989): 18.

34. Committee on Earth Sciences Space Studies Board, National Research Council, *Earth Observations from Space: History, Promise, and Reality* (Washington, DC: National Academy Press, 1994), p. II–5.

35. Frederic Golden, "A Catbird's Seat on Amazon Destruction: Brazil's Space Agency is Playing an Expanded Role in Monitoring the Nation's Environment," *Science* 246, 4927 (October 13, 1989): 201.

36. "Chinese Developing Satellites for Earth Resources Exploration," *Aviation Week and Space Technology* (July 22, 1985), pp. 81–84.

37. UN document A/AC.105/C.2/L.182, April 9, 1991, submitted by Argentina, Brazil, China, Mexico, Nigeria, Pakistan, the Philippines, Uruguay, and Venezuela.

38. N. Jasentuliyana, "Ensuring Equal Access to the Benefits of Space Technologies for All Countries," *Space Policy* 10, 1 (February 1994), p. 11.

39. Molly K. Macauley, "Collective Goods and National Sovereignty: Conflicting Values in Global Information Acquisition," in Proceedings of the Conference on Space Monitoring of Global Change (San Diego: Institute on Global Conflict and Cooperation, 1992), pp. 31–55.

40. Nina Morgan, "Satellites Offer Oil Companies Low-Cost Data Collection," *Petroleum Economist* 61, 8 (August 1994): 16.

41. Peter D. Zimmerman, "Photos from Space: Why Restrictions Won't Work," *Technology Review* 91 (May/June 1988), p. 48. The resolution of Landsat images at the time was 30 meters, while military reconnaissance satellites had a resolution of less than half a meter. See Nicholas Daniloff, "How We Spy on the Russians," *World Politics* Magazine (December 9, 1979), pp. 24–34.

42. Theresa M. Foley, "Pentagon, State Department Granted Veto Over U.S. Remote Sensing Satellites," *Aviation Week and Space Technology* (July 20, 1987), pp. 20–21. In an interesting twist, the Pentagon became a paying customer of SPOT for images of Soviet military installations; while it had millions of its own images, these were classified and so could not be published in its reports. See William M. Arkin, "Long on Data, Short on Intelligence," *Bulletin of the Atomic Scientists* 43, 5 (June 1987), p. 5.

43. Daniel Charles, "US Draws a Veil Over 'Open Skies,'" *New Scientist* 116, 1585 (November 5, 1987), p. 29. Many space experts have argued that commercial ERS can promote peace by lessening military secrets and by promoting the independent verification of arms control treaties. See William J. Broad, "Private Cameras in Space Stir U.S. Security Fears," *New York Times* (August 25, 1987), p. C-12; Michael Krepon, ed., *Commercial Observation Satellites and International Security* (New York: St. Martin's, 1990).

44. Office of the Press Secretary, The White House, "Foreign Access to Remote Sensing Capabilities," *Space Policy* 10, 3 (August 1994), pp. 243–44.

45. Kiran Karnik, "Remote Sensing: The Indian Experience," *UNESCO Courier* 46 (January 1993), p. 17.

46. Molly K. Macauley and Michael A. Toman, "Supplying Earth-Observation Data from Space," *Space Policy* 8, 1 (February 1992), p. 17.

47. Frederic Golden, "A Catbird's Seat on Amazon Destruction: Brazil's Space Agency is Playing an Expanded Role in Monitoring the Nation's Environment," *Science* 246, 4927 (October 13, 1989), p. 201.

48. Christopher Fotos, "Commercial Remote Sensing Satellites Generate Debate, Foreign Competition," *Aviation Week and Space Technology* 129 (December 19, 1988), pp. 49–50.

49. Spector, op cit., p. 16; Group of Experts, UNISPACE 82 Conference, "International Remote Sensing System Proposed by Experts," *UN Chronicle* 22, 2 (February 1985), p. 20.

50. Andrew Lawler, "U.S., Europe Clash over Plan to Set Policy on Data Access," *Science* 268 (April 28, 1995), p. 493.

51. David Rhind, "Geographical Information Systems and Environmental Problems," *International Social Science Journal* 43 (November 1991), p. 662.

52. L. A. Fisk, L. K. Berman, R. Brescia, A. S. McGee, and F. C. Owens, "NASA Takes Lead Role in Earth Observation," *IEEE Technology and Society Magazine* (Spring 1992), p. 11.

53. Thomas W. Becker, "Mission to Planet Earth and Global Space Education Policy," *Space Policy* 8, 2 (May 1992), p. 158. Not surprisingly, many ERS enthusiasts also advocate a crash program in the developing countries aimed at "creating a scientific outlook." See U. R. Rao, Chairman of India's Space Commission, "Space Technology in Developing Nations: An Assessment," *Space Policy* 9, 2 (May 1993), p. 169.

54. James Asker, "Smallsat Pacts Key to NASA Reform," *Aviation Week and Space Technology* 140 (June 13, 1994), p. 56.

55. Graham Harris, "Global Remote Sensing Programmes, Global Science, Global Change: An Australian Perspective," *Space Policy* 9, 2 (May 1993), p. 131. A current example is the struggle that the new one-meter systems face in winning customers who currently use airplanes for mapping or monitoring. Aerial remote-sensing involves "well ensconced relationships with a local pilot, a local customer, [and] local analytical people." See Joseph Anselmo, "High-Resolution Satellite Competition Heats Up," *Aviation Week and Space Technology* 140 (July 11, 1994), p. 56.

56. For instance, see Scientific American, *Managing Planet Earth* (New York: W. H. Freeman and Co., 1990).

57. James R. Beniger, "Information Society and Global Science," *Annals of the American Association of Political and Social Scientists* 495 (January 1988), p. 23.

58. Daniel Clery and William Brown, "Sensing Satellites: Who Calls the Tune?" *New Scientist* 130, 1767 (May 4, 1991), p. 17.

59. Hatoyama-Machi, p. 71.

60. Martua Sirait, et al., "Mapping Customary Land in East Kalimantan, Indonesia: A Tool for Forest Management," *Ambio* 23,7 (November 1994), pp. 411–17; "Cultural Survival," *Geomatics: Who Needs It?* 18,4 (Spring 1995); Jefferson Fox ed., "Spatial Information and Ethnoecology: Case Studies from Indonesia, Nepal, and Thailand," an unpublished manuscript available from the East-West Center in Honolulu, HI. I am grateful to Judith Mayer for her insight into the reterritorializing of political practice at the grassroots level.

61. Nancy Peluso, "Whose Woods Are These? Counter-Mapping Forest Territories in Kalimantan, Indonesia," *Antipoda* 27 (1995), pp. 383–406.

62. Jefferson Fox, "Spatial Information Technology and Human-Environment Relationships," *East-West Center Working Paper* #43 (May 1995), pp. 13–14.

63. Masahide Kato, "Nuclear Globalism: Traversing Rockets, Satellites, and Nuclear War via the Strategic Gaze," *Alternatives* 18 (1993), pp. 344–45.

64. Baumont Newhall, *Airborne Camera: The World from the Air and Outer Space* (New York: Hasting House, 1969), p. 121.

65. This is exactly the kind of issue which bedevils efforts to measure responsibility by formulating a "greenhouse index." See Peter Hayes and Kirk Smith, eds., *The Global Greenhouse Regime: Who Pays? Science, Economics, and North-South Politics in the Climate Change Convention* (Tokyo: Earthscan, 1993).

66. Susan Sontag, *On Photography* (New York: Farrar, Straus and Giroux, 1977), pp. 176–77.

67. For Michel Foucault, Jeremy Bentham's Panopticon, a 1791 design for a model prison, exemplifies modern disciplinary power. Each inmate can be seen by the warden at all times, thereby inducing "a state of conscious and permanent visibility that assures the automatic functioning of power." *Discipline and Punish: The Birth of the Prison* (New York: Vintage, 1979), p. 201. More accurately, ERS furnishes "an inverted panopticon, with the periphery constantly scrutinising the centre from every angle." "A Survey of Space: The Uses of Heaven," *The Economist* (June 15, 1991), p. 17.

68. P.M. Banks and C. C. Ison, "A New Role for Freedom," *Aerospace America* (September 1989), p. 30.

69. Carol Matlack, "Landsat's Slow Death," *National Journal* (July 25, 1987), p. 1903.

70. E. David Hinkley and Gary T. Rosiak, "Instrumenting Space Platforms for Earth Observations," *Proceedings of the Pacific Rim Environmental Research Meeting* (World Scientific Publishing Co. PTE, 1992).

71. Christine Nielsen and Dirk Werle, "Do Long-Term Space Plans Meet the Needs of Mission to Planet Earth?" *Space Policy* 9, 1 (February 1993), p. 15.

72. Global Climate Observation System, *Responding to the Need for Climate Observations* (Geneva: World Meteorological Organization, 1992), p. 12.

73. IPCC, *Scientific Assessment 1995: Policymakers' Summary* (Geneva: World Meteorological Organization, 1995).

74. Langdon Winner refers to this phenomenon as "autonomous technology," whereby technology is experienced as proceeding by its own momentum and driving human choices. See *Autonomous Technology: Technics-out-of-Control as a Theme in Political Thought* (Cambridge, MA: MIT Press, 1977).

75. L. A. Fisk, et al., op cit., p. 14.

76. *The Economist*, op cit., p. 83.

CHAPTER 5

Did Global Governance Create Informational Globalism?

MARTIN HEWSON

This chapter argues that attempts to create global governance have had as a consequence the making of informational globalism. It develops an approach to global governance theory rooted in neo-Weberian world order analysis, in this case focused on the long-term contribution of world organizations to the making of the modern world order. One of the more important features of global change is the rise of informational globalism. The practice of mobilizing information is undoubtedly an ancient one, but today the practice is entangled in networks of informational interaction that have become worldwide in extent. As one significant dimension of the broad trend that has come to be known as globalization, this phenomenon certainly deserves closer attention than it has hitherto received in international relations theory. It would be conventional to explain it as a manifestation of technological development in the context of an evolutionary process of industrialism and postindustrialism. Yet such an account would award to informational globalism a self-levitating quality. Its specific roots, such as in attempts at governance, would be subsumed in the overall trend. Hence there is another line of explanation that I shall pursue in this chapter. I argue that global governance made a significant contribution to the making of informational globalism.

A working definition of global governance is needed as a preliminary statement. Global governance is perhaps best thought of as a process in time and of space. At its core is "a pervasive tendency," in James Rosenau's words, consisting of "shifts in the loci of governance."[1] Rosenau cites as contemporary examples a proliferation of transnational control mechanisms and an increasing worldwide influence of subnational systems of rule. I would add that shifts in the loci of governance are not just a contemporary phenomenon. Relocations of governance have long characterized the modern world, from the building of overseas empires to their disintegration, from the intensifying of geopolitical interaction to the consolidation of transnational agencies. In other words, this is a historicist notion of global governance.[2]

To identify broad patterns of relocation would be a useful element in global governance theory. Amongst all these shifts in the loci of governance, there does seem to be an overall *long-term* spatial trend. Insulated localist forms of governance have not fared well. Localist governances have often been bypassed and dislocated by extensive forms of governance. In retrospect, this is nothing less than a monumental imposition of power upon one of the main primordial forms of life. It is worth bearing in mind this basis of power. Nonetheless, the victor has not been one extensive form of governance but several: territorial, regional, transnational, and global. No one of these has proven itself able to monopolize life; instead they clash repeatedly. Such is the global governance process.

Beyond identifying macropatterns, another useful element of global governance theory would be to sift through potential sources and significances of relocations of governance. This chapter aims to do so by examining how several key relocations of governance shaped informational globalism. The chapter is divided into three main parts. The first examines key preconditions and precursors of informational globalism. The second part argues that global institutions made a contribution to its emergence. Finally, I outline what an approach such as this may mean for global governance theory.

EXTENSIVE INFORMATIONALISM

An evolutionist account would derive informational globalism from prior consolidations of extensive, though not global, informationalism. This is a useful starting point for analysis. But an evolutionary trend to worldwide extension cannot simply be left as a given. In the era before global governance, the contribution of other relocations of governance also needs to be brought in.

One of the more important relocations of governance was the emergence—inserted between prevailing localism and extensive regional space—of a network of geopolitical interconnections. Some elements of governance moved into this geopolitical space, made of permanent linkages among the cities, courts, and powers of early modern times. Concurrently, this relocation shaped an extensive informationalism in its own image.

Consider the spatial shape of some key examples of early modern informationalism. One was the posts. Permanent postal services were created from the fifteenth and sixteenth centuries in western Europe.[3] But they had a curious shape: not national, or even protonational, but best described as geopolitical. The French service bypassed much of France itself in a starlike pattern of main routes. From Paris the main routes went southwest to Madrid, north to London, northeast to Metz, southeast to Naples. Here was the geopolitical space of connections among key power centers. The French posts began in 1470, temporarily collapsed during the civil wars of the late 1500s, were recreated on the same pattern, and lasted in that form into the late eighteenth century.

Similar geopolitical shapes characterized other posts. The German empire franchised its posts to the noble house of Thurn und Taxis. Their routes traversed continental western Europe, connecting key power centers from the Low Countries to Germany and Spain. The Spanish posts, created in the sixteenth century ran from Madrid to Bilbao and thence north to London and Antwep, and from Madrid to Barcelona and thence east to Genoa and Vienna. Even the most national state of the period, England, created posts that were not national but geopolitical. On the one hand, there were localist posts organized by city corporations. On the other hand, the royal posts had four main routes: one north from London to Edinburgh (an independent court), another northwest to Dublin, a third southwest to Plymouth, and a fourth south to Calais and Paris.

Another instance of extensive informationalism following the shape of the relocation of governance into a geopolitical mold was the news. The trade in printed news in weekly newssheets developed in the early seventeenth century. This was a century and a half after the spread of printing itself. A major reason for the delay was that the news trade relied upon the prior development of the posts. Postmasters were a main source of news for printers. They would collect details of events from afar and then sell this to printers. Thus centers of printing, commerce, and diplomacy, such as Amsterdam and Venice, where weekly newssheets were called "gazettes," became also centers of the news trade.[4]

A key feature of the early modern news trade was that it primarily involved foreign news, or foreign intelligence as it was known in England. The world of the news had as much a geopolitical as a local or national shape. This was what the posts supplied. It was often what merchants demanded. And it was what censors allowed. Authorities were more willing to tolerate reports from afar than to allow reports on events nearer to their own concerns. Without anyone intending it, the extensive informationalism of the early modern news followed the relocation of governance.

In addition to the posts and the news, further networks of informationalism took this geopolitical shape. In this era arose networks of permanent agents charged with reporting regularly from distant cities and courts. The mercantile and banking houses of Italy and southern Germany created networks of resident agents in proximity to their clients. Then, after 1450, the Italian city-states followed suit. By the 1530s, the northern monarchies had borrowed the practice and created their own networks of permanent agents in foreign courts. Although it is interrupted by the religious schism, an extensive network of informationalism in a definite geopolitical shape across the continent was in place by the eighteenth century. This was early modern resident diplomacy. The practice of mobilizing information was at the heart of the permanent agent networks. Agents in distant courts were expected to send home regular reports on events and to provide a channel for sending on messages. They also frequently corresponded with one another. In some cases in the more important centers, one report a day would be sent. A Venetian agent sent 472 reports in one year.[5] One historian describes the outcome of these efforts as a "whirlpool of information."[6]

Thus the relocation of governance beginning in early modern times shaped a new practice of mobilizing information into a set of extensive geopolitical networks. Then a new relocation of governance became prominent in the nineteenth century. Localism found itself further bypassed with a shift in the loci of governance more definitely and completely into the space of the nation-state. This had even more profound implications for reorganizing informationalism. Postal informationalism was transformed. Hitherto, localist and geopolitical organization had coexisted. From the 1840s and 1850s, localism decayed and national organization dominated. In 1840, the British Postmaster instigated a major postal reform. The main innovation was to charge a uniform rate for mail sent any distance within the nation. This was supported by prepaid stamps and a lowering of the rate. Once its practical success had been demonstrated in Britain, not least in increasing postal volumes and revenues, France, the US, and Prussia adoped similar models. Now the nation was a uniform, homogenous space of postal informationalism. As with the posts, so with the news trade. The national element in extensive informationalism began to arise alongside the geopolitical element.

Meanwhile, there was a momentous development. Publication bloomed with printed information and statistics on national economies, populations, and societies. An initial episode occurred in revolutionary France. In order to publicize and measure the extent of progress, the revolutionary governors undertook to survey the whole state of the nation in the 1790s. Paris instructed prefects in each department to produce a "statistical topography" of their area. A Bureau of Statistics—the world's first—was founded in 1800. It selected a range of activities (insanity, fairs, land, waterways) and a set of commodities and industries (hemp and flax, tanneries, paper mills, silk) to subject to inquiry. The Bureau did so by sending detailed questionnaires to local officials. Other statistical surveys of the nation inquired into population, mines and forges, commerce, agriculture, arts and manufacturing, and the balance of trade.[7]

Although the French efforts at national informationalism dwindled under the Napoleonic and Restoration regimes, these patterns were later institutionalized in other countries. The British began publishing territorial information on a large scale in the 1830s. Among the results of this reform were the Blue Books used by Karl Marx to reveal the inner workings of the national economy. The US census, established in 1790, began publishing large-scale statistics from midcentury. The 1840 census collected information on five subject areas; the 1880 census had expanded to 215 subject areas. It took nine years for clerks to tabulate this material, by which time the next census was nearly due.

In sum, as governance relocated away from localities into the new nation-states, a new kind of extensive informationalism emerged. Although there were early experiments and temporary reversals, the decisive shift would appear to have taken place between the 1830s and 1880s in leading countries. This turned out to be the fermentation time of an initial phase of informational globalism.

AN INITIAL RELOCATION

A first wave of informational globalism appeared in the late nineteenth century. It could be argued, as in theories of industrial society and postindustrial society, that this was driven by the needs of industrialism. But there is a separate factor to be considered. In the late nineteenth century there was also a new relocation of governance. Global governance in the sense of the activites of world organizations first appeared. To be sure, what shift in the location of governance into global networks there was in the late nineteenth century was slight. Nonetheless it deserves attention as a potential source of informational globalism.

One practice of the earliest world organizations was to promote the connection of emergent national systems of informationalism. The pioneer was the International Telegraphic Union, founded in 1865. Its main influence came from sponsoring common standards that would create a meshing of national telegraph systems. That influence had become worldwide by 1914. The independent states of Asia and Latin America joined. The private telegraph companies of Britain, the US, and Canada adopted its standards. The imperial powers brought their colonies into the regime.[8] Meanwhile, intercontinental cables were being developed. The news agencies led by Reuters followed the wires. As a result, something approaching a worldwide space of informationalism emerged, now disembedded from the limits of physical transport.

The same practice of connecting national infrastructures was followed by the Universal Postal Union, founded in 1874. Built upon the reforms of the 1840s and 50s that innovated uniform national postal spaces, it went some way toward replicating that pattern with an additional layer of uniform worldwide postal space. This was legitimated as service to families separated by migration and to businesses. In truth, though, the picture was mixed. On the one hand, almost all postal administrations joined. A few founding members were non-European (the US, Turkey, Egypt), then the imperial powers pushed to have their colonial postal services admitted, and finally the independent states of Latin America and Asia joined.[9] By about 1900 we can indeed speak of a geographically global network of governance and space of informationalism. Rules were developed not just for letters but also for postcards, books, newspapers, merchandise samples, and money orders. On the other hand, there were some limits to globalism. The agreed price rate for international mail dropped but remained quite high at 20–32 centimes for a fifteen gram letter. A reason for this is that no agreement to abolish payments to countries of transit was possible, so a complicated system of sample weighings and international payments was required.

A second practice pioneered in the initial wave was the attempt to promote the circulation and exchange of many of the products of informational nationalism. The call to share knowledge became a rallying cry at the great international expositions of the age, in the congresses of professional associations, and in the governments of small and medium powers who found in sponsoring information exchanges a source of nonmilitary prestige. The world organizations that resulted could be considered media or channels. After 1875, a series of small world organizations sought to promote the sharing of national statistics, factory reports, tariff schedules, and public health information. Unsuccessful attempts were made to promote the sharing of armaments information.

A third practice was also initiated in the early world organizations: direct production of globalist information. This went beyond linking infrastructures and promoting sharing, toward something more ambitious. One body that pursued this experiment was the International Institute of Agriculture, created in 1905. Its goal was to distribute to farmers, farming associations, and agricultural colleges worldwide information on government food policies, agricultural prices and credit, methods of cultivation, the incidence of plant and animal diseases, and the wages of rural workers. It published yearbooks on agricultural legislation and agricultural statistics as well as a monthly bulletin of "agricultural intelligence." Producing information meant borrowing the techniques developed in the context of informational nationalism, such as sending out questionnaires, collating public sources, and publishing in streams of bulletins and reports. A historian of this episode writes of the "enormous increase in accurate and highly specialized information" produced by several of the institutions of the first shift to global governance.[10]

Thus the earliest attempts to create global governance did contribute to the making of a new informational globalism. One effect of global governance attempts was to link extensive communications infrastructures. A second was to foster the circulation and exchange of the products of informational nationalism. Finally, a third was to engage in the direct production of global information. It is a question whether these three kinds of practice continued beyond the initial phase.

A SECOND RELOCATION

The half-century dominated by the two world wars saw informational globalism both challenged and renewed. In this era, Trotsky's dictum that "war is the locomotive of history" approached the truth. The informational globalism trend was undoubtedly caught in the train. Both wars spawned Grand Alliances that began to sponsor equally grand attempts at global governance before each one split. Both wars spawned momentous revolutions in the civilizations of Russia and China. Yet in this context global institutions continued to develop innovations in informationalism.

The practice of linking information infrastructures declined in significance and innovation between 1914 and 1960. War and revolution removed the universality of the Telegraph and Postal Unions. Meanwhile, attempts at renewal migrated to telephone networks. Before the First World War, the Telegraphic Union had tried to develop standards to connect telephone systems. But national telephone networks had yet to be created. The real work of standard-setting began in the 1920s, now re-lying upon AT&T's model of a extensive system. This came to fruition in a new type of informational globalism only after the development of undersea telephone and telex cables in the 1950s.[11]

In contrast, the practice of promoting information exchange be-came more ambitious. The Grand Alliances had shared military and economic information on an unprecedented scale. The postwar settle-ments in 1919 and 1945 tried to institutionalize and generalize what had been ad hoc and specific to the alliances. In 1919, a provision of the League of Nations treaty encouraged pooling of information on armaments. It committed the members "to exchange full and frank information as to the scale of their armaments, their military, naval and air programmes, and the condition of such industries as are adaptable to warlike purposes."[12] Although it remained just an ambition, the League secretariat sought to follow this aim by publishing an *Arma-ments Yearbook*. After 1919, promoting the circulation of information on "development" began. The mandates system encouraged mandato-ries to compile annual reports on the developmental condition of their domains.[13] After its creation in 1923, the League's health organization endeavored to become an exchange point for collecting and transmit-ting by telegraph news of outbreaks of epidemic disease, particularly cholera and the plague. After 1945, again following the next Grand Alliance's practice, the International Monetary Fund began to promote circulation of information on public finances and national accounts.

Even more than promoting circulation, attempts at producing globalist information were renewed. Most of the new world organizations annexed this as a principal activity. After 1919, the new International Labor Organization sought to survey the condition of the world's workers. This called for a statistical office and publishing operation to make the Labor Organization a world census agency for labor conditions, workforces, and occupational health. Meanwhile, at the League's headquarters there were efforts to monitor the condition of the world economy. These efforts created national income accounting procedures that then became a key component of war planning and postwar Keynesianism.[14] After 1945, one of the first organs of the new United Nations was a statistical office. It endeavoured to gather census reports from across the world, to compile the data, to publish it in a *Demographic Yearbook*, to estimate world population, to judge world population trends, and to compare demographic phenomena of different countries. This era saw the making of incipient statistical bureaus for the world on a similar model to the informational nationalism that emerged in the previous century.

Overall, in the era of the two world wars, the influence of attempts at global governance on the making of informational globalism presents a mixed picture. In contrast to the 1860–1914 era, there were fewer innovations in linking infrastructures than in producing global information. If the main legacy of the earlier period was to initiate each of the three main practices, the main legacy of this subsequent period was to establish the legitimacy of producing globalist information by world organizations. The following era, since the 1960s, would see similarities with both preceding eras.

A THIRD RELOCATION

There has been a resurgence of informational globalism from the 1960s and 1970s to the present. It would be conventional to explain this under the general rubric of a shift to either "postindustrialism" or "postmodernism."[15] The former would be an economistic explanation, the latter a more culturalist one. But there is also a political account to be brought in. It would be rewarding to consider the contribution of global institutions to the newest informational globalism.

The practice of connecting infrastructures turned out to be one source. The moves that had begun early in the century to create standards for linking telephone systems began to have an impact. But more importantly, a move began to link civil communications satellite programs. A new world organization, Intelsat, was formed in 1964 to engage this practice under US sponsorship and with western members. Like the Telecommunication and Postal Unions, its key participants were the national utilities, and it had a leading role in fostering common standards. Unlike the earlier world organizations, it was a consortium that actually owned and operated satellites. National utilities owned the ground stations and shares in Intelsat, the largest shareholding being claimed by Comsat, a US consortium itself largely owned by AT&T. In other words, compared to the nineteenth-century Unions, this was a much more active and direct intervention into promoting linkages in information infrastructures.[16] Not surprisingly, given this investment, results were swift to follow. Its first geostationary satellite was operating in 1965, just three years after the world's first civil communications satellite. By 1967, Intelsat had in place a worldwide network. The Intelsat net came to carry the majority of civil long-distance telephone and television. So if a date were to be chosen as the start of the third phase of informational globalism, it would be 1967.

Meanwhile, there was a further source in the practice of promoting the circulation of information.[17] A disjuncture may be less apparent in this domain than in linking infrastructures, but there was indeed a notable shift. In 1972, the UN created an Environment Program devoted to ambitious programs of global informationalism called Earthwatch and the Global Environmental Monitoring Service. This nomenclature is indicative of a new celebration of informational globalism in its association with the entry of environmentalism into world politics. The outcome was a new round of sponsoring circulation. At the most general level, the Environment Program sponsored what came in the 1980s to be called state of the environment reporting. From 1985, it helped to sponsor an international effort at monitoring climate change. Most recently, in the 1990s it moved into sponsoring satellite monitoring of environmental conditions. By sponsoring circulation, a global institution helped to make the newest phase of informational globalism.

Producing global information by world organizations also entered a new phase. Here a major difference with the earlier phases became clear. The end of the sea-based empires and the emergence of the Third World after 1945 profoundly altered the context of producing global information. It was in the 1970s that the shift began to appear. *Early warning* crept into the lexicon. Famines in the early 1970s led the Food and Agriculture Organization to set up a Global Information and Early

Warning System in 1974. A second boost came with the east African famines of 1985.[18] The attempt at a governance of food production led to monitoring of food stocks and food production trends, surveys of farming, forestry, and fishing, compiling annual harvest assessments on a country-by-country basis, and generating national accounts of food production, imports, and exports. Thus did attempted global governance through early warning lead to informational globalism.

Attempts at global governance arose through "surveillance" and "transparency," as well as through early warning. In the 1970s this became a key legitimation of the International Monetary Fund. Seeking new ways to promote sound public finances after the US had decided to abandon the Bretton Woods rules, the Monetary Fund gave more and more emphasis to "surveillance."[19] This meant, on the one hand, promoting the circulation of information under the label of encouraging "transparency" of national economic information. On the other hand, it meant making the Fund itself into an influential center of production. Crises in public finances in Africa, Latin America, and subsequently East Asia during the 1980s and 1990s only encouraged more efforts at this type of global governance through informational globalism.

In sum, the informational globalism trend has existed for about a century as a prominent strand in the making of the modern world order. Several possible accounts are conceivable. It could be argued that the autonomous power of technology was the key. Alternatively, it could be derived from the inner imperatives of industrialism. Perhaps there was an even longer evolutionary tendency for the practice of mobilizing information to become more and more extended until it ultimately spanned worldwide networks. In contrast, I have sought to show that a satisfactory account would have to bring in the factor of global governance institutions. If so, this claim has interesting ramifications for global governance theory.

CONCLUSIONS: AN APPROACH TO GLOBAL GOVERNANCE THEORY

The most damaging charge against global governance theory is that it lacks a clear focus.[20] According to this challenge, the global governance concept has no obvious reference or limits. As the idea has entered wider circulation in the 1990s, it has become a portmanteau for divergent and ultimately incoherent commitments. Little unites global governance theory. Indeed there is no body of 'theory' in global governance theory, and no 'concept' in the global governance concept.

In this chapter I have offered one way to answer the challenge. The body of the chapter does so not in the abstract but through historical analysis. This conclusion will systematize the response. To begin with, much of the challenge is to be accepted. Global governance theory does need a definite problematic to give it identity, as do all bodies of analysis. But there is a problematic available: the attempt to understand the causes and consequences, the meaning and significance, of worldwide shifts in the loci of governance. To be sure, this is broad, but it is by no means unfocused or incoherent. It can be the 'theory' in global governance theory and the 'concept' in the global governance concept. Any problematic is no more nor less than a cluster of related puzzles or problems linked to a certain empirical phenomenon. I want to suggest that a coherent problematic concerning relocations of governance will have a cluster of three fundamental components.

First comes the issue of space. Relocations of governance are by definition spatial. What have been the spaces created in shifts in the loci of governance? A helpful way of answering this question is, in the first instance, to develop a typology of the most fateful spaces of governance. History displays a bewildering variety of spatial forms of governance. A limited set of "type concepts and generalized uniformities of empirical process," in Max Weber's words, is needed to simplify and concentrate upon the most important.[21]

To begin with, governance might be (a) local or (b) regional. A combination of the two appears to have been the basic pattern for most of written history. A list of the characteristic styles of localist governance would include cities, village-parishes, and many kinds of corporate groupings. Given the logistical limits of premodern times, only localist governance would have been able to undertake the intensive ordering of everyday life. By contrast, those logistical limits made extensive regionalist governance, embodied in empires, leagues, and feudal structures, a relatively thin layer hovering above everyday life. But in the modern world order, localist and regionalist spaces of governance have been supplemented and bypassed if never thoroughly extirpated.

In addition, governance might be located in (c) geopolitical spaces, that is, in the extensive interconnections among distinct power centers. In making this claim, I am modifying the standard realist assessment of geopolitical networks as an absence or void of governance. On the contrary, geopolitical space by definition must be composed of political interaction and hence a certain form of governance. Such a relocation of governance (as suggested in section two of this chapter) challenged and displaced localism and regionalism from the period of the fifteenth through eighteenth centuries onward. Today, a node-and-network space of this kind encompasses the world.

A further shift has been the creation of a series of (d) national or territorial governances. It was in the nineteenth century that the term *nation-state* entered circulation. This suggests that it was in that era that the relocation to national space was consolidated beginning in Europe. The idea that the entire world can and should be organized into a grid of national governances emerged only with the end of the sea-based empires after 1945. That was for a long while a potent and effective organizing myth, even if the actual achievement of the world-wide grid was uneven in the extreme. Today, there is debate on the decline of this space of governance. Yet it may not be the uneven reality but the triumphant myth that is being challenged. National governances standardly shared space with the other forms.

Finally, governance across (e) worldwide or global spaces unquestionably has been distinctive to the modern world. There is little doubt that worldwide governance networks would have been impossible logistically until relatively recently. Only in the late nineteenth century did the limits of movement recede sufficiently to allow such a development, in however limited a form. It was at that time that world organizations were first established with a degree of universality exceeding that of the early to middle twentieth century.[22] Yet, while this space is undoubtedly the most extensive of all, it may be questioned how intensive it has been. What governance there has been of global compass has been a thin layer above everyday life, affecting it only indirectly by relays through states and organized civil society. In addition, since the nineteenth century there is no general process of evolution towards increasing global governance.

This is one line of response to the charge of incoherence in global governance theory. It can and should offer a definite geographical or spatial focus. By contrast, in standard rational choice cooperation theory, regimes and cooperation appear to have a spaceless existence. Yet, it is not possible to tie global governance theory to any one possible relocation of governance. The spatial patterns of governance show no trend to uniformity. On the contrary, they show a trend to proliferation in both the long and the short run.

Relocations of governance are not just spatial. They are also historical processes. Here lies a second area of response to the charge of diffuseness. A definite focus upon the historical time-scales of relocations of governance offers a way forward. There is in some cases a presumption

that global governance theory is concerned exclusively with shifts of a
momentary nature in the current post-Cold War era. An example is the
Commission on Global Governance, whose rhetoric is very much that
of post-Cold War opportunities.[23] But this need not be the case at all.
Relocations of governance are also phenomena of longer term enduring
patterns. Both short and long term perspectives are needed to complement one another.

An exclusive focus upon the short term would seem to lend credence to the charge of diffuseness. After all, in the short-term frame,
many loci of governance that were once thought stable appear to be in
flux. Hitherto prevailing patterns appear to be in question. This sense
of flux is aptly conveyed by Rosenau in his analysis of proliferating
transnationalism.[24] There is a definite need for a "remapping" of world
politics, as Ferguson and Mansbach put it, away from the myth of a
monopoly of the universal grid of national governances.[25] That remapping
is a work of challenging the myth of simplicity with greater complexity.
A long-term perspective searches for some patterns. One is that the
myth of the universal grid has always been a simplification. It would be
false to suppose that a long-term perspective concentrates on the static
and the unchanging. On the contrary, there is a need for a historicist
account of long-term and large-scale patterns of change.

In this chapter I have sought to highlight the longer-term frame.
Let us attempt a deliberate forgetting of the universal grid as the baseline
of analysis for shifts in the loci of governance. The most important
long-term shifts are neither its alleged endurance nor its supposed contemporary decline. What is fundamental is the decay of localist forms
of governance. They have been penetrated, disembedded, and reorganized into nodes within extensive linkages. The obverse is a rise of
extensive forms of governance of several kinds; among the most important have been regionalist, geopolitical, national-territorial, and global.
It is likely that none of these will prove able entirely to subdue the
others. These stand out as the key long-term trends.

The long-term viewpoint carries with it certain risks. It is admit-
tedly one-sided. Yet, it also carries the advantage of answering the
challenge of diffuseness. A long-term perspective cannot encompass
everything, so it must concentrate on identifying the most salient patterns. Pattern searching may be the road to coherence in global governance theory.

So far in this conclusion I have written of shifts in the loci of
governance as if they have significance unto themselves. But they also

have significance for other dimensions of global change. A challenge for global governance theory is to inquire into the implications of shifts in the loci of governance for military, economic, cultural, and (I have argued here) the informational dimensions of the world order. In making this point, I am seeking to underline the importance of taking a multidimensinal, neo-Weberian approach to the analysis of global governance.[26] Hence, in addition to focusing upon spatial shifts in the long-term, the multidimensional element would make global governance theory an important contributor to a much-needed comprehensive account of the making of the modern world order.

It could be argued that relocations of governance have been significant in the making of the modern world economic order. The shift to geopolitical interaction formed one of the principal preconditions for the consolidation of capitalism. "This competitive struggle" among powers, according to Weber, "created the largest conditions for modern western capitalism." This is because, he continues, "separate states had to compete for mobile capital."[27] The shift to global institutions of governance, Murphy argues, promoted the consolidation of large-scale industrialism, first in Europe before 1914 and then across the OECD-zone after 1945. Without the functions of the world organizations, maintains Murphy, firms and states would not have been able to create expanded industrialism alone.[28]

There is also a case to be made that relocations of governance have been important contributors to the making of the modern world cultural order. The shift to territorial governance has been almost everywhere associated with attempts at generating national identities or "nation-building." While this cannot be considered the only source of national identities, it cannot be left out of account.[29] The long-term cultural influence of the world organizations has been both hard to establish and actively challenged. But it could be argued that in their absence the contemporary diffusion of liberal ideology would not have occurred on such a wide scale.

It could be claimed further that the shifts in the locus of governance were significant in the making of the modern world military order. The relocation to geopolitical interaction seems likely to have ensured the spread of the early modern military revolution of standing armies and firearms. A case could be made that there have been several waves of military revolution since then promoted through geopolitical interaction. Has the shift to global institutions been militarily significant? The answer here must be that world organizations have had a negligible

influence upon the development of military power either for the better
or for the worse.

In addition, this chapter has suggested that shifts in the loci of
governance have also had informational implications. What Susan Strange
calls the "knowledge structure" has been "the most overlooked and
underrated" of the major aspects of the modern world order.[30] One aim
of this chapter is to counteract that overlooking and underrating. But
instead of a static structure it is more helpful to focus upon practice: the
practice of mobilizing information for social goals. The usefulness of
informationalism for extensive organization is at the root of its importance in the modern world order.

How did informational globalism arise? How did the practice of
mobilizing information become entwined in worldwide networks? Although technology and economy, as well as ideology and culture, made
contributions, this chapter has focused upon the role of shifts in the
locus of governance. This factor brought two main preconditions without which informational globalism would have been unlikely if not
impossible. First, the emergence of intensive geopolitical interaction
fostered a distinctive kind of extensive informationalism. Then, even
more intensive patterns of informationalism were promoted by the
consolidation of national governances. It is worth pointing out that
these were two distinct developments, even though they have often been
conflated in international relations theory.

One of the main consequences of the shift to the making of world
organizations was a series of intended and unintended contributions to
informational globalism. The makers of the earliest world organizations
developed a set of new practices. One was to link together technical
infrastructures formed by telegraph and post, telephone and satellite.
Another was to encourage the wider circulation of information through
states and civil societies. A third was for the staffs of world organizations themselves to produce globalist information. Although the focus
and balance changed between the late nineteenth and late twentieth
centuries, each of these basic practices continued to be at the forefront.

The earliest wave of informational globalism owed much to the
world organizations of the late nineteenth century. The Telegraphic and
Postal Unions achieved virtually universal membership in linking together different national and imperial communications systems. Other
early international unions promoted a sharing of public information.
Some sought to develop the capacity to produce globalist information.
Still, it has to be concluded that the overall bandwidth of these efforts

and projects was relatively narrow. The second wave of informational globalism, in the early twentieth century, saw some reversals and some efforts at deepening following the two world wars, but no decisive expansion. The Telecommunications Union began to link national telephone systems. The League of Nations-era and United Nations-era world organizations continued to promote wider circulation. Where they differed from the early phase of international unions was the undertaking to become larger producers of social and economic statistics. Then a third and contemporary wave of informational globalism crystallized in the 1960s and 1970s. The Telecommunications Union's linking of telephone systems had become intercontinental, and Intelsat's linking of satellite systems became global in 1967. Other world organizations experimented with both producing and fostering the circulation of public information in new areas such as the environment and public finances. In these ways, global governance did contribute to the making of informational globalism.

NOTES

1. James N. Rosenau, "Governance in the Twenty-First Century," *Global Governance: A Review of Multilateralism and International Organization* 1, 1 (1995), p. 17.

2. On historicism in the context of international relations theory, see Robert W. Cox, "On Thinking about Future World Order" and other essays in Cox with Timothy J. Sinclair *Approaches to World Order* (Cambridge: Cambridge University Press, 1996).

3. This description draws on one general historian who emphasized the significance of the posts in early modern times, George Clark, *The Seventeenth Century* (New York: Oxford University Press, 1961), ch. 4.

4. Anthony Smith, *The Newspaper: An International History* (London: Thames and Hudson, 1979).

5. Garrett Mattingly, *Renaissance Diplomacy* (Boston: Beacon Press, 1955), p. 110.

6. Joycelyne G. Russell, *Peacemaking in the Renaissance* (London: Methuen, 1986), p. 69.

7. Stuart J. Woolf, "Towards the History of the Origins of Statistics," in Jean-Claude Perrot and Stuart J. Woolf, *State and Statistics in France* (Chur, Swizerland: Harwood, 1984).

8. George A. Codding, *The International Telecommunication Union* (New York: Arno Press, 1952); also see Mark W. Zacher with Brent A. Sutton, *Governing Global Networks: International Regimes for Transportation and Communications* (Cambridge: Cambridge University Press, 1996), Chapters 5 and 6.

9. George A. Codding *The Universal Postal Union* (New York: New York University Press, 1964) pp. 34–72.

10. F. S. L. Lyons, *Internationalism in Europe, 1815–1914* (Leyden: Nijhof, 1963), p. 37.

11. George A. Codding and Anthony M. Rutkowski, *The International Telecommunication Union in a Changing World* (Dedham MA: Artech House, 1982), pp. 84–87.

12. Covenant of the League of Nations, Article 8, Section 6.

13. Raymond F. Betts, *Uncertain Dimensions: Western Overseas Empires in the Twentieth Century* (Minneapolis: University of Minnesota Press, 1985).

14. Marilyn Waring, *If Women Counted: A New Feminist Economics* (San Fransisco: Harper and Row, 1988).

15. Krishan Kumar, *From Post-Industrial to Post-Modern Society: New Theories of the Contemporary World* (Oxford: Blackwell, 1995).

16. This was a model for the Soviet bloc's Intersputnik (1971) and the maritime satellite organization Inmarsat (1979).

17. See Ernst B. Haas and John G. Ruggie, "What Message in the Medium of Information Systems?" *International Studies Quarterly* 26, 2 (1982), pp. 190–219.

18. Rosemary Righter critizes it in *Utopia Lost: The United Nations and World Order* (New York: The Twentieth Century Fund Press, 1995), pp. 236–37.

19. Louis W. Pauly, "The Political Foundations of Multilateral Economic Surveillance," *International Journal* XLVII (1992), pp. 293-327.

20. A. J. R. Groom and Dominic Powell, "From World Politics to Global Governance: A Theme in Need of a Focus," in A. J. R. Groom and Margot Light, eds., *Contemporary International Relations* (London: Pinter, 1994); Lawrence S. Finkelstein, "What Is Global Governance?" in *Global Governance* 1, 3 (1995) pp. 367–72.

21. Max Weber, *Economy and Society* (Berkeley: University of California Press, 1978) vol. 1, p. 19.

22. Craig N. Murphy, *International Organization and Industrial Change: Global Governance since 1850* (New York: Oxford University Press, 1994).

23. Commission on Global Governance, *Our Global Neighborhood* (New York: Oxford University Press, 1995). See also Michael G. Schechter, "Our Global Neighborhood: Pushing Problem-Solving Theory to Its Limits and the Limits of Problem-Solving Theory," in this volume.

24. James N. Rosenau, "Towards an Ontology for Global Governance," in this volume.

25. Yale H. Ferguson and Richard Mansbach, "History's Revenge and Future Shock: the Remapping of Global Politics," in this volume.

26. For a fuller account, see Martin Hewson, "Historical Sociology of Global Governance," *Review of International Political Economy* 3, 1 (1996), pp. 186–93.

27. Max Weber, *General Economic History* (London: George Allen and Unwin, 1927), p. 337.

28. Craig N. Murphy, *International Organization and Industrial Change: Global Governance since 1850* (New York: Oxford University Press, 1994), pp. 120–35 and 227–42.

29. John Breuilly, *Nationalism and the State* (Chicago: The University of Chicago Press, 1994).

30. Susan Strange, *States and Markets: An Introduction to International Political Economy* (London: Pinter, 1994), p. 115.

CHAPTER 6

Governance and the Nation-State in a Knowledge-Based Political Economy

EDWARD A. COMOR

With the development of complex transnational and subnational systems of rule, the capacity of national governments to control their domestic policy environments appears to be in decline.[1] In assessing these changes, James Rosenau has made an important contribution. While not denying that nation-states remain "the central loci of control," Rosenau believes that "states have lost some of their . . . dominance . . . as well as their ability to evoke compliance and to govern effectively."[2] Dynamic developments involving international communication and information activities, says Rosenau, are core factors directly shaping the emerging character of governance. A seemingly paradoxical trend has ensued: governance is becoming both more pervasive and disaggregated.

The role played by contemporary communication and information developments in relation to this paradox is the underlying focus of this chapter. By applying a relatively precise conceptualization of the relationship of these developments to governance, the following pages argue that the analysis provided by Rosenau and others now requires elaboration through a more concentrated evaluation of the qualitative features of the emerging knowledge-based political economy. More specifically, this chapter explains why a qualitative analysis—focusing on how information becomes knowledge—directs the student of governance toward markedly different conclusions from those suggested by Rosenau. Rather than a world order in which the liberation of political and economic power is becoming more possible, an entrenchment of powers already held by dominant transnational corporations, international elites, and perhaps even the United States (through its assertion of a new form of hegemonic dominance) appears more probable.

In developing these arguments, this chapter first provides a theorization of the relationship between information and knowledge. This is presented in order to clarify key, but still under-assessed, aspects of contemporary communication and information-based developments. The next section builds on this theorization by addressing qualitative issues related to governance and the continuing centrality of the nation and the nation-state. Recent and successful efforts of US state officials to secure America's longstanding free flow of information policy are outlined in the third section. This brief case study is provided in order to directly redress assumptions that current communication and information-related governance developments necessarily presage a decline in the powers of nation-states. Rather than the relative decline of the nation-state, it is suggested that what is underway is a shift in the form in which states relate to "the global" and "the local." In the final section of what follows, a more general point is made: quantitative developments are not necessarily analogous to qualitative. Through this and other observations, I conclude that a sharpening of social-economic inequalities and reactionary forms of politics are probable and problematic features of the world order now taking shape.

HOW INFORMATION IS RELATED TO KNOWLEDGE

A fundamental step toward understanding the role of communication and information-based activities in governance is the articulation of how human beings sort out and process information into what is known. In this task, what a person knows of his/her life and world can be represented as a complex set of conceptual systems. These conceptual systems are constantly applied in ongoing efforts to perceive and interpret. These systems not only mediate reality, they are themselves subjected to continual reaffirmations or modifications in accordance with individual and collective experiences. Information flows, in whatever form, thus are continually subjected to interpretation. Simply put, culture—defined in relation to the individual as "a general state or habit of the mind" and for a community as "the whole way of life, material, intellectual, and spiritual"[3]—provides an environmental-contextual reference point or social compass on which conceptual systems are applied or modified to interpret information.[4]

To some degree, institutions, organizations and even technologies are reifications of complex historically based constructions. Institutions, organizations, and technologies also play a mediating role in the ongoing interaction and modification of conceptual systems and cultures. This way of understanding information and its relationship to knowledge directs the analyst beyond assumptions that a predominantly one-way flow of information from a capitalist metropole, for example, inevitably will infuse a receiving population with consumerist desires and/or liberal ideals. Instead what this alternative suggests is that a concern with the capacity of individuals and collectivities to interpret and make use of information constitutes a more significant analytical task.

A focus on information flows and their assumed cultural effects therefore represents only the beginning of this concern with knowledge as a process. In this, the term *cultural power* can be used to refer to the direct or indirect ability to shape conceptual systems. The rapid growth in recent years of information as commoditized products and services (facilitated by new technologies) suggests that this concern with cultural power involves not just what is thought about but, more essentially, why people think in the ways in which they think. While the production and distribution of information-based commodities, for instance, implies the capacity to modify human perceptions and habits (as the multibillion-dollar international marketing and advertising business indicates), the pervasiveness of such commoditization activities modifies cultural environments most cogently through their intergenerational reshaping of conceptual systems.

It is in this context that emerging transnational communication systems not only constitute vehicles through which ideas are exchanged and worldwide markets accessed, they also are media through which commercial free speech and the ideal of individual choice can be promulgated. This takes place most directly through the individual's day-to-day use of such systems, providing a seemingly open relationship between the individual and the outside world. Human beings are neither the passive recipients of information nor innately capable of processing information in necessarily rational, critical, or creative ways. Conceptual systems and cultures—forged and modified through institutional, organizational, and technological mediators—thus constitute key nodal points shaping what is known and imaginable and, conversely, what is unreal and unimaginable.[5] Information in and of itself is meaningless without the presence of conceptual systems that facilitate particular understandings and applications.

In what Harold Innis referred to as the monopolization of knowledge, the capacity of some individuals or groups to shape directly how such conceptual systems are formed and used by others is fundamentally important. More generally, Ian Parker writes that "changing social economic conditions and the changes in structures of power that accompany them alter social definitions of reality and unreality. . . . The boundaries of reality are inextricably linked to the capacity to exclude the irrational, as defined principally by those with the power to enforce their definition."[6] Fundamental in the construction of such realities is the ability to manipulate knowledge, not merely through the supply and distribution of information but more essentially through the day-to-day modification of conceptual systems by means of institutional, organizational, and technological mediators. With this in mind, my critical assessment of Rosenau on global governance can begin.

QUALITATIVE ASPECTS OF GOVERNANCE

In "Governance in the Twenty-First Century" Rosenau states that governance "encompasses the activities of governments, but it also includes the many other channels through which 'commands' flow in the form of goals framed, directives issued, and policies pursued."[7] In relation to the conceptualization outlined above, there is a problem with this definition: it virtually ignores the process through which information is communicated, mediated, and subsequently transformed into knowledge. It is a definition concerned with communication relationships rather than processes. Rosenau thus assumes that the emergence of new trade partnerships, the formation of crossborder coalitions among environmental or labor groups, and the formulation of international commercial policies by cities rather than nation-states "will ripple across and fan out within provincial, regional, national, and international levels as well as across and within local communities."[8] This is true, of course, but conclusions regarding the qualitative effects of such relationships are far from obvious, particularly in the absence of some understanding of the process through which communication, over time, shapes conceptual systems and more general cultural capacities.

Observing the rapid development of new relationships that are seemingly divorced from spatial and temporal limitations, Rosenau concludes that "[t]here is no single organizing principle on which global governance rests, no emergent order around which communities and nations are likely to converge."[9] Given the absence of a theory of process, this statement is premature. Moreover, in using the analytical tools outlined above, and in light of the contemporary role played by the United States, it is dubious. Before addressing this directly, a central paradox rarely discussed in this period of enthusiastic communication and information development should be underlined. On the one hand, relatively advanced capitalist countries are experiencing an unparalleled rise in the absolute density of information becoming available to mass publics. On the other hand, however, specialized forms of information have attained unprecedented levels of concentration in the hands of national and international elites.

Much of the information now being produced and becoming more and more available (i.e., information available at relatively low costs or through predominantly indirect methods of payment) can be characterized as infotainment-type materials—mass market products and services such as television programming and advertising. Increasingly, however, relatively intellectual or valuable forms of information (i.e., information useful to specialized professional or business interests) are typically being produced and distributed on direct pay-per-access bases. If the information has a potential market among the wealthy or entrepreneurial, such as information contained in a specialized database or newsletter, it typically is more expensive to access. As such, a minority population of information "haves" is emerging relative to information "have-nots." Those possessing the wealth, education, and time required (or those able to employ specialist info-workers) to take full advantage of expanding and increasingly commoditized information resources typically are utilizing these resources to generate more wealth and, ultimately, deepen existing social-economic power disparities.[10]

The benefits of late-twentieth century communication and information developments are not being shared universally. Even if the personal computer and modem—or some future variation thereof—become relatively inexpensive and user-friendly, questions involving intellectual abilities (i.e., functional literacy rates) and temporal opportunities (i.e., the time needed to participate) must be raised in relation to nonelites and their capabilities.

Rosenau's argument that "global governance is likely to become increasingly pervasive and disaggregated in the years ahead" may well be correct.[11] However, the process and character of this reformulation of identity and authority remain undertheorized. Rosenau therefore can only assume that new social movements will act as potentially progressive forces amidst globalizing processes: "They pick up the pieces, so to speak, that states and businesses leave in their wake by their boundary-crossing activities."[12] Rosenau goes on to quote Joseph Camilleri who writes that "antisystemic movements . . . articulate new ways of experiencing life, a new attitude to time and space, a new sense of history and identity."[13] The evidence for this kind of radical departure from the past, particularly among nonelites, is largely anecdotal. In fact, by applying the approach suggested above, a different outlook is warranted.

Human beings are not intellectual sponges. The conceptual systems that mediate a person's use of information and subsequent interpretations of reality constitute ongoing products of complex socialization processes. Importantly, however, who we are and how we think about our worlds, while ongoing constructions, tend to be relatively inelastic. The sediments of experience accumulate and harden. Human biases thus often become entrenched. These constructed conceptual systems, in turn, directly mediate interpretations of new relationships and information flows. As such, even those relationships and flows that overtly challenge established perspectives rarely generate significant modifications to established ways of seeing. Put in another way, human intellectual and cultural capacities are products of how people are raised, their significant relationships, their day-to-day social-ecological environments, how they work, eat, and love. How people have lived and are living their lives, which includes what information they are exposed to and who they communicate with, is of primary importance in forging conceptual systems.

In this context, two related questions need to be addressed. First, can contemporary impulsions toward both the globalization and localization of human relations significantly modify the role of the nation as the nodal point par excellence of mass identity? And second, will these impulsions significantly modify the role of the nation-state as the focal point of the international legal-political order?

On the first question, one lesson that the twentieth century provides is that human beings continually require answers—at least imagined ones—to suffering, sickness, and death. On this, Benedict Anderson has provided a powerful theorization of the saliency of the nation in modern history.[14] Nationalism, says Anderson, is not an ideology, not a coherent doctrine, not some kind of pernicious false consciousness. The nation, instead, is a historically produced but nevertheless real social identity. Rather than some sort of territorially and linguistically disparate form of world religion, the nation is an inclusive but largely anonymous extended family. It includes a broad range of peoples under a seemingly disinterested form of solidarity. The nation thus serves tangible ongoing human needs in a complex, crowded, and often lonely world. This point has particular saliency at the turn of the century, a time in which post-1945 patterns of political and economic life are undergoing extraordinary transformations. In this historical environment characterized by rapid change and, hence, psychological insecurity, social movements and transnational or local groupings tend to come and go. With few but significant exceptions, these remain relatively peripheral to the political, economic, and cultural lives of the world's nonelites. The nation—its history, culture and influence on individual conceptual systems—remains uniquely pervasive and powerful.

On the second question, as Rosenau recognizes, the nation-state is still the focal point of the international legal-political order. Moreover, this status will not and indeed can not decline, despite the ongoing obliteration of time and space through communication and information technologies—will not and indeed can not decline. As discussed below, the World Trade Organization (WTO), for example, now constitutes the essential legal basis for the continuing proliferation of transnational communication and information activities. It is a treaty organization of nation-states. Given the rather predictable outcome of the new free trade regime (neoliberal economic idealism notwithstanding) involving the emergence of competitive winners and losers, the medium through which capitalists, workers, women, minority groups, and others will most directly and effectively address their fears, aspirations, and grievances will remain the nation-state. Relating this to the status of nationalism when future international crises and conflicts take place, the base point of individual and collective identities relative to external threats will remain the nation and its complex of institutions.

Regardless of the possible but distant realization of information highway linked, mass-scale global organizations and identities or some type of sustained mass discovery of community-based forms of activism, it is the nation and the nation-state that will constitute the linchpins of individual and collective political economic identities. French or South Korean or Mexican capitalists, while sharing certain roles, goals, and perspectives, will most probably mediate political and economic conflicts and crises through their meaningful positions as privileged citizens of their respective countries. Economic, legal, and sociological reasons underline the ongoing centrality of both the nation and the nation-state.

THE UNITED STATES AS COMPLEX MEDIATOR

The contemporary role of the United States in establishing an international free flow of information through international trade treaties underlines the ongoing centrality of nation-states. Not only has the United States acted as the core mediator through which mostly large-scale American and foreign corporations secure free flow and requisite international intellectual property rights, the institutionalization of these reforms constitutes the legal basis on which a global division of information haves and have-nots is being elaborated. Rather than acting as a primary stimulant to new forms of transnational and local governance, this liberalization and commoditization of international communication and information activities paradoxically is accommodating a new form of US hegemony. In arguing that the material capabilities of nation-states are in decline, Rosenau is on firm ground. But in not recognizing the unique and central role that has and will continue to be played by the United States, and the long-term qualitative implications of contemporary global information economy developments, the ground on which Rosenau's argument proceeds becomes less certain.[15]

To some extent, American private and public sector interests only recently have come to recognize that future US hegemonic capacities increasingly are becoming dependent on the internationalization of liberal and consumerist ideals. This understanding has evolved in the context of a more general recognition that US-based corporations hold dominant world positions in most information-based commodity activities. These industries are primarily engaged in the production and dissemination of copyrighted materials, including newspapers, periodicals, books, broadcasting, cable television, audio recordings, motion pictures, advertising, computer software, and data processing, and in real value-added terms, they grew from $93.8 billion in 1977 to $206.6 billion in 1991. As measured in relation to national Gross Domestic Product (GDP), these industries constituted 2.2 percent of US GDP in 1977 and 3.55 percent in 1991.[16] Employment in these industries rose from 1.5 million jobs in 1977 to 2.9 million in 1991. Also from 1977 to 1991, employment in information-based industries grew by an average of 4.5 percent each year, while employment in the US economy as a whole grew at an average rate of 1.6 percent.[17]

By 1986, American-based companies already were responsible for over forty-three percent of world revenues in this sector. This dominance was particularly strong in information-based services where US corporations generated forty-seven percent of international revenues.[18] Not only was the United States the world's largest services exporter prior to the signing of the Uruguay Round General Agreement on Tariffs and Trade (GATT), it also held the largest services trade surplus. While from 1987 to 1992 the US trade surplus in services increased almost fourfold, reaching $60.6 billion in 1992, the US trade deficit in goods was reduced from $159.5 billion in 1987 to $96.2 billion in 1992. As a result of the services surplus, in 1987 the US trade deficit was lowered by eight percent, and in 1990 services exports reduced this by thirty-six percent. In 1992, the US trade deficit was reduced by sixty-three percent as a result of America's relative strength in services.[19]

In the early 1980s, in response to the emerging discrepancy between domestic service sector capabilities and international legal-political communication superstructures, US-based transnational corporations (TNCs) orchestrated a global elite-targeted "consciousness raising" campaign. Financial services executives and other corporate officials recognized that the United States was unlikely to change foreign attitudes toward information-based free flow activities through a unilateral attempt to reform existing international institutions. American Express Vice President Joan Edelman Spero, for instance, said that to be successful, Americans had to convince foreign governments that a free flow of information was in their long-term economic interests also. This would be possible only through a concerted effort to promote the righteousness of neoliberal trade ideals concerning information-based activities.[20]

Compelling this corporate activism was a policy vacuum in Washington. In foreign communication policy, given both the US constitution's separation of powers and the growing dependency of domestic corporate activities on international communications, the legal supremacy of the executive branch in foreign policy generated intrastate conflicts. Moreover, private sector dominance over a broad range of communication and information activities for many years had been institutionalized through commercially oriented judicial interpretations of the First Amendment.[21] In the United States, therefore, an activist state had been structurally inhibited while interagency (and to some extent intraagency) conflict was perpetuated in part due to the enormous economic stakes involved in policy decisions related to the information economy.[22]

In sum, at the very time that an increasing number of US-based corporations required a stable international free flow of information regime, the US public sector lacked the means to work with private sector interests to redress what had become an international impasse.

Faced with its relative economic decline and unable to neuter the legal authority of foreign states to control information activities within their own borders, US officials faced a foreign communication policy crisis in the mid-1980s.

European, Japanese, and Canadian-based TNC executives became the primary targets of American corporate efforts to modify the perspectives of foreign governments. As service providers, some of these overseas corporations presumably would be opposed to US competition in their domestic markets. To counter this, US-based TNCs promoted the recognition among foreign corporations that they are service consumers and emphasized the potential benefits available to those able to access US advertising, consultancy, financial, and other relatively advanced services.[23] US private sector interests subsequently pushed ahead of American state officials in efforts to modify how foreigners perceived both free flow and free trade. In this project, US-based TNCs forged a strategic policy infrastructure through which their interests could be identified, formulated, and promoted.[24] American state officials followed this lead by beginning the process of reconceptualizing the free flow of information to involve free trade issues.[25]

Just prior to the start of US-Canadian free trade negotiations, a complex overlapping of US trade policy with foreign communication policy had emerged. The relative decline of the US economy, the recognition that its information-based service corporations constituted its most competitive international sector, and the realization that longstanding law-based free flow of information efforts had run their strategic course, all converged on Washington, where a policy vacuum enabled the free trade solution to unfold.

In the context of aggressive efforts by American state officials to redress UN-based resistance to free flow through free trade, as early as 1987 an International Telecommunications Union (ITU) legal symposium examined international telecommunications issues as trade issues in order to coordinate these concerns with those emerging in the GATT. In part, this GATTization of the ITU was a response to TNC and US suggestions that the technical regulations set by the ITU since the nineteenth century now should be evaluated as trade facilitators or impediments. In 1988, the ITU's World Administrative Telegraph and Telephone Conference (WATTC-88) produced an agreement in which privately owned networks, to some extent were exempted from future ITU regulations. Most remarkably, WATTC-88 formally recognized that future telecommunication services regimes should be negotiated as trade regimes.[26]

The services issue as trade issue equation placed United States Trade Representative (USTR) officials in the unexpected role of America's central foreign communication policy agents. Recognizing that other countries would need to be pulled toward the reconceptualization of communication and information issues as trade issues (rather than just being pushed into it), the Reagan White House, with Congressional support, instructed the USTR to pursue bilateral service and intellectual property rights agreements. Through the establishment of trade treaties with Israel and Canada and industry-specific deals with Japan and the EC, precedents and standards were set for future GATT negotiations. Importantly, these agreements would compel GATT members to take part in multilateral negotiations or face potential exclusion from the US market.

The GATT Uruguay Round negotiations were completed at the end of 1993. Last-moment resistance by France resulted in the temporary exclusion of its television and film industries. While the Clinton administration was berated by the Motion Picture Association of America and related interests for this exemption, the more general provisions in the agreement on services, telecommunications, and intellectual property, in conjunction with ongoing developments involving digital technologies and telesatellites (among others), almost certainly will facilitate the ongoing globalization of most information-based commodity activities. While the principle of national sovereignty still reigns supreme in international law, digital and miniature technologies nevertheless are making national borders porous to information transmissions. More importantly, the Uruguay Round agreement provides information producers and distributors with new mechanisms through which they now can demand both market access and remuneration for their transnational services.

COMMUNICATION, INFORMATION, AND US HEGEMONY

In its ongoing role as the complex mediator of emerging information economy interests and its ability to act as the core agent through which an international free flow/free trade regime has been forged and the common sense of liberalization promoted, the United States is different. What American officials have established dramatically enlarges the rights of commercial interests in relation to public sector concerns. The United States, in effect, has institutionalized the international free flow of commercial information—the type of information that, for the most part, serves the interests of the world's information haves rather than its increasingly marginalized have-nots.

As a result of the resuscitation of the free flow of information through free trade and the collapse of Soviet and East European communism, officials directly involved in US foreign communication policy now generally recognize information-based commodity exports to have implications that directly shape policy developments overseas. According to the Department of Commerce, "it appears that the global dissemination of electronic media and technology is playing an increasingly significant role in promoting US foreign policy by fostering demand for democratic reforms internationally."[27] The reception of West European television and radio signals in Eastern Europe, the distribution of mostly pirated US-produced videotapes, and the longstanding activities of the Voice of America, Radio Liberty, and Radio Free Europe are rightly or wrongly cited as important components facilitating the end of the Cold War. The mushrooming availability of in-home communication technologies and other forces facilitating the expansion of transnational information activities will generate, it is believed, both consumerism and ongoing demands for democracy.[28] Moreover, the use of terms like *radical perestroika,* at least in some Washington circles, reflects a belief among some officials that international exposure to corporate-produced information and entertainment itself undermines popular support in foreign countries for apparently anticapitalist (and, to some extent, anti-American) policy developments. According to one of the USTR's North American Free Trade Agreement negotiators, "we [US trade officials] have gotten a lot further away from counting beans and pairs of shoes . . . [to explicitly focusing on] the overall environment that creates our competitiveness."[29]

American-based TNCs directly involved in information-based products and services, such as IBM, AT&T, and Disney/ABC-Capital Cities, have since the early 1980s promoted the assumption that communication technologies will facilitate the development of new economic opportunities leading to greater national wealth. Over this period, virtually every sector of the international economy has been influenced by technological change involving the convergence of computers and telecommunications. Through the application of digital technologies, a broad range of integration opportunities continue to develop. To survive, TNCs must undertake ongoing modifications involving massive investments and efforts to control the environments in which production, distribution, and consumption take place. The monetary and nonmonetary costs that these entail themselves stimulate the pursuit of stability and predictability. This, in turn, encourages collusion rather than competition on an increasingly global scale.[30]

As transnational communication systems become essential tools in the globalization of marketing and consumption, the commercial, short-term, and acritical biases generated through their use among nonelites will contribute to the weakening capacities of the world's social-economic peripheries to mount sustained counterhegemonic challenges. The producers and distributors of information-based products and services that have been and will be made available to mass consumers, contrary to notions equating greater quantity with genuine choice, seek little more than the sensual engagement of audiences. More generally, when information becomes thought of and treated as little more than a commodity, national and international laws and regulations increasingly treat publics as consumers rather than as citizens. And while virtually all that is sellable will be made available to the consumer possessing adequate monetary and nonmonetary resources, there exists little substantive evidence to indicate that most of the world will not remain marginalized and/or massified over the course of this information revolution. From this qualitative perspective, which involves human intellectual capacities rather than legal and/or technological opportunities alone, non-elite or have-not individuals and groups stand little chance of developing and practicing the critical and creative intellectual capacities needed to become fully engaged in governance.

Given that information is always mediated through conceptual systems and that these tend to be ingrained through cultural contexts and the accumulated sediments of day-to-day experience, the potential for long-lasting and radical shifts in global governance practices appears limited. The resources needed to take full advantage of emerging transnational communication and information opportunities are money, education, and time. As such, there is little reason to believe that these developments will significantly benefit the lives of nonelites. The growing disparity in what information is becoming available to mass populations, relative to what is becoming available to elites, signals little hope that the information revolution will result in much more than the liberation of the already powerful. Given the role of conceptual systems, a significant quantitative rise in individual or collective access to information by itself will not produce significant advances in critical governance capabilities. In fact, given the predominance of infotainment-type services in emerging mass markets, rather than the promotion of sustained democratic participatory opportunities, contemporary information and communication developments more probably will facilitate reactionary forms of mass politics.

Both through the mediation of the United States and the application of new technologies, an international regime has emerged through which an almost limitless range of information activities are being commoditized. As something that now can be readily manipulated and packaged, and its distribution largely controlled, information is being produced and sold like most other commodities. The WTO has become the legal means through which such activities are being globalized. More fundamentally, these developments, in conjunction with the ongoing saliency of neoliberal mythologies, are modifying nation-state public policy in relation to the production and distribution of information. Rather than a public good or something valued for its educational, cultural, or spiritual worth, information is becoming more and more valued as something that can be sold or as a vehicle through which consumers may be attracted to consider purchasing another commodity. In other words, contemporary US-mediated international developments have modified the way state officials and publics think about information and communication. The price system, in effect, is colonizing and reshaping not just what information is being produced and will be made available, it is modifying how humankind conceptualizes information itself.

In "Governance in the Twenty-First Century," James Rosenau writes that "there is no magic in the dynamics of self-organization." He continues to explain that

> Circumstances have to be suitable, people have to be amenable to collective decisions being made, tendencies. toward organization have to develop, habits of cooperation have to evolve, and a readiness not to impede the processes of emergence and evolution has to persist.[31]

In this chapter, I have addressed what is perhaps the most fundamental circumstance influencing these crucial points—the intellectual and cultural capacities of individuals and collectivities. Students of global governance do their subject a disservice if they fail to address why people think in the ways in which they think. While it is clear that the effectiveness of nation-state policies is "likely to be undermined by the proliferation of emergent control mechanisms both within and outside their jurisdictions,"[32] the structural bases for this decline is rarely articulated beyond mostly anecdotal discussions and subsequent assumptions concerning the globalization or localization of political or economic activities. Related to this is the need for more research focusing on the processes underlying the recent and increasingly universal acceptance of private sector actors as natural and Godlike arbiters of international political, economic, and cultural life. More than the study of the flow and quantity of information, this requires analyses of how information becomes knowledge and how what we know to be realistic or imaginable becomes ingrained.

I have argued that such questions require both an investigation of the microprocesses of human knowledge formation, involving the role of conceptual systems, and of macro processes, involving, for instance, the role of the American state in the construction and maintenance of the international free flow of commercial information. As discussed, large-scale capitalist interests have gained significant new capabilities to commoditize and exploit information-based products and services. This centralization of power in the hands of information haves will have the long-term effect of rendering more public sector producers and distributors of information comparatively inefficient and less desirable given ongoing state deficit crises in conjunction with the price system's resurgent colonization. Little evidence exists to support the belief that these commercial priorities will accommodate, either quantitatively or qualitatively, the democratic governance capabilities of most people.

In response to Rosenau and in light of the analysis presented above, Stephen Gill's point that the United States remains "the political and military guarantor of disciplinary neo-liberalism" is too modest.[33] Given that recent trade-based agreements constitute the legal bases of ongoing free flow of commercial information developments, for the forseeable future the American state will remain the complex mediator of the globalization of private sector communication and information activities.[34] An essential response to this involves the very capacity to conceptualize and forge ideas as realistic alternatives. Without this potential to develop sustained critical and creative intellectual capacities, the globalization of information-based commodities will tend to promote the perpetuation of neoliberal or acritical conceptions of reality.

The form in which the nation-state is mediating the demands of capitalist and other interests is being modified. Beyond its political and military leadership, the United States not only has shown itself to be the essential mediator of globalization developments, but the US-based private sector is positioned to be their chief economic benefactor. Beyond even this, the qualitative implications of these developments suggest that out of the long-term promotion of acritical mass publics, the commoditization of information, and the subsequent disparity between international information elites and information have-nots, the conditions in which hegemonic consent can be forged are now taking shape. Out of contemporary uncertainties and transformations, a new Pax Americana is possible for three fundamental reasons. Capitalism, as has always been the case, needs the nation-state to act as its political, legal, and military mediator. The United States has been in recent years and will continue to be this mediator. And—given that the essence of hegemony is consent, the divided or acritical qualities perpetuated by commoditization of information-based activities indicate little potential for the world's economic and geographic peripheries either to organize themselves on a mass scale or to even conceptualize alternatives to existing or emerging orders.

James Rosenau's work on global governance constitutes a rich point of departure for a vigorous and critical assessment of the issues raised above. What Harold Innis observed over sixty years ago in the North American context may now be true for the international political economy: "No one can say we have not solved the problem of circuses, whatever may be said as to the problem of bread."[35] The focus must be on capitalism, as the complex and ever-problematic agent of contemporary and future developments, and the nation state—particularly the United States—as its core and equally complex mediator. It is in this context that the qualitative dimensions of governance and the processes shaping human communication involving the construction and possible reconstruction of shared realities should be pursued.

NOTES

1. Another version of this chapter was published under the title "Governance and the Commoditization of Information," *Global Governance* 4, no. 2 (1998). The author thanks James Rosenau and the editors of this book for their critical contributions.

2. James N. Rosenau, "Governance in the Twenty-First Century," *Global Governance* 1, no.1 (1995), p. 39.

3. Raymond Williams, "Culture and Civilization," *The Encyclopedia of Philosophy*, Paul Edwards, ed. (New York: Macmillan and The Free Press, 1967) Volume Two, 273.

4. See L. David Ritchie, "Another Turn of the Information Revolution, Relevance, Technology, and the Information Society," *Communication Research* 18, no. 3 (June 1991), pp. 412-27.

5. On this general perspective, see Paul Levinson, *Mind at Large: Knowing in the Technological Age* (Greenwich: JAI Press, 1988).

6. Ian Parker, "Myth, Telecommunication, and the Emerging Global Informational Order: The Political Economy of Transitions," *The Global Political Economy of Communication: Hegemony, Telecommunication, and the Information Economy*, Edward A. Comor, ed. (London: Macmillan, 1994), p. 47.

7. Rosenau, "Governance in the Twenty-First Century," p. 14.

8. Rosenau, p. 15.

9. Rosenau, 16.

10. Ian Parker, "Commodities as Sign-Systems," in *Information and Communication in Economics*, Robert E. Babe, ed. (Boston: Kluwer, 1994), pp. 75–76.

11. Rosenau, "Governance in the Twenty-first Century," p. 23.

12. Rosenau, p. 24.

13. Camilleri quoted in Ibid.

14. Benedict Anderson, *Imagined Communities* (London: Verso, 1991).

15. A full elaboration of arguments made in this section can be found in Edward A. Comor, *Communication, Commerce and Power* (London: Macmillan, 1998).

16. Stephen E. Siwek and Harold Furchtgott-Roth, *Copyright Industries in the U.S. Economy*, 1993 Perspective (Washington, D.C.: International Intellectual Property Alliance, October 1993), p. 8. If industries producing and disseminating a product that is only partially copyrighted are included, such as architectural services; industries that distribute copyrighted materials, such as libraries; and related industries that produce and maintain equipment used exclusively for copyrighted materials, such as computer and television manufacturers, the scale and relative importance of these activities increase substantially.

17. Recent estimates of US information-based commodity exports for the core industries listed above indicate that $26.5 billion in revenue was generated in 1989, $34.0 billion in 1990, and an estimated $36.2 billion in 1991. See Siwek and Furchtgott-Roth, pp. 8, 10, and 12.

18. UNESCO, *World Communication Report* (Paris: UNESCO, 1989), p. 83.

19. Coalition of Service Industries, *The Service Economy* 7, no. 3 (July 1993), p. 13.

20. Joan Edelman Spero, "Information: The Policy Void," *Foreign Policy* 48 (Fall 1982), p. 155.

21. Robert Horwitz, "The First Amendment Meets Some New Technologies," *Theory and Society* 20, No. 1 (February 1991), pp. 21-72.

22. Jeremy Tunstall, *Communications Deregulation* (Oxford: Basil Blackwell, 1986), pp. 198-199.

23. William J. Drake and Kalypso Nicolaidis, "Ideas, Interests, and Institutionalization: 'Trade in Services' and the Uruguay Round," *International Organization* 46, no. 1 (Winter 1992), p. 49.

24. Karl P. Sauvant, *International Transactions in Services: The Politics of Transborder Data Flows* (Boulder: Westview, 1986), p. 199.

25. For example, see US Department of Commerce, "Long-Range Goals in International Telecommunications and Information," National Telecommunications and Information Administration (Unpublished 1983), and Jane Bortnick, "International Telecommunications and Information Policy: Selected Issues for the 1980s," report prepared for the US Senate Committee on Foreign Affairs (unpublished 1983).

26. Despite these concessions, American interests criticized the conference for not formally recognizing that PTTs constitute unacceptable institutional barriers to the development of international services. See R. Brian Woodrow, "Tilting Towards a Trade Regime, the ITU, and the Uruguay Round Services Negotiations," *Telecommunications Policy* 15, no. 4 (August 1991), p. 331.

27. US Department of Commerce, "Comprehensive Study of the Globalization of Mass Media Firms," notice of inquiry issued by National Telecommunications and Information Administration (February 1990), p. 7.

28. See ibid, pp. 51–59.

29. Personal interview with Emory Simon, Deputy Assistant United States Trade Representative, Office of the United States Trade Representative, Washington DC, 9 September 1992.

30. Edward A. Comor, "The International Economic Implications of the United States Telecommunications Act," *Journal of Economic Issues* 31, no. 2 (June 1997), pp. 549–56.

31. Rosenau, "Governance in the Twenty-First Century," p. 17.

32. Rosenau, p. 17.

33. Stephen R. Gill, "Neo-Liberalism and the Shift Towards a US-Centered Transnational Hegemony," *Restructuring Hegemony in the Global Political Economy*, Henk Overbeek, ed. (London: Routledge, 1993), p. 278.

34. For example, in 1997 the Clinton administration announced its Global Electronic Commerce initiative. Among other things, the United States is pushing to make Internet commercial activities tariff-free.

35. Harold A. Innis, *Staples, Markets, and Cultural Change*, Daniel Drache, ed. (Montreal and Kingston: McGill-Queen's University Press, 1995), p. 451.

PART THREE

KNOWLEDGE, MARKETIZATION, AND

GLOBAL GOVERNANCE

CHAPTER 7

The Late-Modern Knowledge Structure and World Politics

TONY PORTER

The implications of the knowledge intensity of contemporary life for global governance have received increasing attention in recent years. Rosenau, for instance, has highlighted the way in which the growing knowledgeability of citizens has increased their interest and competence in world politics. Regime analysts have pointed to the need for particular types of knowledge as a reason for states to engage in cooperative institution building. State interests may even be altered through the actions of knowledge-producing epistemic communities. More generally the importance of information flows has been seen as undermining territoriality as the organizing principle of the states system.[1]

Despite this recognition of the relevance of knowledge, there has not been a systematic effort to understand the distinctive characteristics of knowledge production and dissemination in our contemporary period. A useful starting point in such a project is Susan Strange's notion of the knowledge structure. Strange defines the knowledge structure by its effects: it "determines what knowledge is discovered, how it is stored, and who communicates it by what means to whom and on what terms."[2] Strange usefully highlights the relative autonomy of the knowledge structure and gives as examples the medieval Christian church and science as the two most important forms that this structure has taken in this millennium. She points out that knowledge can confer power on some and exclude others and that this political aspect of knowledge is becoming a

more important source of conflict as the economy has become more
knowledge intensive. Unfortunately Strange's analysis and the discipline
of international relations more generally have lagged behind other disciplines to some degree in understanding more recent changes in the
knowledge structure that have been signified by the terms *postmodern*
or *late-modern*. Strange's analysis itself basically ends with "the scientific
state."

This chapter seeks to contribute to addressing this analytical gap
by applying key concepts from a growing literature which treats late
modernity or postmodernity as a particular historical period with distinctive political, economic, and social characteristics and which sees
alterations in the structuring effects of knowledge as central to this
period.[3] This literature includes most notably Harvey's *Condition of
Postmodernity*, Lash and Urry's *Economies of Signs and Space*, Giddens'
Consequences of Modernity, Baumann's *Intimations of Postmodernity*,
and Beck's *Risk Society*.[4]

I focus in particular on the increased speed and intensity with
which new abstract knowledge is transformed into routine unquestioned
practices which can then be taken as commonsense reality. I distinguish
two characteristic features of this knowledge structure. The first effect
is ontological: there is an increasing tendency to negotiate or rework the
fabric of understandings that constitute our notion of what is real. The
second is decentralizing: this reworking becomes effective not through
centralized controls and directives but through its acceptance and reproduction at the micro-level. Traditional political conflicts in world politics and the frameworks we use to understand them have been organized
around the state, either in the form of interstate conflict or challenges
to sovereignty, but in distributional and ordering conflicts associated
with the postmodern knowledge structure the power of the state shifts
from a central focus to an element in the broader institutional character
of the knowledge-production process.[5]

There are three particular implications of these changes for world
politics that will be illustrated in the second part of this chapter with
examples from global finance. First, once knowledge is recognized as
having, in late modernity, an enhanced constitutive and structuring
capacity relative to its more passive representational role, and that this
takes place in an increasingly decentralized fashion, then its more dramatic effects are rendered more visible. Second, once this altered role is
made more visible, then it becomes apparent that the state, by intervening more effectively in the decentralized constitutive process of knowl-

edge production and dissemination, can exercise more effective influence than would be the case if it relied solely on older conceptions of the knowledge structure. Third, a focus on the distinctive character of the late modern knowledge structure reveals new ways that citizens can shape and have been reshaping the fabric of the international system. Taken together these points imply that it is not just differentials in the possession of knowledge that have political consequences, but also differentials in the knowledge about knowledge—the awareness of and capacity to take advantage of the knowledge structure—that matters.

It is important not to overstate the differences between the older knowledge structure and that of late modernity. I am not suggesting that there will be a wholesale replacement of the former by the latter. The goal is rather to identify certain significant shifts in the relative importance of the two types of knowledge structures.

THE DISTINCTIVENESS OF THE POSTMODERN KNOWLEDGE STRUCTURE

As is well known, our late-modern world is characterized by the proliferation of abstract systems—"systems of technical accomplishment that organize large areas of the material and social environments."[6] Time, for instance, operates as an abstract system to coordinate activity.[7] Abstract systems such as insurance are used to coordinate future activities as well—a "colonization of the future," to use Giddens's term.[8] History is continually reworked and re-presented in simulations and spectacles.[9] Abstract systems are a form of knowledge, but knowledge that produces our reality and does not simply reflect it.

The effects on the subject of this proliferation of abstract systems are ambiguous. Contrary to the pessimistic image of Luke in which the subject is relentlessly colonized, the literature upon which this chapter is focusing stresses the creative ability of agents to monitor and alter their own practices—a process termed *reflexivity*.[10] As Beck puts it, "biographies become self-reflexive; socially prescribed biography is transformed into biography that is self-produced and continues to be produced."[11] Giddens similarly emphasizes the liberating side of the expansion of abstract systems:

> the construction of the self as a *reflexive project*, an incremental part of the reflexivity of modernity; an individual must find her or his identity amid the strategies and options provided by abstract systems . . . a *concern for self-fulfilment*, which is not just a narcissistic defence against an externally threatening world, over which individuals have little control,

but also, in part, a *positive appropriation* of circumstances in which globalised influences impinge upon everyday life.[12]

The paradox, however, is that this intensified reworking of identity draws on abstract systems over which the individual has little influence. The private sphere becomes "the outside turned inside and made private, of conditions and decisions made elsewhere." Indeed in Beck's *Risk Society* our lives are increasingly influenced not by the distribution of wealth but by the distribution of sometimes potentially catastrophic risks, such as nuclear war or toxic spills, which are an unintended byproduct of the knowledge-production process: "in class positions being determines consciousness, while in risk positions, conversely, *consciousness (knowledge) determines being.*"[13]

Science itself becomes more reflexive and is forced to apply its skepticism to its foundations by the often contradictory character of its proliferating claims: "science becomes more and more *necessary*, but at the same time, *less and less sufficient* for the socially binding definition of truth." Science becomes increasingly politicized: "the doubled, constructed reality of risk politicizes the objective analysis of its causes."[14]

The paradoxical effects of a simultaneous loss and increase in control which are a feature of a knowledge-intensive late modernity are not simply random, however. Some forms of control are decreasingly effective relative to others. Highly centralized systems radiating from a single center are being displaced by more decentralized ones. Borrowing from Baudrillard, we can trace a metaphorical progression in the way in which knowledge achieves its effects: from mechanical reproduction, to generative models, to the virus. This last is a complex construction that operates by circulating through networks.[15]

Rights play an increasingly important role in this transformation. As Beck notes, "constitutional rights . . . are hinges for a decentralization of politics with long-term amplification effects. They offer multiple possibilities for interpretation and, in different historical situations, new starting points to break up formerly prevalent, restrictive, and selective interpretations."[16] Human rights are not simply entitlements conferred by centralized states but rather exist independently of them and are sustained by our shared late-modern conceptions, our *knowledge* of what it means to be human. These conceptions emerge from a multitude of varied practices, only some of which involve traditional centralized political activity.

The ability to bridge differentiated bodies of knowledge is becoming more important than simply imposing abstract systems from a position of power. Bauman traces this through an analysis of culture: in the previous period "the intellectual ideology of culture was launched as a militant, uncompromising and self-confident manifesto of universally binding principles of social organization and individual conduct."[17] Culture at this earlier stage was linked to the state and assisted it in remaking society:

> Popular, locally administered ways of life were now constituted, from the perspective of universalistic ambitions, as retrograde and backward-looking, a residue of a different social order to be left behind; as imperfect, immature stages in a overall line of development toward a 'true' and universal way of life, exemplified by the hegemonic elite.[18]

By contrast, in the present,

> Interpretation between systems of knowledge is recognized...as the task of experts armed with specialist knowledge, but also endowed, for one reason or another, with a unique capacity to lift themselves above the communication networks within which respective systems are located without losing touch with that 'inside' of systems where knowledge is had unproblematically and enjoys an 'evident' sense.[19]

Laclau and Mouffe's 1985 analysis of hegemony provides a useful focus on the symbolic political negotiation that is the counterpart to this new role of interpretation. Rather than ideologies and hegemonies being simply imposed from the top down, order involves the creation of "articulations," to use Laclau and Mouffe's term. Articulations are interpretations of signs that establish relations between differential social positions. These articulations are always open to alternative interpretations due to the indeterminacy of these signs: "every antagonism, left free to itself, is a floating signifier, a 'wild' antagonism which does not predetermine the form in which it can be articulated to other elements in a social formation."[20]

The above analysis has suggested that there is a fundamental difference in the way in which knowledge affects social practices in late modernity relative to the state-scientific knowledge structure that Strange discusses. I will now illustrate these concepts by applying them to a particular issue area, global finance.

GLOBAL FINANCE AND THE POSTMODERN KNOWLEDGE STRUCTURE

In this section I focus on three developments in global finance which are illustrative of the above changes in the knowledge structure and, in turn, illustrate the three political implications of these changes noted earlier: rendering more visible the knowledge structure's more dramatic effects, the potential for designing regulatory tools which are more consistent with this structure, and the increased potential for citizens to shape the fabric of the international system. The first illustration focuses on the production of new financial instruments, the second on the increased use of decentralized techniques in bank and transfer pricing regulation, and the third on the politics of defining capital.

THE CREATION OF NEW FINANCIAL INSTRUMENTS

The emergence of complex new financial instruments was a distinctive feature of global financial markets during the 1980s. Note issuance facilities (NIFs) are an example. The value of NIFs increased from zero to $1 billion in 1981, the first year they were produced, and then to $50 billion in 1985. Similarly, the value of the interest-rate swap market grew to an estimated $100 billion in 1985 and $2 trillion in 1989.[21]

The process by which markets in such new financial instruments were created fits the generalized account of postmodern knowledge production in several respects. First, production of these instruments is highly knowledge-intensive, involving complex mathematical modelling of risks, but once created they function to coordinate expectations as much as.to crystallize and communicate information exogenous to the relationship among the participants. The coordinated expectations are evident in definition of an NIF as "a medium-term legally binding commitment under which a borrower can issue short-term paper in its own name, but where underwriting banks are committed either to purchase any notes which the borrower is unable to sell, or to provide standby credit."[22]

Once established, these practices rapidly become routine, as is evident in their widespread adoption, and the ordering effects of these expert systems are readily apparent. These instruments move from a mathematical model in a financial analyst's computer to being the basis of vast markets in the space of a few years. Once the instruments are accepted as routine, these markets come to be taken for granted as the baseline reality around which other practices are oriented. In short, the knowledge created has a powerful ontological effect.

Also striking is the decentralized way in which these instruments reorganize practices. To a large degree they replace the functions carried out by states under the Bretton Woods regimes. In that earlier historical period, states took the responsibility for coping with the potential disruptions resulting from payments imbalances. Coordination was highly centralized among central bankers and in meetings at the International Monetary Fund and the Bank for International Settlements. The new financial instruments are a market-based and very decentralized substitute for the earlier state-based coordination. As is well known, they also seem to be easily able to bypass or undermine the more centralized coordination of states. For instance, swaps were first initiated as a way to get around exchange controls imposed by states.

The above examples of new financial instruments are in fact merely a small subset of an increasingly complex proliferation of derivatives. Derivatives grew from $2 trillion at the end of 1986 to $20 trillion at the end of 1994, an average annual growth rate of 140 percent.[23] Indeed even more generally the degree to which financial transactions dwarf real transactions in the international political economy has been widely remarked on. For instance, by the end of the 1980s one estimate put financial flows at fifty times the size of trade flows.[24] Concern has been expressed from many quarters at the degree to which financial volatility can wash out the price signals generated in real goods markets. This example illustrates the dramatic capacity of knowledge production processes to create powerful markets which then constitute a new and very real systemic feature of the international system.

DECENTRALIZED REGULATION

It has been widely noted that states appear to have lost their ability to control the flow of capital across borders. Capital controls, which were common in the immediate postwar period, are now regarded as impractical. In this section I provide examples of the way in which states can develop decentralized regulatory techniques which are more compatible with the late-modern knowledge structure illustrated in the previous section and thereby enhance their regulatory capacity.

Along with the production of new knowledge-intensive products by private firms comes an increased need and capacity of those firms to exercise control over those products; this can be influenced or in some cases even harnessed by states. Sinclair, for instance, has highlighted the prominent role of debt rating agencies in monitoring financial markets.[25] These ratings increasingly are incorporated into official regulatory standards.[26] Similarly, the Fédération internationale des bourses en valeurs (International Federation of Stock Exchanges, or FIBV) provides an increasingly institutionalized form of private regulation for stock markets. This is a private initiative, and indeed the FIBV has explicitly stated that one of its goals is to preempt state regulators. Yet such preemption indicates that the FIBV's intergovernmental counterpart, the International Organization of Securities Commissions (IOSCO), can stimulate regulatory activity at the FIBV. Much of the standards work of IOSCO and the FIBV overlaps so much that it is almost indistinguishable.[27]

In other cases states are able more directly to alter the knowledge producing process in markets to control firms. For instance, the Basle Committee on Banking Supervision's capital adequacy agreement of 1988, which considerably strengthened the regulatory capacity of the Committee's member state regulators, did so not by intrusive centralized monitoring but by altering the rules so that markets enforced more prudent behavior. This market enforcement was carried out first by shareholders who had been forced by the requirements to put more of their capital at risk (the standards increased requirements for capital relative to assets such as loans) and second by ratings agencies and the financial press which adopted the new capital standards in their own monitoring. The regulations led to the reworking of internal routine procedures in banks to monitor risk in ways that matched the state-initiated standards.[28] Knowledge production, in the form of the monitoring capacity of private actors, was critical in each part of this process.

The Basle Committee has subsequently strengthened its regulations in a way that further illustrates the potential of decentralized regulation. Faced with the proliferation of new financial instruments, the Committee initially worked on complex regulations to address a variety of new risks. Ultimately it found this to be too cumbersome for monitoring the most innovative banks. It therefore has adopted a new policy which allows banks to use data generated by their own internal risk management systems in the determination of the minimum levels of capital which they must maintain. This revolves around the concept of 'value-at-risk': the bank's estimate of its maximum loss over a given time period. Required capital levels will be a multiple of this value-at-risk. The multiple will be increased for banks which underestimate their value-at-risk over time; in other words, a penalty will be imposed if banks fail to monitor their own compliance with standards.

Recent new US regulations on transfer pricing offer a further example of decentralized regulation. Transfer pricing, which can involve the manipulation of internal prices to shift profits to low-tax jurisdictions, has long been regarded as a sign of the power of multinational corporations relative to the state. In the new US regulations, the onus has now been placed on multinational corporations to justify their choice of among six alternatives. Doing so will require high costs for firms in terms of producing data and employing tax lawyers. Penalties for non-compliance are regarded as high by MNCs: from 20 to 40 percent of the additional tax depending on the size of the adjustment.[29]

While there is little doubt that each of the above examples involves some degree of increased monitoring or regulation, there is room for dispute about the relative control of firms and states over the process. An inevitable difficulty in analyzing the use by states of market forces to discipline firms is in disentangling the relations of influence in a relationship that has become more complex. This, of course, has been a longstanding debate with respect to concepts such as 'regulatory capture' in domestic politics. Despite this difficulty, the instances cited in this section do indicate that decentralized forms of regulation which alter the knowledge production process in markets may allow states to regain some part of the control that has been lost as centralized regulation is abandoned.

REDEFINING CAPITAL

Capital has a variety of meanings. In part this reflects the various uses to which the concept is put. A Marxist concern for social equality, for instance, might lead one to emphasize the control over the means of production which is inherent in the notion of capital, while accountants, with their concern about insolvency, might treat capital as simply the difference between assets and liabilities. These meanings circulate around a common referent, but as the *International Dictionary of Finance* puts it, "the term has no precise meaning out of context."[30] These differences in meaning hint at the degree to which the notion of capital is not produced by a single underlying essence or deep structure but is rather discursively constructed—produced by the intersection and articulation of meanings attached to it. This would then suggest that the ontological and ordering effects of a shift towards a postmodern knowledge structure would be visible in the meaning of capital.

A widely recognized turning point in the history of capital is the emergence of professionalized management and dispersed shareholding, first identified by Berle and Means in their classic 1932 *Private Property and the Modern Corporation*. The role of knowledge in this transformation was primarily centralizing. This is most evident in the way in which scientific management codified tacit knowledge from observation of the practices of craft workers and then used this knowledge to exert an intensive control over the bodies of employees.[31] This centralizing professionalized knowledge also increased the control of managers relative to shareholders; the gap that had opened up between the two was evidence for Berle and Means of a profound change in the meaning of capital as two of the defining characteristics of capital, that is, ownership and control, were no longer necessarily integrated.

Although the gap between ownership and control can be regarded as the origin of a decentralizing tendency in the Berle-Means corporation, this was offset in practice in two key ways. First, a continued inequality in the distribution of share ownership across the population allowed a relatively small class of owners to continue to exercise effective control. This was reinforced by other social institutions, including private clubs, interlocking corporate directorships, elite schools, and the central organizational role of banks. Second, corporation law unequivocally held that the rights of shareholders must be the guiding criterion in judging the performance of boards of directors and executives in their fiduciary and managerial duties.

Three contemporary developments in corporate governance mark the undermining of these centralizing tendencies by changes in knowledge. First, the institutionalization of investment has involved a decentralization of the knowledge that previously had been concentrated in the hands of professional managers. Second, the growth of intangible assets as a proportion of total corporate assets has challenged conventional conceptions of capital. Third, political struggles have enlarged the concept of 'stakeholder' relative to 'shareholder,' greatly expanding the range of rights to which capital refers. The first and third of these changes is most pronounced in the United States but nevertheless is relevant internationally because of the weight of US capital markets in the world economy and because of the spread of US practices beyond its borders. I shall briefly look at each of these three tendencies in turn.

INSTITUTIONALIZATION OF INVESTMENT

The institutionalization of investment involves the creation of institutions, such as mutual funds and pension funds, which professionally manage the savings of those who invest in them.[32] These institutional investors have displaced to significant degree both bank intermediation, which channeled funds from small depositors to borrowers, and individual dispersed investors in stock markets. They provide an alternative monitoring capacity to that of the corporations they invest in, and in so doing weaken the hold of professional managers over corporations. In practice most institutional investors monitor corporations by analyzing stock prices rather than the detailed information about managerial performance, and this has led to concern about short-termism in those markets, most especially the US, where this is most common. At the same time, these investors provided the funds for the hostile takeover wave of the 1980s, which challenged the entrenched management of the largest corporations and is seen by many economists as a sign of increased competitiveness in the 'market for corporate control,' which in turn is a key source of discipline for corporate managers. In short, the preeminent influence of bureaucratic corporations, enhanced by the systematic appropriation and centralization of knowledge through scientific management, is being displaced by a more decentralized arrangement in which alternative sites for producing knowledge about the management of corporations have emerged and have begun to exercise influence.

GROWTH OF INTANGIBLES

The growth of intangibles as a proportion of total assets has posed challenges for the laws and accounting practices which define capital.[33] The lay image of property as unproblematic exclusive ownership by an individual of an object has become increasing irrelevant in the actual practice of law in late-modern societies. Indeed a significant current in legal scholarship and practice sees both ownership and property as relatively meaningless concepts that should be replaced by bundles of rights. Grey has argued that the 'thing-ownership' conception of property was in part appropriate to an earlier period in which most wealth was possessed in discrete material units such as plots of land, and in part an ideological weapon in the hands of the bourgeoisie in its fight against the complex and overlapping ownership system of feudalism. Presently the increasing importance of intangible assets, such as trademarks and goodwill, has highlighted the degree to which property is about complex and interdependent relations between people rather than individual ownership over things. Rights over things are rarely held by single individuals but are shared and limited by a variety of regulations.[34] Examples of well-developed legal practices that limit and divide ownership rights include various rights of access by the public to property such as hotels and bus lines, the separation of rights through licenses for use, the rights of tenants, the rights of borrowers against mortgage foreclosure, laws against unjust dismissal of employees, laws regarding the disposition of property in divorce, and restrictions on wills.[35]

These changes in law are accompanied by an ongoing deliberation among accountants about how to account for intangibles. Traditionally intangibles were called 'goodwill' and could be measured only when the firm was sold and a difference between the selling price and the value of tangible assets appeared. This approach is now widely recognized as inadequate given the high proportion of firm assets that intangibles now represent. For instance, it has been estimated that only 6 percent of IBM employees work in factories, with the rest producing intellectual services.[36] Accountants have therefore begun to develop detailed procedures for estimating the value of intangible assets. The need for expanding the range of human activities covered by accounting practices is also evident in the concern on the part of governments with human capital and how to measure and foster it,[37] and in the effort to measure the social costs of pollution.[38] Both of these involve the development of expert systems to measure and influence intangibles; in the first, the thing measured is a knowledge-based activity as well.

In short, the growth of intangible assets has provided a challenge to traditional conceptions of capital as physical property to which was attached a single set of rights. In part the efforts of accountants can be seen as rescuing this traditional conception by providing techniques for treating intangibles as comparable to tangible assets. At the same time, by revealing the constructed nature of this process, they are undermining the naturalness of the earlier conceptions.

STAKEHOLDERS VERSUS SHAREHOLDERS

The sharing of rights over property, to which the previous section referred, has also been evident in the increased prominence of the notion of 'stakeholder' relative to 'shareholder' in corporation law. Particularly in the United States corporation law has held, in the words of a classic statement of a court with regard to the Ford Motor Company,

> A business corporation is organized and carried on primarily for the profit of the stockholders. The powers of the directors are to be employed for that end. The discretion of directors is to be exercised in the choice of means to attain that end and does not extend to a change in the end itself, to the reduction of profits, or to the nondistribution of profits among stockholders in order to devote them to other purposes.[39]

In recent years, however, there has been a sea change in corporate governance as the rights and well-being of other constituencies, including the community, employees, and creditors, have been recognized as relevant ends of corporate policy. By 1991, at least twenty-eight states in the US, had adopted "nonshareholder constituency" or "stakeholder" statutes,[40] and these covered many Fortune 500 multinational corporations, such as Exxon, Standard Oil, General Electric, IBM, and Union Carbide.[41] Moreover, the courts are beginning to take the interests of nonshareholder constituencies more seriously. For instance, in a decision regarded as a landmark by many, Justice Horsey of the Delaware Supreme Court suggested that the Board of Directors owed its duty to a metaphysical *corporate entity* rather than to the shareholders, at least in a takeover context.[42]

The above examples are drawn exclusively from the United States but are relevant for international politics for two reasons. First, the US-based MNC has been an important actor in the international political economy. Second, there is growing interest in the issue of international harmonization of corporate governance, in part due to the increased pace of cross-border trading of stock. A recent report of the International Task Force on Corporate Governance of the International Capital Markets Group (ICMG), prepared jointly by the International Federation of Accountants, the Section on Business Law of the International Bar Association, and the Fédération Internationale des Bourse de Valeurs, explicitly focused on criteria relevant to the constituency or stakeholder concept:

> We have focused on the processes used to direct and manage the business and affairs of the company with the objective of balancing:
>
> • the attainment of corporate objectives
> • the alignment of corporate behavior with the expectations of society
> • the accountability to recognized stakeholders[43]

Although the report, recognizing the diversity of traditions, eschews prescribing common standards, it does identify a tendency to convergence across the six major OECD countries that it studies. Indeed the traditional concern of countries such as Germany and Japan with the interests of constituencies other than shareholders is likely to further contribute to the enhancement of the concept of stakeholder at the international level.

The concept of stakeholder is consistent with the "rights revolution" which has been evident not only in the US but in international negotiations as well. In an extensive review of international law, Franck refers to "the post-ontological search for fairness," in which international law has become so complex and well developed that "lawyers no longer need to defend the very existence of international law. Thus emancipated from the constraints of defensive ontology, international lawyers are free to undertake a critical assessment of its content."[44] A key component of this assessment is fairness, which in turn involves the expansion of rights.[45]

The changes in the meaning and practices associated with capital that have been discussed in this section have not been brought about by the type of centralized political intervention that has been used historically, such as nationalization. Rather they result from a more decentralized process of negotiation and conflict, expressing and facilitated by the late-modern knowledge structure. As noted, for instance, the expansion of the narrow conception of capital embodied in shareholders' property rights is facilitated by the increased legal recognition that capital involves intangible knowledge and relationships and not simply possession of material resources. It would be a mistake to overstate the impact of this shift. Clearly shareholders continue to exercise a high degree of control over capital, and initiatives such as the Multilateral Agreement on Investment enhance their rights internationally. Nevertheless, ignoring the ways in which a key element of the international system, such as capital, is being altered by a political but decentralized renegotiation of its meaning, would be to miss a way in which the late-modern knowledge structure offers new avenues for citizen involvement in governance.

THE POSTMODERN KNOWLEDGE STRUCTURE
AND GLOBAL FINANCE: CONCLUSION

The above three sections have each addressed aspects of global finance that have been affected by the shift from the more centralized scientific knowledge structure discussed by Strange to a postmodern knowledge structure. In the first section the relevance of Giddens's notion of expert systems to the creation of markets of new financial instruments is striking. These new financial instruments are increasingly detached from underlying real assets. Moreover, the knowledge that creates them does not simply measure features of an external environment but rather simultaneously structures and orders the conduct of market actors; the coordination of expectations about the future is a central feature of these instruments. In the second section I turned from market activity to regulation. While centralized regulation is becoming decreasingly effective, new decentralized techniques are being adopted by regulators to regain control over global financial markets. These, like the financial transactions they seek to regulate, are based on the creation of generalized principles that structure the flow of information. The third section focused on the way in which the expansion of knowledge was undermining traditional conceptions of capital, once regarded as a solid foundational category of capitalism. The importance of human capital in a knowledge-intensive economy undermines the apparently natural connection between property rights and the possession of corporate assets. Challenges to the narrow conception of property rights embodied in shareholder-based systems of corporate governance are being transformed by the expansion of other rights.

In all three of the above areas the ontological and ordering effects of the postmodern knowledge structure are apparent. The production of knowledge is increasingly entering into the constitution of objects (such as tradeable products) and relationships (property rights in capital) that conventionally have been regarded as natural or material. Moreover, the ordering effects are ambiguous; control is both enhanced and eroded as knowledge evolves. Indeed the knowledge-production process has, consistent with Beck's approach, become more politicized, although this is often not recognized.

CONCLUSION

In this paper I have argued that Strange's concept of a knowledge structure is useful but that we need to explore the possibility that we are witnessing a transition from the more centralized, state-supported scientific stage that her account ends with to a more decentralized, postmodern knowledge structure in which knowledge enters with ever-increasing speed and intensity into the creation of those aspects of daily life that we take for granted. The distinctions between material and ideational, or between the real and imaginary, have become increasingly attenuated in those issue areas most affected by the postmodern knowledge structure.

Knowledge production can either enhance or undermine control. Indeed struggles over the decentralized effects of expert systems increasingly are displacing conventional centralized political struggles over state policy. The proliferation of rights both domestically and internationally is the vehicle through which these struggles are pursued. Approaches that ignore the role of the knowledge structure entirely, or that do not acknowledge the unique features of the knowledge structure in late modernity, run the risk of overlooking the significance for world politics of these developments.

NOTES

1. James N. Rosenau, *Turbulence in World Politics* (Princeton: Princeton University Press, 1990); Robert O. Keohane, *After Hegemony* (Ithaca and London: Cornell University Press, 1983); Peter Haas, "Introduction: Epistemic Communities and International Policy Coordination," in *Knowledge, Power, and International Policy Coordination*, special issue of *International Organization*, 46(1), Winter, 1992, pp. 1–35; Timothy W. Luke, "From the Flows of Power to the Power of Flows: Teaching World Politics in the Informationalizing World System," in Lev S. Gonick and Edward Weisband, eds., *Teaching World Politics* (Boulder: Westview, 1992), pp. 39–60.

2. Susan Strange, *States and Markets* (New York: Basil Blackwell, 1988), p. 117.

3. While there have been numerous insightful analyses of world politics that could be associated in varying ways with the notion of postmodernity, the tendency has been to focus on postmodernism as a type or attribute of scholarly approaches, rather than treating postmodernity as a longer-run socio-historical trend that is evident in nonscholarly practices in world politics. This tendency is evident in James Der Derian and Michael J. Shapiro, eds., *International/Intertextual Relations: Postmodern Readings of World Politics* (Lexington: Lexington Books, 1989). An important exception to this tendency is John Gerard Ruggie, "Territoriality and Beyond: Problematizing Modernity in International Relations," *International Organization*, 47(1), Winter, 1993, pp. 139–74, which seeks to "historicize postmodernity." The knowledge structure is not the primary focus of Ruggie's article, however.

4. Zygmunt Bauman, *Intimations of Postmodernity* (New York: Routledge, 1992); Ulrich Beck, *Risk Society: Toward a New Modernity* (London: Sage, 1992); Anthony Giddens, *The Consequences of Modernity* (Stanford: Stanford University Press, 1990); David Harvey, *The Condition of Postmodernity* (Oxford: Basil Blackwell, 1989); Scott Lash and John Urry, *Economies of Signs and Space* (London: Sage, 1994).

5. An important question is the role of knowledge in enhancing the capacity of international firms to complement or usurp the rule-making capacity of states. This theme is explored in A. Claire Cutler, Virginia Haufler, and Tony Porter, eds., *Private Authority and International Affairs* (Albany: SUNY Press, 1999).

6. Giddens, p. 27.

7. Roger Friedland, Roger and Deidre Boden, eds., *NowHere: Space, Time, and Modernity* (Berkeley: University of California Press, 1994); Stephen

Kern, *The Culture of Time and Space, 1880–1918* (Cambridge: Harvard University Press, 1983).

8. Anthony Giddens, *Modernity and Self-Identity* (Stanford: Stanford University Press, 1991).

9. Jean Baudrillard, *L'illusion de la fin* (Paris: Editions Galilée, 1992).

10. Luke argues that the transformations in the family and self-identity are driven by the extension of commodification and corporate mechanisms of control into new areas of daily life. He labels this as a shift from "Fordism" to "Fondaism," to a system which educates individuals "to view themselves as appreciating or wasting 'capital assets' in the corporate economy . . . even the deepest personal insecurities and self-doubt can be reified, labeled, and then subjected to the commodified therapies of disciplinary training programs," p. 118.

11. Beck, p. 135.

12. Giddens, *Consequences*, p. 124.

13. Beck, p. 133.

14. Beck, pp. 156, 170.

15. Jean Baudrillard, *The Transparency of Evil: Essays on Extreme Phenomena*, trans. James Benedict (London/New York: Verso, 1993), p. 6.

16. Beck, p. 195.

17. Bauman, p. 11.

18. Bauman, p. 7.

19. Bauman, p. 27.

20. Ernesto Laclau and Chantal Mouffe, *Hegemony and Socialist Strategy: Towards a Radical Democratic Politics*. Translated by Winston Moore and Paul Cammack (London: Verso, 1985), pp. 105–14, p. 171.

21. Group of Ten Study Group, *Recent Innovations in International Banking* (Basle: Bank for International Settlements, 1986).

22. Group of Ten, p. 19.

23. International Monetary Fund, *International Capital Markets: Developments, Prospects, and Policy Issues* (Washington: IMF, September 1995), p. 18.

24. Joan E. Spero, "Guiding Global Finance," *Foreign Policy* 73, Winter, 1988/89, pp. 114–34.

25. Timothy Sinclair, "Between State and Market: Hegemony and the Institutions of Collective Action Under Conditions of Capital Mobility," *Policy Sciences*, 27(4), 1994, pp. 447–66.

26. "Rating the Ratings Agencies," *Economist*, July 15, 1995, pp. 53–54.

27. For a more complete discussion of the themes in this paragraph, see Tony Porter, "The Transnational Agenda for Financial Regulation in Developing

Countries," in Leslie Elliott Armijo, ed., *Financial Globalization and Democracy in Emerging Markets* (Basingstoke: Macmillan, forthcoming, 1998) and Fédération Internationale des Bourses de Valeurs, *Annual Report*, 1994.

28. The Basle Committee on Banking Supervision, a Committee of the Group of Ten, is the leading body concerned with international bank regulation. See Tony Porter, *States, Markets and Regimes in Global Finance* (Basingstoke: Macmillan, 1993). The information in this and the next paragraph is based on various issues of the Basle Committee's *Report on International Developments in Banking Supervision*.

29. Ken Kral, Jack Serota, Carmen Johnson, and Price Waterhouse LLP International Tax Services, "Complying with Global Transfer Pricing Rules," *Journal of Accountancy*, September 1995, p. 28.

30. Graham Bannock and William Manser, *International Dictionary of Finance* (London: The Economist and Hutchison Business Books, 1989), p. 38.

31. Harry Braverman, *Labor and Monopoly Capital* (New York: Monthly Review Press, 1972).

32. Helen Garten, "Institutional Investors and the New Financial Order," *Rutgers Law Review* 44, 1992, pp. 584–674.

33. Gordon V. Smith and Russell L. Parr, *Valuation of Intellectual Property and Intangible Assets* (New York: John Wiley and Sons, 1989).

34. Thomas C. Grey, "The Disintegration of Property," in J. Roland Pennock and John W. Chapman, eds., *Property*, Nomos XXII (New York: New York University Press, 1980), pp. 69–85.

35. Joseph William Singer, "The Reliance Interest in Property," *Stanford Law Review* 40, February 1988, pp. 611–751.

36. Tom Peters, "Crazy Times Call for Crazy Organization," *Success*, July/August 1994, p. 56A. This management guru (p. 24D) quotes an executive as saying "if you can touch it, it's not real."

37. This has been a concern in the Organization for Economic Cooperation and Development. See, for instance, Riel Miller and Gregory Wurzburg, "Investing in Human Capital," *The OECD Observer* No. 193, April–May 1995, pp. 16–19. See also the *Economist*'s "Putting a Value on People," June 24, 1995, p. 69, which comments, "economic theory suggests that better human capital is an important source of growth. Measuring it is devilishly difficult."

38. See Daniel Blake Rubenstein, "Beyond the Clear-Cut," *CA Magazine*, October. 1994, pp. 22–29.

39. Dodge v. Ford Motor Co. 1919, cited in James J. Hanks, Jr., "Playing with Fire: Nonshareholder Constituency Statutes in the 1990s," *Stetson Law Review* XXI(1), Fall 1991, p. 99.

40. Steven M. H. Wallman, "The Proper Interpretation of Corporate Constituency Statutes and the Formulation of Director Duties," *Stetson Law Review* XXI(1), Fall 1991, pp. 163–96.

41. Hanks, pp. 119–20.

42. Trevor S. Norwitz, " 'The Metaphysics of Time': A Radical Corporate Vision," *The Business Lawyer* 46(2), February 1991, pp. 378–79.

43. International Capital Markets Group, *International Corporate Governance: Who Holds the Reins?* (London: ICMG, 1995), p. viii.

44. Thomas M. Franck, *Fairness in International Law and Institutions* (Oxford: Clarendon, 1995), pp. 6–7.

45. The increasing tendency in international negotiations and jurisprudence to recognize nongovernmental organizations has been cited by Shell as evidence of a stakeholder model at the international level. While this refers to an intergovernmental context, not private capital, it does signify a comparable decentralization of the right to be involved in decision making. See Richard G. Shell, "Trade Legalism and International Relations Theory: An Analysis of the World Trade Organization," *Duke Law Journal* 44(5), March 1995, pp. 830–927.

CHAPTER 8

Synchronic Global Governance and the International Political Economy of the Commonplace

TIMOTHY J. SINCLAIR

The world revolves around great decisions taken in high places, or so most international political economists would have us believe.[1] This is a zone of Michelin's three-star restaurants, first-class air travel, ministerial decisions, and globe-spanning treaties. In this view, global governance is an elite concern, a process in which decision-makers fashion the practices and understandings of our world. Rather than international political economy (IPE), a more appropriate name for the study of these phenomena might be something like international economic diplomacy, or possibly international public policy. Each approach has its merits. When reconfigured with a broader and deeper analytical focus, IPE has much more to offer. This chapter is about that potential.

A central argument in this chapter is that the substance of global governance is not exhausted by the activities of state decision makers and the usual trappings of sovereignty. It is also about everyday phenomena in our lives which support the incursions of processes of change, including globalization. This infrastructural view of global governance requires a different sort of international political economy analysis from the established approaches. This new international political economy will be one that links the changes at the broadest level with transformations in the lives of workers, consumers, and citizens. The significance of commonplace experience within IPE must be revalued to achieve this development. The commonplace world of everyday experience is important because this is where conflicts of interest are actually experienced and where change is most widely felt.

Beyond making this point about where to look for global governance, the chapter argues that contemporary global governance is characterized by a specific semantic content. Sets of core or metropolitan social practices—ways in which things are thought and done—are being internationalized, based on alliances of interest between dominant social forces in the core and those in the periphery. These signals from the center are not, however, passively received and adopted in the periphery, but become a dimension in the construction and corrosion of social alliances there.

What are these norms? At the center of global governance there is an assumption that all social situations are (or should be) much the same in their essentials and that political rule and capital investment have universal functional needs. Fundamental to this form of global governance, therefore, is the expectation that diverse societies will adjust themselves to the functional requirements of global capital. These global governance pressures are transmitted (and received) in commonplace, everyday ways, making shopping malls and mass media the central socioeconomic institutions alongside the more familiar subject matter of IPE. The homogeneity of the messages that constitute global governance compete with longer-standing but less organized sets of practices and habits, in which at least fragments of economic and political life remain embedded in pre-existing social arrangements, where time horizons are longer, concrete situations are deemed specific rather than interchangeable, and the emphasis is on generating growth through production rather than extracting profits by market trading. Of crucial importance to this contest between global governance and what I term local governance is the dialectical potential of the commonplace arena in which these pressures compete. Global governance is challenged because of the contradictions and crises which develop from time to time in everyday experience, reflecting the failure, thus far, of global governance to become hegemonic in the Gramscian sense of combining coercive power with a measure of consensus.

This chapter is organized in four parts. The first considers the conditions of possibility which have underpinned global governance as I understand it. In the section which follows, the notion of global governance is discussed and its characteristics elaborated. Part three of the chapter argues that full understanding of what I will call synchronic global governance requires a transformation of international political economy analysis away from exclusive focus on state-centric macroscopic concerns to include everyday socioeconomic experience. Some of the main features of this commonplace or prosaic approach to international political economy are sketched. In the final substantive element of the chapter I consider three examples of global governance processes: the global capital markets, deficit discourse, and what I have termed the global information economy. In the conclusions which follow I ponder potential countertendencies and implications for the emerging world order.

CONDITIONS OF POSSIBILITY

At least four conditions have given rise to the ascendance of global governance as I conceive of it. These conditions relate to the transactional volatility, the tendency to authority reallocation, and the transformations of working life which lie at the heart of the phenomenon called globalization. These conditions of possibility have made global governance a feasible development, although none have made it inevitable. The conditions include the return to austerity after the post-World War II long boom, the perceived failure of state activism, everyday hypercompetitiveness and its effects on individual and collective consciousness and behavior, and the absence of elite agreement on significant global problems.

The first condition, austerity, has undermined the established ensemble of hegemonic social relationships which underpinned the postwar world order. This order was premised on critical side payments between leading social forces and the subordinate ones which had been brought into alliance with them, such as established or semiskilled industrial workers.[2] These side payments assumed growth and constant productivity improvement. Mass production (and consumption) systems grew out of this set of social arrangements, organized around highly routinized work processes. However, with the onset of inflation in the late 1960s, this system became less able to deliver the sort of growth that was necessary to its maintenance. Rising unemployment in the 1980s and 1990s challenged established welfare norms enshrined in this set of social alliances by increasing the costs of the system, just as the fiscal capacity to support the existing level of transfers fell. The effect of these circumstances was the gradual development of a sense of pervasive crisis and growing demands for new solutions in most countries of the West.

If this first condition created a sense of ongoing crisis that would, it was understood, not find ready solution in the strategies of the past, the second condition destroyed the idea that socially mediated solutions are even possible. A widespread crisis of confidence developed in the practice of state intervention in most western economies during the late 1980s. Possible causes for the development of this scepticism about the social utility of the state lie in the persistence of low rates of growth, despite repeated efforts to refire the postwar growth dynamic through corporatist wage arrangements, large infrastructure and energy projects, and the nationalization of strategic assets. The reversal of many of these "Think Big" initiatives in places as diverse as Alberta and New Zealand in the second half of the 1980s only reinforced the sense that states were impotent in the face of the new conditions.[3] More recently, the re-emergence of international capital mobility has made states behave in ways which demonstrate to both hegemonic and subordinate social forces that states are no longer necessarily the supreme source of effective social and political authority.[4] Although states retain the legal means to exercise direct power, the substance of their action supports the view that their capacity to act in ways which refocus social organization toward collective goals has substantially diminished. The reassertion of orthodox economics since the early 1980s has further strengthened this cross-class understanding by promoting the argument that states do not have the capacity to make effective choices in markets because they lack information and are driven by political imperatives which are not conducive to sound business decisions.[5] This view has become the point of departure for policy initiatives in the central bureaucratic institutions of western societies. It is no longer possible to make convincing arguments about the benefits of state action in ways which were conventional in the postwar era. The audience is dubious about the activist state and its plans and schemes.[6]

The third condition which has promoted the form of global governance I identify relates directly to the population's sense of how to survive. Hypercompetitiveness has become a central feature of everyday experience in the West, and increasingly in what was the communist bloc too. This phenomenon is related directly to what we typically think of as globalization: plant closures and the relocation of industrial capacity to low-wage countries, expanded trade flows, increased investment mobility, and so forth. But these material developments are importantly matched by an intersubjective understanding that the old regime of postwar expectations is no longer operative in the post-Cold War order.

This regime of forty-hour weeks and work rules, of demarcation lines, of mass production and large volumes of cheap, standard goods for consumption, had its own logic which valued the individual's reproduction as both a worker and consumer. This established set of expectations, which contained protective dimensions, has of course been replaced by fierce competition of a zero-sum kind, often between workers, which varies depending on industry sector and type of work. This means that for many individuals in the West, the workplace is a zone of potential dangers, in which other employees are likely enemies in the struggle for a semblance of security. This hypercompetitiveness is evident both extensively, in terms of longer hours of work, and intensively, in heightened instrumentalism about work relationships. Importantly, hypercompetitiveness reduces the propensity of individuals mentally to place themselves in the position of others, thus reducing their own tolerance for taxation and for the trade-offs inherent in representative politics. Individualization has been greatly enhanced, and forms of collectivization have increasingly moved outside the set of feasible possibilities for the atomized. Again, this is an ideal-typical situation, and is less true of some places than others (and some sorts of work than others). In Germany, for example, more competitive business conditions like longer shopping hours have met a wall of hostility (from workers) and indifference (from consumers).[7]

The lack of a robust intra-elite consensus is also an important condition making everyday forms of global governance possible. This condition concerns social and political leadership and its role in a well-functioning system of trade-offs between diverging and converging social interests. Although certain policy options seem to have been effectively ruled out in globalized conditions, there is an absence of agreement on solutions to large-scale problems of the biosphere, of financial volatility and market panics, of endemic European unemployment, and of perpetual misery in peripheral zones such as sub-Saharan Africa. Susan Strange has lamented the increasingly unilateral nature of US policy in a number of these contexts.[8] Within western societies themselves there is another form of unilateralism. It is also a reflection of this lack of agreement and the power of certain interests to dominate in the absence of more consensual conditions. Stephen Gill has discussed this narrower, disciplinary mode of social regulation.[9] This reflects an inability on many issues to establish a genuine and lasting set of trade-offs between competing interests. As a consequence, differences over economic policy, say, generated by economic crisis, increasingly have come to be solved by the imposition of solutions rather than more corporatist means. This way of dealing with intra-elite differences of view has had a chilling effect on public debate. The scope of political contestation has diminished as economic policy is made increasingly independent of electoral politics on the grounds that these are technical matters. The origins of the decay of agreement, and the more disciplinary world order that accompanies it, lie in the causes of the austerity discussed above.

FORMS OF GLOBAL GOVERNANCE

Let us now consider how these conditions of possibility have actually shaped the experience of global governance. The world we live in reflects the ascendancy of particular interests and their associated ways of thinking and acting, combined with the subordination of other habits and practices. The nature of this global order, how it was created and what implications it has, constitutes the study of global governance. This is an historical, concrete matter, and one in which the interests of particular social forces must be taken into account. Global governance is not, therefore, in any sense above human social relations. It is the structuring of these relations into particular patterns that make up the subject matter of global governance.

What is global governance then? Considered most broadly, global governance can be understood as the various means that social forces employ to realise particular forms of world order, where world order denotes "an historically specific configuration of power" permeating a global system comprising at least three main components: a global political economy, an interstate system, and the biosphere.[10] It is the means of world order realization that is the substance of global governance.

The historically specific form of governance I am interested in I term synchronic global governance. The term *synchronic* comes originally from Saussure's linguistic thought.[11] He distinguished the synchronic study of language from what he called the diachronic. The synchronic referred to the current logic of a language, or the relations of coexistence between its elements. The diachrony of language sought the origins and processes of language development. Understanding the former requires ignoring the complexity of the latter, suggested Saussure. These ideas were subsequently applied to social analysis by Sorel and, later, Piaget. Sorel linked the prominence of the synchronic study of all things with the maximizing proclivities of the newly emerging middle classes of his time.[12] Synchronic thought, Sorel argued, is best understood as a technology of accumulation. Piaget makes the case for the necessity of understanding both the synchronic and the diachronic, but argues that although interconnected, one does not necessarily follow the other. The origins of social practices do not, for example, necessarily explain their current operation, as practices may be integrated into new orders which change their operation altogether.[13]

Cox appropriates these ways of thinking about social phenomena and applies them to world order in two ways. The first follows Saussure, Sorel, and Piaget in drawing the distinction between the synchronic and the diachronic, and Piaget in seeing the importance of both elements in developing an understanding of social life. The second sense in which Cox appropriates these ideas develops Sorel's insight about mentalities as technologies of accumulation. Particular orders, suggests Cox, are characterised by the dominance of synchronic or diachronic mentalities. These mentalities are linked by Cox to blocs or alliances of social forces.[14] It is in this second sense of a technology of accumulation that I want to characterize the dominant form of global governance as synchronic. This technology remains dominant, not hegemonic, because of its more disciplinary, less consensual character.

What are the characteristic elements of the synchronic form of global governance? I argue that there are three central principles. The first principle is the universalization of self-regulating markets and exoticization of other modes of social interaction. Although it is not realized in the concrete, the notion of a self-regulating market, free from state interference and redistributive costs, has again become a central organizing focus in western societies. Other forms of social organization, it seems, will increasingly be judged against this norm. This tendency has developed to the point where George Soros, probably the most successful financial speculator the world has seen, warned—seemingly without irony—of the risk to an open society posed by laissez-faire thinking.[15] The resurgence of the self-regulating market norm makes any sense of intentional community action open to question not on its merits, but more importantly, in principle.

The second principle or aspect of synchronic global governance to highlight is its tendency to identify time and space as obstacles or matters of no value, and therefore as problems to be overcome. This intolerance of the material world is related to the development of the low-growth dynamic in developed countries since the end of the long boom, and the resulting heightened business competition. Synchronic global governance is centrally concerned with faster turnover, just-in-time practices, and efficiency gains. Time horizons are shortened, and little thought is given to creating stable arrangements for social reproduction over the long run. There is a prevailing sense that there is no point in establishing such habits when the nature of the competition is likely to shift tomorrow, making these practices redundant. Schumpeter's "creative destruction" is thus taken to its extreme by being fed into the very logic of governance.[16]

The last feature of synchronic global governance I want to comment on here is the narrower nature of relationships and the institutions they are built on. The means employed by the leading social forces to remake the world order leads individuals increasingly to think they do not need community or other support to prosper, that such phenomena are just further taxes on them. This atomizing tendency inherent in the prevailing form of global governance is perhaps its most profound effect. Our expectations, resistances, and capacities for organization are limited by this mentality. This is not simply a response to helplessness. Some privileged social forces, such as Lasch's elites, embrace atomization. Increasingly they "have removed themselves from the common life."[17]

INTERNATIONAL POLITICAL ECONOMY OF THE COMMONPLACE

The argument I now wish to make is that the explanation of synchronic global governance and an understanding of its significance requires a very different type of international political economy. Mainstream or problem-solving IPE starts with a state-centric ontology and considers how changes in state capacity have impact on other states.[18] Private agents are formally outside the set of phenomena to be explained. However, as I have shown elsewhere, this public-private dichotomy is unsustainable in IPE, because authority cannot be allocated simply to public or state institutions but also permeates private institutions and social relations in a globalized world order.[19]

Braudel sought a similar goal in the study of history. "Is it possible somehow," he asked, "to convey simultaneously both that conspicuous history which holds our attention by its continual and dramatic changes— and that other, submerged history, almost silent and always discreet . . . ?"[20] Campbell, too, has explicitly advocated the importance of the everyday in international relations because of its status as the site of political conflict in which all manner of social determinations meet.[21] It is here that the truly infrastructural changes that are part of synchronic global governance can be found.

What features will an international political economy of the commonplace (IPEC) have? Only a very tentative answer can be given here. An open ontology and a refutation of transhistorical certainties will be central. More specifically, IPEC will break with the 'states and markets' view of the world, in which specific domains are allocated to politics and economics respectively. A feature of the new thinking will be sensitivity to the existence of authority outside the context of the state and to new types of authority other than those defined by law. There will likely be a general extra-state character to IPEC work.

The second major characteristic of IPEC that can be anticipated here is an interest in drawing links between ordinary lives and major structural change. The only reason to understand the latter is to illuminate the former, but the former also reveals much about broad change. Consumer behavior, tax revolts, and education are all important places to develop understanding of the emerging world order for those with an IPEC commitment.

The last characteristic of IPEC thinking I want to outline is a commitment to an ontology in which the world is understood to be socially constructed. What I am pointing to here is the importance of intersubjectively held beliefs in the making of social life. These collective views become a basis for action because agents think out their strategies with these beliefs concerning what others are up to uppermost in their minds. This is how financial markets work, as traders place bets on what they anticipate others will be thinking and planning. Implicit in this is a denial of a static social world. There is no fixed material order in social terms, but only the world we construct mentally and act upon. This being the case, a static, nonsocial analysis is insufficient, and IPEC must be built on a constant juxtaposition of synchronic and diachronic modes of investigation of the material and ideational. The social world is not sufficiently fixed *in situ* for a synchronic, functional analysis alone.

THREE EXAMPLES

I now want to illustrate my concern with the synchronic form of global governance and with developing an international political economy of the commonplace to investigate it by considering three brief examples drawn from my own research program.

The first case I discuss is financial disintermediation. Financial intermediation occurs when a party, usually a bank, takes deposits and makes loans, providing an investment opportunity for lenders and credit for borrowers. The intermediary solves the information problem that exists for both parties. However, this comes at a price which roughly amounts to the cost of the bad loans plus the remainder of the bank's overhead. Because of these costs, and the financial vulnerability of many banks during the 1980s, a different way of borrowing money has developed in which borrowers and lenders have met directly in capital markets, cutting the bank out of the picture. Money market accounts, for example, allow the advantages (and risks) of disintermediation to be experienced by the consumer as well as by major borrowers.

Disintermediation is a prime example of synchronic global governance. It gives rise to a distancing of borrower and lender rather than a closer relationship, as might at first be thought. The reason for this is that holders of bonds and stocks are well positioned to trade their way out of any relationship with the firms and governments that borrowed their money by using secondary markets. Banks, by contrast, tend to be stuck with their loan portfolios. The fact that banks are in a sense prisoners to their borrowers makes them somewhat more patient and willing to think through the growth dynamics required to repay the loans. German banks have taken this most seriously, as Zysman shows.[22]

An important feature of disintermediation is the movement from an institutionalized world of legal authorities to a de-centered, marketized world. At the wholesale level we see the development of epistemic authorities such as bond-rating agencies, which substitute their information and expertise for bank judgments. Where does the commonplace come into this? Considering the dynamics of markets and institutions themselves is, by comparison with the orthodox IPE ontology centred on sovereignty, to bring the commonplace into the frame (even if it is still at rather an elevated level). Beyond this sphere, we can see analogous processes of social disintermediation in ordinary lives generated by privatization and hypercompetitiveness. Individuals are empowered by the advent of synchronic global governance only to the extent that they have the resources to take advantage of it. Increases in the public perception of insecurity in the West reflect the realization by many that they do not have these resources.

An example of synchronic global governance which reaches into the very pores of western society is associated with the development of what I have termed the deficit discourse.[23] What I am referring to here is the complete turn around in thinking within OECD states about public deficits over the past decade. Where public sector deficits were thought to be useful ways of stimulating economies during the postwar era, they have increasingly fallen into disrepute despite the fact that there is actually disagreement about the impact of deficits in the public finance and economics literature.[24]

The deficit discourse has been built upon an analogy between public expenditure and the private checking account. Purveyors of this view of things have claimed that just like the individual, the state must live within its means. This is a highly synchronic view of state finance, as it leaves out of the picture the fact that in general states are the most attractive, lowest risk borrowers in any market, far more so than corporations or individuals. It also eliminates the possibility of the state having a social purpose of any kind if the nature of its spending is equated with private expenditure.

The IPE of the commonplace is relevant in this situation because transnational ideologies such as deficit discourse acquire power through the efforts made to connect broad policy changes to the everyday experience of millions of citizens and taxpayers. What also comes through in this example is the significance of presentation or staging in the subject matter of IPEC.[25] State-centric IPE ignores these sorts of crucial synchronic moments in global governance.

The Global Information Economy (GIE) provides my final example of synchronic global governance and the need for an IPE of the commonplace. The GIE can be defined very broadly as an emerging complex of information and knowledge production, distribution, and consumption, which is tending to displace the material mass production economies of the postwar era.[26] I want to make two points about the GIE as a mechanism of synchronic global governance. The first point is about the tendency it generates to homogenize thought, which I have termed cognitive centralization. Cognitive centralization is much more significant than the mere emulation of American popular culture. Its significance goes beyond consumption. What I am identifying here is not the reduction of all practices and habits to those of American capitalism. I argue instead that what is developing is a tendency for the delegitmization of alternate ways of solving problems, of thinking through issues, and of anticipating mechanisms for economic and social adjustment. Over the long haul, even if alternative cognitive practices emerge and compete with the epistemically authoritative, I suggest that the basis for that competition will be steadily narrower and increasingly permissive only of cultural expressions, especially where such expressions can be commodified. The places to look for cognitive centralization are in accounting practices, in the organization of schooling and university research, in privatization programs, in the use of foreign consultants and advisers, and in models of corporate organization, amongst others. These are contexts in which local or national expertise is especially vulnerable to the predations of cognitive centralization. Crowding out diversity is characteristic of synchronic global governance.

My second point about synchronic global governance and the GIE is that the emerging information complex seems to be predicated on a very unequal society in which a small group of knowledge workers obtain great benefits, and a vast pool of service workers struggle to make ends meet. This is the world described by Drucker.[27] Such an order acts as a considerable discipline upon the lives of ordinary people, who must work very hard to have a chance at employment in "good" knowledge-based jobs. However, such a situation is unstable and prone to fall into crisis as victims express their discontent. Is this the situation in much of Western Europe today? This failure to attend to the basic reproduction of the population is one of the most significant vulnerabilities of synchronic global governance.[28] An IPE of the commonplace is best placed to reveal the sorts of work-based tensions suggested here. IPE, as it is, systematically ignores such matters.

CONCLUSIONS

In this chapter I have tried to demonstrate how what has come to be called global governance is best understood in a particular form, as synchronic global governance, and is most effectively investigated through a new International Political Economy of the Commonplace. I illustrated the utility of this approach by briefly sketching some applications to my existing research program. Not considered here, but a priority for further work, is a more systematic elaboration of the ontological and epistemological basis of IPEC. I would now like to offer three prognoses for the emerging world order based on these considerations.

My first point is that the focus of future global change will be infrastructural and that the emerging world order will reflect a more unified operating system than ever before. I am not suggesting here that some sort of global culture is developing. However, beneath the surface is a slow change in expectations which will bring with it pressure to standardize around common business practices.

We can expect the nature of challenges to globalization to change, too. The more infrastructural character of synchronic global governance is not likely to be lost on antiglobalization forces, and it seems probable that they will target their efforts with this in mind. Standards and codes are likely to become hot sites of political contestation in the future. The EU is a good place to look for such conflicts.

Increased personal exposure to risk will dominate the future as intermediating institutions try to withdraw and as social arrangements become increasingly dominated by the discourse of efficiency. Whether aggregate risk itself is likely to increase or not is unclear. However, the formation of an intersubjective sense that aggregate risk has increased is perceivable. Given this, we can expect considerable social mobilization around avoiding exposure to risk. This could be a boom time for insurance and pensions in compensation for what people see as the unsupportive nature of the social system. Perhaps it is only if such individual responses come unstuck that society and the diachronic ethos can reassert themselves against synchronic global governance.

NOTES

1. This chapter was first presented as a paper at the annual meeting of the International Studies Association, Toronto, March 1997. For comments, I thank Bud Duvall, J. Ann Tickner, Jacqui True, Martin Hewson, and the anonymous reviewers of this volume.

2. See the essays in *Post-Fordism: A Reader*, edited by Ash Amin (Oxford: Blackwell, 1994) for an elaboration of these issues.

3. Roger Douglas and Louise Callen, *Roger Douglas: Toward Prosperity* (Auckland: David Bateman, 1987), pp. 151–66.

4. There is a large and growing literature on this theme. An interesting place to start is Susan Strange, *The Retreat of the State: The Diffusion of Power in the World Economy* (Cambridge: Cambridge University Press, 1996).

5. See, for example, Murray J. Horn, *The Political Economy of Public Administration: Institutional Choice in the Public Sector* (Cambridge: Cambridge University Press, 1995).

6. It would be a mistake, of course, to insist that this is always the case. Countertendencies exist. In the United Kingdom, for example, a number of sporting events remain listed by the state and must be shown on free broadcast television rather than pay cable or satellite channels. However, the point to be made is that such policies look increasingly anachronistic.

7. Ralph Atkins, "Longer Hours Leave Consumers Cold: German Retailers are Disappointed by the Response to an Extension of Opening Hours," *Financial Times*, November 1, 1997, p. 2.

8. Susan Strange, "The Persistent Myth of Lost Hegemony," *International Organization*, Volume 41, Number 4, Autumn 1987, pp. 551–74.

9. Stephen Gill, "Structural Change and Global Political Economy: Globalizing Elites and the Emerging World Order," *Global Transformation: Challenges to the State System*, Yoshikazu Sakamoto, ed. (Tokyo: United Nations University Press, 1994).

10. Robert W. Cox with Timothy J. Sinclair, *Approaches to World Order* (Cambridge: Cambridge University Press, 1996), p. 494.

11. Ferdinand de Saussure, *Course in General Linguistics* (La Salle, IL: Open Court, 1983).

12. Georges Sorel, *Reflections on Violence*, translated by T. E. Hulme and J. Roth (New York: Collier, 1961), p. 141.

13. Jean Piaget, *Sociological Studies* (London: Routledge, 1995), p. 50.

14. Cox, 1996, pp. 181–88.

15. George Soros, "The Capitalist Threat," *The Atlantic Monthly*, February 1997, pp. 45–58.

16. Joseph A. Schumpeter, *Capitalism, Socialism, and Democracy* (London: Allen and Unwin, 1976).

17. Christopher Lasch, *The Revolt of the Elites and the Betrayal of Democracy* (New York: Norton, 1995), p. 45.

18. A good discussion of this orthodoxy can be found in Craig N. Murphy and Roger Tooze, "Getting Beyond the 'Common Sense' of the IPE Orthodoxy," in *The New International Political Economy* (Boulder, CO: Lynne Rienner, 1991).

19. Timothy J. Sinclair, "Passing Judgement: Credit Rating Processes as Regulatory Mechanisms of Governance in the Emerging World Order," *Review of International Political Economy*, Volume 1, Number 1, Spring 1994, pp. 133–59.

20. Fernand Braudel, *The Mediterranean and the Mediterranean World in the Age of Philip II*, Volume I, translated by Sian Reynolds (London: Collins, 1972), p. 16.

21. David Campbell, "Political Prosaics, Transversal Politics, and the Anarchical World," *Challenging Boundaries: Global Flows, Territorial Identities*, edited by Michael J. Shapiro and Hayward R. Alker (Minneapolis: University of Minnesota Press, 1996), p. 23. Also see Randall D. Germain, "The Worlds of Finance: A Braudelian Perspective on IPE," *European Journal of International Relations*, Volume 2, Number 2, 1996, pp. 201–30.

22. John Zysman, *Governments, Markets, and Growth: Financial Systems and the Politics of Industrial Change* (Ithaca, NY: Cornell University Press, 1983).

23. Timothy J. Sinclair, "Deficit Projections: The Global Construction of Mental Frameworks of the Orthodox," paper presented to the annual meeting of the International Studies Association, San Diego, CA, April 1996.

24. See, for example, Robert Eisner, *The Misunderstood Economy* (Boston: Harvard Business School Press, 1994).

25. For elaboration of this point, see Bruce Lincoln, *Authority: Construction and Corrosion* (Chicago: University of Chicago Press, 1994), p. 11.

26. Timothy J. Sinclair, "The Global Information Economy and the Generation of Cognitive Centralization," paper presented to the annual meeting of the American Political Science Association, San Francisco, CA, September 1996.

27. Peter F. Drucker, *Post-Capitalist Society* (New York: HarperBusiness, 1993).

28. Ethan B. Kapstein, "Workers and the World Economy," *Foreign Affairs,* May/June 1996, pp. 16–37.

CHAPTER 9

Borrowing Authority;
Eclipsing Government

M. MARK AMEN

In various places and times, innovations in credit have transformed the devices and levers that release "the great mass of elementary economic activity" trapped in everyday life. Italian merchant-bankers unleashed commercial trade when they created bills of exchange circa 1300. Shortly after 1550, Europe was further integrated when Genoa's bankers combined silver, gold, and bills of exchange to finance the Spanish crown and the Italian economy. The Rothschild conglomerate spurred the expansion of international trade and investment during the nineteenth century when it constructed financial networks for transnational activities. Tinkering with computers in the latter part of the twentieth century, financial analysts commodified the credit activities of market economies by inventing derivatives. People responded to these inventions and began to participate in the lender-borrower relations these discoveries required. As time passed, these new credit relations were repeated in the everyday life of various locations. Some endured, became routine, and led to further transformations of credit markets and economic relations. In its repetition, each device and lever that endured created what Braudel has referred to as "a generality or rather a structure. It pervades society at all levels, and characterizes ways of being and behaving which are perpetuated through endless ages."[1]

Credit is one of many sites where people govern their social relations. Classical, Marxist, and liberal traditions in political economy accept Genoese merchant bankers, the Rothschilds, inventors of derivatives, and others like them as important players in the governance of political economic life. These traditions have nonetheless developed a rich and diverse analysis of how institutions, structures, and other forces mold and lead such people in shaping power and governing many social sites. Notwithstanding the agency/structure debate in which some have participated, these efforts tend to treat people as representations of underlying market, political, or natural forces and laws rather than as inventors of their own lives. They do not attend to people in historical situations and explain how they affect power and governance in particular settings. The entire classical tradition, from Smith through post-Keynesian economics, has never suspended its central tendency to explain economic life by referring to market forces and structures. People are seen through the lenses of investment, production, and consumption. Marxism also has retained a commitment to detecting those forces that denote the essence of humans. In this tradition, a historicized human nature is tied to the organization of social life. Liberal theory has fared no better. Its conceptions of sovereignty, human nature, and inalienable rights have allowed liberalism (and its neorealist variant) to assess political economy and people in relation to the structure of the state and institutions of government. The search for ultimate explanations also deters those who are outside these three traditions from exploring the extent to which people represent themselves. The Frankfurt School, for instance, presumed that humans have true (unchanging?) interests even though they are often misled in pursuing them. Even Foucault maintained a central focus on the importance of institutional life. In his assessment of the transformation of government's role from "ruling" to "guiding" the population, he was still concerned with government's innovative strategy of using disciplines like the market to mold and shape human beings. Consequently, these traditions neglect the effect people have on power and governance—one that is independent of market, government, social, and teleological forces.

People make more than an intervening and passive contribution to their fates. They are active in governance, or the social process of distributing power that results from the ways in which people and their institutions exchange knowledge. People govern when they congregate and form ways of "being and behaving" concerning interests they hope to satisfy. Their particular efforts at these sites make a difference for governance, regardless of whether they have their own "right" interests in mind and independent of any guidance the market and government may provide. People bring and subject their thoughts, communications, and practices to the purposes that attract them to places of governance. In time, enough people conform to new ways of being and behaving to establish norms and routines in these places. The transformation to mercantilism, for instance, was initiated by relations among people rather than by the feudal system of government and religion. The "introduction of new methods in international trade . . . business by correspondence and the establishment of the Italians in Flanders near the centers of cloth production" were the determining factors in creating the commercial revolution that led to mercantile capitalism.[2] After merchant bankers introduced bills of exchange in the late feudal period, new ways of governing trade and finance were set in motion. Feudal law was replaced by a system of self-regulation and arbitration designed and run by the merchants themselves. The prohibitions of usury were suspended to advance merchant interests. New social relations emerged as these merchants came to terms with a feudal system ill-suited to economic development. City-states formed and were governed by tradesmen and merchants rather than by the feudal aristocracy.[3] Other people joined these merchant bankers in the venture that ultimately led to mercantilism. How did power function throughout this transitional period in the political economy of Europe? Each theoretical tradition will construct a response that is tied to one or a combination of the following factors: the feudal class system; the pursuit of natural interests; sovereignty; individual entrepreneurship; new methods and structures (or disciplines) in international trade, finance, and other areas; or the power of religion.

I approach the answer from a different perspective by looking at people as agents of power rather than as representations of some other and ultimate source of power. I suspend final claims concerning the power and governance of credit relations and explore the possibility that people have an effect on two aspects of credit relations: how power functions in them and why their governance persists. I begin the first topic by assessing the relationship between power and knowledge.[4] My claim is that people are the original source of knowledge, and that their use of it affects how power functions in the governance of credit relations. While people affect power in governing themselves, their response to knowledge does not account for the persistence of governance. I therefore turn to the second topic by introducing the notion of authority to explain how people's actions allow their governance of credit to last. I do not propose to explain how power functions and governance persists in either particular or general historical periods. Instead I situate the impact people have on power and governance in isolated places and times for the purpose of illustrating ways in which people affect credit relations. In each section, I also consider the implications for government's role in the governance of credit relations when this perspective is taken.

THE POWER OF KNOWLEDGE

People affect power in governance through their relation to knowledge. How power functions in credit relations is determined by the ways in which people reconcile four interrelated conditions of knowledge: that it is finite, fixed, paradoxical, and hierarchical.

KNOWLEDGE IS FINITE

First, knowledge offers no freestanding platform from which to determine how power functions in credit relations. Without final knowledge, people are still required to govern a complex, pervasive, and abstract set of relations that entail "two promises separated in time: I will do something for you, you will pay me later."[5] These promises complicate governance because every credit relation requires connecting less than innocent knowledge about the present (and uncertain) world with even less certain knowledge about tomorrow. The risk involved, as Keynes pointed out, is only overcome by mass psychology.[6] Since knowledge is finite, people package it to suit their interests. They select pieces of information, assign meaning, make factual claims, and render particular interpretations and understandings. The power people have in credit relations is therefore first and foremost guided by what everyone claims to know about the purposes for which these relations are formed. What people claim to know about financing trade, home mortgages, or credit cards is neither absolute nor final; instead, it is selective and contingent upon the goals they hope to attain when they enter these credit relations.

Although knowledge is never complete, people use it to invent new routines in credit relations. In the early 1990s, people changed credit relations when they created derivatives.[7] Jeff Spies, Treasurer for the City of St. Petersburg, Florida, was one of many municipal money managers who contributed to this innovation. He began investing in derivatives in 1991. His investments were in collateralized mortgage obligations (CMOs), bonds created by pools of home mortgages, inverse floaters that pay higher returns as interest rates fall, and floaters to hedge a declining return on inverse floaters. When the inverse floater bond rates began to rise at the end of 1994, Spies bought floaters to offset declining returns from the inverse floaters. He eventually placed thirty-seven percent of the city's portfolio (i.e., $85 million) in derivatives by purchasing these three instruments. Although the portfolio of the City of St. Petersburg suffered a $40 million paper loss in February 1995 as a consequence of his actions, Spies was able to act outside the norm and assist in the market's innovation.[8]

Unique talents and abilities are at play when people use their knowledge to create new credit opportunities for themselves and others. People acquire power in credit relations in part by the way in which their individual traits influence how they acquire and apply knowledge. One such trait is the capacity to learn causally. Individuals are causal learners when they think about how their own resources and preferences interface with what they know about the market. This self-awareness need not employ an analytic, systematic, or calculating process; but it must include learning about oneself in the social context. Credit card indebtedness illustrates that many lack this trait. United States revolving credit, primarily credit card debt, has increased over the last thirty years from $30 billion in 1977 to well over $444 billion. It is projected to increase to over $660 billion by 2000.[9] Only 35 percent of United States credit card holders pay off their balances in full each month. A record 1.3 million Americans filed for bankruptcy during the fiscal year ending June 30, 1997. The Consumer Credit Counseling Service (CCCS), an affiliate of the National Foundation for Consumer Credit, began creating local agencies in the early 1980s "to help consumers understand the trammels of the credit system and show them how to better manage money and credit."[10] CCCS centers have grown from 200 in 1984 to more than 1,300 branches today. These agencies do not address the psychological, social, and cognitive causes of chronic indebtedness. Instead, they negotiate a realistic payment plan for the client in exchange for receiving from the creditors a percentage of what is collected. Individuals thus are left to themselves. If they do not act as causal learners, they cannot remain debt-free and acquire power in credit card markets.

A second indicator of causal learning is the capacity to understand other individuals and institutions in the market and to understand when and how to respond to them. This element of causal learning presupposes that humans possess what Onuf has described as the "recursive" capacity "of knowledge agents to refer to their own or others' past and anticipated actions in deciding how to act."[11] Understanding others requires that they be taken on their own terms—that knowledge about them be considered within their particular historical, socioeconomic contexts. Todorov and Nandy have shown, in their respective works on the Spanish conquest of the Americas and on the British conquest of India, that the need to know others on their own terms is derived from a historical separation of the world into "us" versus "them."[12] This separation allows people to understand or disregard "the other." Some banks have recently shown, by changing the lending terms so that women and minorities can receive microloans, that they have the capacity to understand others who normally do not qualify for credit.

John Meriwether's activities in 1988 illustrate that understanding others also occurs in institutional settings. Meriwether and his colleagues at Salomon Brothers noticed that mortgage-backed securities were paying 1.5 rather than 1.0 percentage points more than Treasury securities. Meriwether and his partners bet $10 billion that the spread would narrow to traditional levels. They were right and made a quick profit of $275 million. Merely knowing about the spread was not sufficient. Meriwether needed to know the glitches in the market. As Hamilton notes, "Finance is information—or misinformation. He who hears the news first stands to gain most. For money is made in the markets. . . .by being ahead of market sentiment."[13] While timing and resources were crucial, Meriwether also had to know the market sufficiently to be ahead of its sentiments.

KNOWLEDGE IS FIXED

Although knowledge is finite, it is also firmly in place at the sites of governance to which people come. People encounter this second condition of knowledge when they come to credit. There they find fixed knowledge in the ways of being and behaving that characterize governance of credit. At this point, people can submit to a process of learning, conform to what is expected of them, and even change their activities to comply with the norms. This is the case when individuals change their spending patterns to maintain good standing with their credit card company. Conformance to routines is not unique. As forms of credit have multiplied and spread, people have reconciled the potential dilemma between what they know and fixed knowledge by complying with the expectations contained in various credit instruments: bank notes, promissory notes, letters of credit, joint stocks, bonds, mortgages, securities, and more recently, junk bonds, interest rate swaps, collateralized mortgage obligations (CMOs), inverse floaters, and other forms of commodified credit.[14]

While people may learn the routines of credit and even conform to them, they may not be aware of either the detailed knowledge about themselves or how that knowledge may affect them. In the case of the home mortgage industry, for instance, mortgage companies are turning to mathematical default-risk scoring techniques that 'tag' homeowners after their closing date. Scores determine how the industry treats individuals who are delinquent on a monthly payment. The scores are based on public and private data about people that is on file with the major credit reporting agencies in the United States (i.e., Equifax, TRW, and TransUnion). Mortgage companies assume a low score is more likely to lead to delinquency and foreclosure, and they therefore treat the borrower with greater scrutiny than if he or she had a high score.[15] Since homeowners do not know their scores, they have no idea if or how they should prepare themselves for any action the mortgage companies may take. As Gill has noted, this detailed knowledge about and 'sorting' of people based on their credit behaviors also is prevalent in the credit card surveillance and ratings system.[16]

It is not surprising, then, that people do not automatically advance their interests when they comply with the routines of credit. Credit swap outcomes illustrate that even corporations may be unaware of market operations. As Sassen notes, these financial instruments are part of "commodity markets, where the value of the instrument lies in its resale potential."[17] Swaps are exchanges of credit commodities that are used for a variety of purposes, such as reducing the cost of borrowing or the loss of profits. In April 1994, Procter and Gamble Company lost $102 million due to bad investments in interest rate swaps. Interest rate swaps are contracts in which two parties agree to swap different types of interest payments on a principal amount that is not exchanged. Like other companies with global operations, Procter and Gamble used swaps to reduce the likelihood that its profits in foreign countries would be hurt by interest rate and currency differentials when it converted profits into US dollars. The company incurred losses from two leveraged swaps derived from complex formulas that assumed US and German interest rates would fall. When they rose, the swaps backfired. According to Erik Nelson, senior vice president for Procter and Gamble, "the individuals involved didn't fully understand what they were up against in terms of the swaps presented to them, and for that reason they got themselves into something they didn't fully understand."[18]

KNOWLEDGE OPENS A PARADOXICAL AVENUE TO POWER

In both its finite and fixed forms, knowledge is active and as such "is linked to power... as the unavoidable result of its own activity."[19] Power distributions in credit relations result from the ways in which these two forms of knowledge are reconciled. A third aspect of knowledge, therefore, is that the resolution of these two knowledges resides in people. They must contend with a paradoxical relationship between competing knowledge claims. Governance assumes "human beings as agents, and thereby involves them as mediums of power in the very exercise of power upon themselves." People have knowledge that empowers; and they are also empowered by submitting to the knowledge of others whose routines prevail. Knowledge entails "subjectification to power that is empowering."[20] Humans have power to act as agents of knowledge, and they are subject to the power of knowledge contained in the routines they learn at the sites of governance. Every credit card holder experiences both the limits of having a card as well as the opportunities previously unavailable. They both subject themselves to power and are empowered by this subjection.

Every credit relationship entails an exchange of knowledge between borrowers and lenders. The knowledge exchanged is a mixture of new and routine information. Lenders generally operate from the power of categories that require prospective borrowers to provide relevant information about qualifying for a loan. Lenders determine what information is relevant to obtain a home mortgage, letters of credit for trade, or a credit card. In each of these instances, borrowers have no direct control over setting the qualifying categories. This is not to say that lenders always and automatically disadvantage borrowers by the control they have over setting the categories for loan qualification. It simply illustrates that the power to determine what information is relevant in credit relations is unevenly distributed in favor of lenders. Routines can change. Historically, women have not been able to qualify for small enterprise loans. Recently, however, The Grameen Bank in Bangladesh, South Shore Bank in Chicago, and the United States Social Investment Forum have given microloans to women and other minorities who normally would not qualify for small enterprise loans.[21] Another sign of collaborative exchanges of information is a pamphlet for women distributed by the United States Federal Trade Commission. The pamphlet offers advice to women on ways to build their credit histories so they can have better access to credit.[22]

The activities of Genoese merchant bankers during the sixteenth century illustrates that social learning skills can integrate new and routine knowledge. By modeling their own behavior after the Fuggers (a social learning skill), Genoese lenders were able to assume financial backing of the Spanish crown after it went bankrupt in 1557.[23] At that time, the Genoese learned from mistakes the Fugger firm had made and took advantage of the crown's need for credit resources they possessed. Bills of exchange gave the Genoese a means with which to finance the Spanish crown's trade. The bills "were only worthwhile if the money-markets between which they circulated had different discount rates; a bill had to acquire value on its travels."[24] Hence, Genoese bankers were required constantly to watch changes in the volume and value of bills circulating in several money-markets. As the crown's undertakings drew the merchant bankers into a complex web of international finance, the Genoese continued to monitor and learn from their activities. In 1568 they secured their wealth for the rest of the century by abandoning trade finance and advancing loans to the king.

Over time, credit relations have been slowly abstracted, and intersubjectivity has become opaque. Whereas barter required a physical presence of subjectivity in a particular place, credit depersonalized exchange and constructed a reality independent of physical space. Subject and place were dissolved. Credit, like money, disassociated itself from any "specific subjectivities."[25] The abstraction of people in credit relations has confounded the way they resolve the encounter between finite and fixed forms of knowledge. Although power is attained through both innovation and conformance, the abstraction of credit has predisposed people to seek power by submitting to that which they may not understand.

KNOWLEDGE IS HOUSED IN A HIERARCHICAL SETTING

Abstract credit relations increase the likelihood that the hierarchical setting in which knowledge is exchanged will itself affect the distribution of power. The routines of any governance site predispose some people to defer to fixed knowledge. This predisposition can be an advantage for those who advocate the knowledge claims on which credit routines are based. It is generally easier for credit card issuers than for applicants to determine both the kind and content of knowledge that is necessary to conclude negotiations for a credit card. The hierarchy of credit also allows a collaborative approach to sharing knowledge and distributing power, as indicated by microloans to women and other minorities, credit cards for impoverished people, and efforts to assist women in the development of their credit histories. The hierarchical context of credit can also be used to privilege knowledge and power. When this occurs, power is tied to position rather than to either finite or fixed knowledge. The relationship between knowledge and power is severed, and power distributions are derived from structural and institutional sources. Refusal to provide borrowers with their credit rating scores is an example of how hierarchy itself can be a source of power. In this sense only, some approaches (e.g., neorealism or structurationist ontologies) are correct in holding that social structures and systems must be considered independently of human agency when explaining how power functions.[26]

We live in a world where position has its privileges, one of which is accessing information. Information is not always equally accessible to all the players. A case in point has been the repeated practice of having and using insider information to buy and sell stocks. The activities and successes of the Rothschild banking conglomerate in the early nineteenth century derived from the bank's sophisticated information network that supported coordination of its activities across separate stock exchange markets. After the Congress of Vienna, the Rothschild brothers quickly reorganized themselves to a postwar economy in which governments became dependent on them to finance state activities.[27] In 1818 they positioned themselves to underwrite the second French loan when the leaders of Europe met at Aix-la-Chapelle. The meeting was called to arrange a loan that would help France pay off its war indemnity. In order to do so, the Rothschilds had to undercut the value of the first French loan stock, held by its competitors Ouvrards in Paris, Hopes (the Anglo-Dutch bank), and Baring of London. Rothschild financial agents in Frankfurt, Paris, and London bought up all loan stock entering the market. As the price rose, investors sold until, at a prearranged time, the Rothschilds dumped their shares simultaneously. As a consequence, they became a major holder of the second French loan. After 1818, they were regularly courted by all the major and minor European powers and became the leader in arranging states loans and cash transfers.

Borrowers and lenders in the credit card industry are also not guaranteed equal access to or control over information. Gill has convincingly demonstrated how that industry has been able to reduce risks by accessing information about prospective customers.[28] The industry has used this information to normalize a set of surveillance mechanisms related to various categories of creditworthiness. Credit card holders and applicants in the United States have been fighting with Congress for several years to amend the Fair Reporting Credit Act of 1970 so that they can have greater control over what information is collected on them, the sources of that information, and how the information will be used to affect their opportunities in the marketplace.[29] Currently consumers do not have access to credit scores or any other risk scores or predictors relating to themselves. Nor do credit reporting agencies have to disclose their sources of information unless a consumer takes legal action.[30] Consumers also do not have a surveillance mechanism in place to assess credit reporting agencies.

KNOWLEDGE AND GOVERNMENT

How is government affected by the various ways in which people reconcile knowledge and distribute power in credit relations? When it joins in governance of credit, government must also contend with the four conditions of knowledge. Its position as political sovereign does not free government from the risk and uncertainty of knowledge. This reality often is not understood, particularly by those in international relations theory who hold that the state's position is determined independently of historical practice. Such an essentialist view of the state first posits that the system and the units (i.e., states) are structurally prior to the limits of knowledge (e.g., the centrality of the state in power relations).[31] State interests in and knowledge concerning credit relations (e.g., the interests of central bankers) are privileged.[32] Strange, for instance, confined her analysis of prior knowledge structures to the structures of political power that prevailed (i.e., medieval Christendom and the scientific state of the seventeenth century).[33] For others, what state institutions know is deemed "high-quality" and carries with it the capacity to surmount uncertainty and foster cooperation. Keohane inferred such a relationship between state institutions and credit markets when he made the general claim that the state's conception of its interests was based on " . . . the quantity, quality, and distribution of information."[34]

Peter Haas took a similar approach to the contingency and uncertainty of knowledge when he defined epistemic communities as those containing "authoritative claims to policy-relevant knowledge." States control uncertainty by privileging the epistemic community's depiction of social and physical processes. According to Haas, the information states demand from these communities is based on the assumption that "state actors are uncertainty reducers as well as power and wealth pursuers."[35] In his analysis of knowledge and power, Ernst Haas closed the problem of knowledge for the state by merging the knowledge claims of science and politics. Haas reduced the contingent nature of knowledge in politics by claiming that "human aspirations and human institutions" are caused by a marriage between politics and science.[36] These approaches to the state displace the problem of knowledge by claiming that choice can be calculated on the basis of an identifiable set of rational procedures. This forces the fixed parameters of choice to be imposed on knowledge, thereby relegating uncertainty and risk to the periphery rather than to the core of knowledge claims.[37] If government considers itself to be as free from the constraints of knowledge as some scholars do, it is also likely to free itself from the authority that governs credit relations.

To summarize, power in governance functions through its relation to knowledge. Since knowledge is not final, power is distributed in credit relations through the ways in which people reconcile knowledge's finite and fixed bases. People are required to resolve knowledge within the hierarchical context of credit, where knowledge is usually unequally accessible and hierarchy can affect the outcome. They do so by using various social and personal skills. The combined impact these factors have on the construction of knowledge and power can promote either collaboration or privilege. While these relations help us understand how power functions in credit relations, they fail to account for why people's actions allow governance to persist. The answer to this can be found by assessing the authority with which people act.

AUTHORITY AND GOVERNANCE

Governance persists in the face of two challenges to knowledge: competing knowledge claims and abuses of hierarchical position. It endures because people navigate finite and fixed knowledge by accepting each other's decisive actions in daily life. This human process of management, action, and acceptance constitutes what I refer to as authority. Governance thrives because people act with authority. By acting decisively every day, people manage knowledge and become the instruments of authority. Today people have the authority to complete their purchases by using a credit card. When they make airline reservations by phone, both the agent and the ticket purchaser conclude the sale by mutually consenting to accept a valid card. On the many occasions in a given hour when any kind of reservation is made by phone, thousands of people exercise the authority of credit cards.

The history of credit is far more complex, all-encompassing, and abstract than the negotiation of credit card transactions. For a brief period, merchant bankers used their knowledge of the Northern European trade fairs to introduce bills of exchange and begin the transformation to mercantilism. Since then, many other forms of credit activity have been invented: insider trading; electronic transactions in NASDAQ stock exchanges; credit cards; Procter and Gamble's leverages interest rate swaps; Jeff Spies's investments in CMOs and inverse floaters; recent government initiated rescue plans for the currencies of Mexico, Thailand, and Indonesia; CCCS's negotiations with indebted credit card holders; and Meriwether's $10 billion bet on the spread between mortgage-backed and Treasury securities.

THE AMBIGUOUS EFFECT OF KNOWLEDGE ON AUTHORITY

These anecdotes of credit activity leverage an even greater mass of daily economic life that lies underneath feudal, mercantile, and market systems. While knowledge has been the catalyst for the ways in which power functions in these relations, its paradoxical relation to itself and therefore to power creates an uncertainty and contingency that would not allow governance to persevere if knowledge were its only foundation. Yet governance thrives, despite this first challenge to its persistence, because people act with authority. Authority has been the tool people use to organize the combination of men and things into a unit that, in the case of credit relations, "is a grid of insistent calculation, experimentation, and evaluation concerned with the conduct of conduct."[38]

The human struggle with finite and fixed knowledge spills over into action. Although there are many ways in which this struggle can transform practice, action occurs. It does so despite the inactivity knowledge might otherwise cause. On one hand, people act with certainty by "construing 'reality' as calculable, problematizing it as amenable and accessible to technologies of knowing, and constituting it as a domain of calculable subjects and calculable spaces."[39] On the other hand, what is claimed as calculable must be acknowledged as uncertain and contingent, that is, subject to social and institutional contexts. People reconcile the various aspects of knowledge and transform what they know into decisions about what to do. They decide to act and thereby form and are reformed by credit institutions whose routines are themselves subjected to empowering subjects.[40]

People act decisively. They agree to engage in a wide range of authoritative activities in many places. They must accept these activities without the arbitration of final knowledge that might otherwise denounce or determine the power of authority. When their decisiveness is accepted by others, people become the instruments of authority. Genoese merchant bankers were one source of authoritative action in sixteenth-century Europe. These bankers positioned themselves in the market, empowered themselves, subjected others to their own routines, and adapted to particular historical contexts. Twenty to thirty bankers oversaw Genoa's financial system. Most of them resided in Madrid, appeared at court, handled royal contracts, acted as advisers and collaborators of the king, intermarried, and acted as a single voice whenever the Spanish king posed a threat to their interests.[41] But position was not the sole source of their authority. Access to information about the market increased their confidence about what to do. Unlike ordinary people, they knew the art of foreign exchange, the vagaries of Mexican silver mines, tax income for Castile, financial developments in Amsterdam, political developments between Charles I and Spain, and changing economic conditions in Italy. But they were never finally certain that their course of action was guaranteed. Learning from social practice also enhanced their chances of being authoritative. Genoese merchant bankers learned how to execute the role of financier for the Spanish crown by knowing the successes and failures of the Fuggers. People saw these Genoese bankers as authorities because they used their traits and skills effectively. Having gained entry to the crown, Genoese bankers could sustain their authority only by continual assessment of the situation, one result of which was their decision to stop financing trade. The Genoese also were required to understand what others were doing. The network was small, as " . . . throughout Europe a small group of well-informed men, kept in touch by an active correspondence, controlled the entire network of exchanges in bills or specie, thus dominating the field of commercial speculation."[42] In time, they failed and were replaced by other authorities: the Rothschilds, John Meriwether, Jeff Spies, CCCS counselors, Equifax reporters, FTC employees, and IMF staff.

Legitimacy, juridical power, and sovereignty do not replace knowledge as the source of persistent governance. The liberal tradition, for instance, suggests that government exists because people freely consent to enter a social contract founded on inalienable rights and interests. This view certainly provides a rationale for the presence of government in credit relations, yet daily credit relations are not conducted on the basis of inalienable rights. In the governance of the credit card industry, for instance, some may object to the finance charge system, the credit rating system, or lack of access to credit. Others become delinquent or default on their loans. Yet government does not guarantee their rights to credit independent of market conditions. For this, people turn instead to the site of governance where market routines create a range of options. Of course, this range is part of a routine that may be negotiated with individual lenders. Government may participate and act as one of many authorities. It does so when it regulates the range on finance changes, but government itself is subject to a negotiation process with both issuers and holders. In credit cards, as in other instances of credit, people construct, diffuse, and spread authority among reporting agents, issuers, regulators, counselors, and users. These people reflect a range of accommodation concerning the conduct of the industry they have joined. While all have subjected themselves to the routines of the industry, on occasion they also may not agree about what happens at various points in governing the site. While dissent may serve as a catalyst for change in authority, dissent does not prevent others from engaging in authoritative activity.

HIERARCHY'S IMPACT ON AUTHORITY

Hierarchy has been a second challenge to the persistence of governing credit. Authority in credit relations occurs on a less than level playing field. Braudel noted the hierarchy that was apparent even in early credit relations: "[c]ertain groups of privileged actors were engaged in circuits and calculations that ordinary people knew nothing of. Foreign exchange for example . . . was a sophisticated art, open only to a few initiates at most."[43] Hierarchy expanded as credit spread. Although governance of credit relations has endured, the unfavorable impact of hierarchy on these relations has been considerable. Gill's work on credit is particularly insightful in pointing out the constraints to collaboration that hierarchy poses. He suggests that the new technologies of capitalism "are being used to increase exploitation and oppression" rather than to create a democratic civil society.[44]

Hierarchy in credit relations is frequently detached from its knowledge bases. For instance, signs of detachment and disregard for others are widespread in the credit card industry. When CCCS counselors are concerned with putting their clients on realistic payment plans rather than with addressing the underlying causes of chronic indebtedness, this represents CCCS's detachment from the debtor's perspective. Can the debtor understand the creditor's perspective? Muson and Sadowski note that "consumers have been lulled into thinking that as long as they pay the minimum amount required on each month's statement, they are in good shape. It's really the banks that are in good shape: they keep lowering the minimum required payments, and consumers carry more debt and pay more interest."[45] This is but one of many ways in which credit relations can be based on a hierarchy detached from its knowledge base. When position alone guides the outcome, hierarchy determines how power is distributed. Consider, for instance, occasions when credit is not extended based only on gender, race, age, nationality, religion, ethnicity, or credit risk scores. These categories are constructed by those in power who enforce them without knowledge about the creditworthiness of particular people fitting these categories. They are able to deny credit because of the position they occupy rather than because of the knowledge they have.

HIERARCHY, SOVEREIGNTY, AND AUTHORITY

Government is present in the governance of credit relations. The difference it can make there is better understood by distinguishing between authority and juridical power. Government, like all of us, has knowledge and power. It can act with authority, but only when complementarity exists between its sovereignty and authority. Government becomes an authority in credit relations through the population's surveillance of it. Government can earn a place at the site of governance as one of many players acting under the conditions of knowledge. It can also be outside governance, allowing for "governance without government."[46] This is the case when it relies on the exercise of a juridical power which does not complement governance.[47] In this instance, government's proximity to governance is detached from authority, and it wields a legitimacy born of law, order, and hierarchical position. Signs of such a presence would be government's reliance on coercive regulatory and legislative mechanisms to force social consensus or efforts to manage these relations through rules and institutional procedures typical of bureaucracies. On these occasions, people may opt to assert their authority. They may monitor themselves outside the juridical power of the state and act as such in the daily life of credit inventions and routines they authorize.

Government also has relied on its hierarchical position and frequently used its political authority to act in the governance of credit relations. Some believe governments have directed credit markets.[48] They claim, for instance, that " . . . the US and British governments . . .

allow[ed] the growth of the Eurocurrency markets in London in the 1960s . . . ," or that the US and Britain were "midwives at the birth" of Eurocurrency markets.[49] If such views of the Euromarket's origins are correct, they are justified only if one believes that juridical power promotes the governance of credit relations. Government activity in other markets offers compelling evidence of its attempts to advance its hierarchical position in credit relations through use of its juridical powers. For instance, the International Monetary Fund (IMF) has tried routinely to assert such power over the market (e.g., the fixed exchange rate system, the General Agreement to Borrow, Swaps, Special Drawing Rights, and various stabilization mechanisms).

Governments in the industrialized world, together with the IMF, the Bank for International Settlement, and the World Bank, have also exercised their juridical powers on other governments. The rescue plans for the currencies of Mexico ($47.5 billion in January 1995), Thailand ($17.5 billion in August 1997), and Indonesia ($23 billion in November 1997) prescribe that these countries adopt liberal economic, fiscal, monetary, and trade policies as a condition for receiving the loans. These requirements are the result of political economic practices in advanced industrialized societies. The historical and social contexts of Mexico, Thailand, Indonesia, and others are opaque to the industrialized world.[50] The Mexican plan, for instance, allowed Mexico to extend its costly short-term debt by collateralizing Mexican oil revenues, regardless of what impact this might have had on Mexican society. In the process, Mexican credit markets were integrated into a liberal, global credit market through mechanisms such as variable rates on outstanding loans and domestic stabilization policies administered by the IMF and the United States.[51]

In general, international relations scholars do not distinguish between authority and sovereignty when they analyze the role of the state in the governance of credit relations.[52] They assume that sovereignty provides government with the tools it needs to act in credit markets. This view privileges the hierarchical position government occupies in credit relations. It reinforces the unfavorable contribution hierarchy can make to the persistence of governance and does not provide guidance for ways in which government might overcome its own unfavorable tendencies. In attending to governance, these scholars consider government in the "functional" sense, in "the capacity to regulate arrangements so that they remain routinized" in the absence of "centralized authority," or in the performance of "functions normally associated with governance ... [that] are performed "without the institutions of government." Consequently, governance and government are synonymous, and order is viewed as "both a precondition and a consequence of government.[53] These approaches concentrate on the state's effective subjectification of governance to sovereignty. Order, rules, institutions, regimes, law, and regulation become central concepts to explain the activity of government in credit relations. The scholarly invention of epistemic communities privileges the state's knowledge. The language and knowledge of these communities become normalized in government's contribution to credit relations.

Government's capacity to play an effective role in governance is further compromised by Foucault's distinction between the state and the art of government: "the state is governed according to rational principles which are intrinsic to it." The state, "like nature, has its own proper form of rationality ... " whereas government "must find the principles of its rationality in that which constitutes the specific reality of the state."[54] This link between the state and artful government reinforces a sovereign role for government, albeit in historicized form. Such a view is not far from that of neorealists like Buzan, Jones, and Little. They claim that the "essence" of politics is its concern with "the shaping of human behavior for the purpose of governing large groups of people" and its right to do so through law and policy.[55] Such a view supports government's tendency to adopt a juridical role in governing credit relations. Buzan, Little, and Jones offer this support by asserting that the practice of government entails managing people by "coercion in the case of power, legitimacy in the case of authority, and administration in the case of organization."[56]

Governance persists and power functions in credit relations independently of coercion, legitimacy, and government's administration and as a consequence of the ways in which people respond to knowledge with authority. People are able to manage these relations in spite of ambiguous knowledge and misuses of hierarchical position. While credit relations cannot be understood without making people a central part of the analysis, is attention only to them sufficient? Can a more complete picture be drawn that warrants returning to classical, Marxist, liberal, or other lines of thought and analysis? The risk involved in returning to explanations that treat people as representations of larger forces is that a central focus on people in their historical settings will not be sustained. They will be incorporated and made to fit with the forces and structures essential to all these traditions. Instead, one ought to consider the possibility of reconstructing these traditions from the ground up by questioning the extent to which markets, governments, social, and te-leological forces exist independent of people in their particular histori-cal contexts. The outcome of this reconstruction might extinguish human nature, natural law, or systemic forces rather than the people who rep-resent these intangibles.

NOTES

I would like to thank Tim Sinclair, Mark Marone, Scott Turner, and Raymond Duvall for their helpful comments and suggestions on earlier drafts.

1. Fernand Braudel, *The Structures of Everyday Life*, translated by Sian Reynolds (Berkeley: Univ. of California Press, 1992 [1979]), p. 29.

2. Raymond de Roover, *Money, Banking, and Credit in Mediaeval Bruges* (Cambridge: The Mediaeval Academy of America, 1948), p. 12.

3. John F. Chown, *A History of Money: From AD 800* (New York: Routledge, 1994), pp. 116ff.

4. The term *knowledge* refers to claims based either on the possession of information (i.e., data and factual claims) or on a comprehensive view of the world that includes the assignment of meaning or interpretation to information, assumptions, causal assertions, and presumed consequences.

5. Braudel, *The Structures of Everyday Life*, p. 470.

6. John Maynard Keynes, *The General Theory of Employment, Interest, and Money* (New York: Harcourt Brace Jovanovich, 1936 [1964]), p. 170.

7. Financial contracts whose value depends on price or interest rate movements in some other financial market. Derivatives may be a method of hedging against extreme swings in prices or of making quick gains from other securities. Their constantly changing value is determined by interest rates, stock indexes, commodities, mortgages, or other securities. Since these contracts are ties to the value of other financial instruments, they differ from the options traded by Dutch merchants on the Amsterdam market in the seventeenth cen-tury or the futures contracts purchased by farmers through The Chicago Board of Trade beginning in the middle of the nineteenth century.

8. Robert Trigaux, "Burned by Derivatives," *St. Petersburg Times*, 5 February 1995, p. H1; Mary Rowland, "Yes, You Own Derivatives, "*St. Peters-burg Times: Bloomberg Personal*, February 1995, p. 24.

9. United States Deptment of Commerce, Bureau of the Census, *Statisti-cal Abstract of the United States* (Washington: GPO, 1996), p. 515. See also the statement by Janet Yellen (Member, Board of Governors of the Federal Reserve System) to the US Senate Subcommittee on Financial Institutions and Regula-tory Relief of the Committee on Banking, Housing, and Urban Affairs, 24 July 1996.

10. Howard Muson and Wiktor Sadowski, "The Mind of the Debtor," *St. Petersburg Times: Bloomberg Personal,* January 1995, p. 7.

11. Nicholas Onuf, *World of Our Making: Rules and Rule in Social Theory and International Relations* (Columbia: University of South Carolina Press, 1989), p. 6.

12. Tzvetan Todorov, *The Conquest of America* (New York: Harper Perennial, 1984); Ashis Nandy, *The Intimate Enemy: Loss and Recovery of Self under Colonialism* (New Delhi: Oxford University Press, 1988 [1983]).

13. Adrian Hamilton, *The Financial Revolution* (New York: The Free Press, 1986) p. 40.

14. Saskia Sassen, *The Global City: New York, London, Tokyo* (Princeton: Princeton University Press, 1991).

15. Kenneth R. Harney, "Electronic Credit Scoring Makes Its Debut," *St. Petersburg Times,* 25 March 1995, p. 8D.

16. Stephen Gill, "The Global Panopticon? The Neoliberal State, Economic Life, and Democratic Surveillance," *Alternatives* 20, no. 1 (Jan.–Mar. 1995), pp. 20–27.

17. Sassen, *The Global City,* p. 111.

18. "Deals Lose Millions for Procter and Gamble," *St. Petersburg Times,* 13 April 1994, p. E6.

19. John S. Ransom, *Foucault's Discipline: The Politics of Subjectivity* (Durham: University Press, 1997), p. 19.

20. Michael Dillon, "Sovereignty and Governmentality: From the Problematics of the 'New World Order' to the Ethical Problematic of the World Order," *Alternatives* 20, no. 3 (July–Sept. 1995), p. 324.

21. Paul Eking, *A New World Order: Grassroots Movements for Global Change* (London: Routledge, 1992), pp. 122ff.

22. United States Federal Trade Commission, Bureau of Consumer Protection, Office of Consumer and Business Education, "Women and Credit Histories" (Washington: GPO, October 1993).

23. Eric Wolf, *Europe and the People Without History* (Berkeley: University of California Press, 1982), pp. 114ff; Fernand Braudel, *The Perspective of the World,* translated by Sian Reynolds (New York: Harper and Row, 1992 [1979], pp. 164–70, 208–09.

24. Fernand Braudel, *The Wheels of Commerce,* translated by Sian Reynolds (New York: Harper and Row, 1982 [1979]), p. 394.

25. Michael Shapiro, *Reading "Adam Smith": Desire, History, and Value* (Newbury Park: Sage, 1993), p. 18.

26. Alexander Wendt and Raymond Duvall, "Institutions and International Order," in *Global Changes and Theoretical Challenges: Approaches to World Politics for the 1990s,* Ernst-Otto Czempiel and James N. Rosenau, eds. (Lexington, MA: Lexington Books, 1989) , p. 59.

27. Derek Wilson, *Rothschild: The Wealth and Power of a Dynasty* (New York: Charles Scribner's Sons, 1988).

28. Gill, "The Global Panopticon?"

29. The effort died when the Senate failed to take action on a House of Representatives proposal in the summer of 1994. See Andrew Taylor, "Credit Act Update Passes House After Key Hurdles Cleared," *Congressional Quarterly* (Washington: GPO), 18 June 1994, pp. 1585–86.

30. United States Federal Trade Commission, "The Fair Credit Reporting Act," http://www.ftc.gov/os/statutes/fcra.htm, 17 March 1997.

31. Examples of such an approach include Kenneth N. Waltz, "Realist Thought and Neorealist Theory, "*Journal of International Affairs* 44, no. 1 (Spring 1990), pp. 21–37; John Ruggie, "Territoriality and Beyond: Problematizing Modernity in International Relations," *International Organization* 47, no. 1 (Winter 1993), pp. 139–74. See Bahman Fozouni, "The Confutation of Political Realism," *International Studies Quarterly* 39, no. 4 (December 1995), pp. 479–510, who offers a critical epistemological and empirical refutation of such approaches.

32. Examples of those who have signaled the state's knowledge base in other areas include John Odell, *U.S. International Monetary Policy* (Princeton: Princeton University Press, 1982), who analyzed the impact of the state's "ideas" on international monetary issues during the 1960s and 1970s, and John Steinbruner, *The Cybernetic Theory of Decision* (Princeton: Princeton University Press, 1974), who assessed the extent to which the "cognitive processes" of policy makers reflected causal versus constrained learning in the case of the multilateral force issue.

33. Susan Strange, *States and Markets* (London: Pinter Publishers, 1994, 2nd edition). Strange claims that "power and authority are conferred on those occupying key decision-making positions in the knowledge structure—on those who are acknowledged by society to be possessed of the 'right,' desirable knowledge and engaged in the acquisition of more of it, and on those entrusted with its storage, and on those controlling in any way the channels by which knowledge, or information, is communicated. . . . " (p. 121)

34. Robert Keohane, *After Hegemony* (Princeton: Princeton University Press, 1984), p. 245.

35. Peter Haas, "Introduction: Epistemic Communities and International Policy Coordination," *International Organization* 46, no. 1 (Winter 1992), p. 4.

36. Ernst Haas, *When Knowledge Is Power* (Berkeley: University of California Press, 1990), p. 11.

37. An example of this is Barry Buzan, Charles Jones, and Richard Little, *The Logic of Anarchy: Neorealism to Structural Realism* (New York: Columbia University Press, 1993). See also Robert Powell, "Anarchy in International Relations Theory: The Neorealist-Neoliberal Debate," *International Organization* 48, no. 2 (Spring 1994), pp. 313–14, where structure subsumes preference.

38. Dillon, "Sovereignty and Governmentality," p. 330.

39. Dillon, p. 325.

40. Anthony Giddens, *Central Problems in Social Theory* (London: Macmillan, 1979).

41. Braudel, *The Perspective of the World*, pp. 168–69.

42. Fernand Braudel, *The Mediterranean and the Mediterranean World in the Age of Phillip II*, translated by Sian Reynolds (Berkeley: University of California Press, 1995 [revised edition 1966], p. 321.

43. Braudel, *The Structures of Everyday Life*, p. 24.

44. Gill, "The Global Panopticon?" p. 4.

45. Muson and Sadowski, "The Mind of the Debtor," pp. 6–7.

46. James Rosenau, "Governance, Order, and Change in World Politics," in *Governance without Government: Order and Change in World Politics*, James Rosenau and Ernst–Otto Czempiel, eds. (New York: Cambridge University Press, 1992), p. 5.

47. Contra Dillon, "Sovereignty and Governmentality," pp. 334ff.

48. Karl Polanyi, *The Great Transformation: The Political and Economic Origins of Our Time* (Boston: Beacon Press, 1957 [1944]); Susan Strange, "An Eclectic Approach," in *The New International Political Economy*, Craig N. Murphy and Roger Tooze, eds. (Boulder: Lynne Rienner Publishers, 1991), pp. 33–49; Strange, *States and Markets*; Ethan B. Kapstein, "Between Power and Purpose: Central Bankers and the Politics of Regulatory Convergence," *International Organization* 46, no. 1 (Winter 1992), pp. 265–88; Philip G. Cerny, ed., *Finance and World Politics: Markets, Regimes, and States in the Post-hegemonic Era* (Brookfield: Edward Elgar, 1993).

49. Strange, "An Eclectic Approach," p. 35.

50. Jorge G. Castaneda, "Ferocious Differences," *The Atlantic Monthly* (July 1995), pp. 68–76; David E. Sanger, "U.S. Is Set to Lend $3 Billion to Help Bolster Indonesia," *The New York Times*, 31 October 1997, p. 1; "IMF Okays $23 Billion to Rescue Indonesia," *St. Petersburg Times*, 1 November 1997, pp. 1A, 7A.

51. David Adams, "Dragged Down by Debt," *St. Petersburg Times*, 27 November 1995, pp. A1–4.

52. Peter Haas, "Introduction," actually discounts the importance of such an understanding when he states that governments do not need information that "guesses about others' intentions. . . . ," p. 4.

53. Rosenau, "Governance, Order, and Changes in World Politics," pp. 6–8.

54. Michel Foucault, "Governmentality," *The Foucault Effect: Studies in Governmentality*, Colin Gordon and Peter Miller, eds. (Chicago: University of Chicago Press, 1991), p. 97.

55. Buzan, Little, and Jones, *The Logic of Anarchy*, pp. 35, 37.

56. Buzan, et al, pp. 35–36.

PART FOUR

POLITICAL IDENTITY, CIVIL SOCIETY, AND GLOBAL GOVERNANCE

CHAPTER 10

History's Revenge and Future Shock

The Remapping of Global Politics

YALE H. FERGUSON and RICHARD W. MANSBACH

For several hundred years theorists and practitioners of global politics have regarded the sovereign state as the focus for humanity's highest loyalties and source of its most important values.[1] This assumption masks the fact that human beings have multiple identities and, often, loyalties to a variety of political authorities, which sometimes are entirely compatible, conflict, or are mutually exclusive. During the epoch of European ascendancy, territorial states claiming exclusive rights over territory within their boundaries and freedom from external interference—legitimated by the treaties of Augsburg (1555) and Westphalia (1648)—dominated European politics and conquered much of the rest of the world. Nevertheless, even during this "state-centric" era, "the actual content of sovereignty," declares Stephen Krasner, was repeatedly "contested" and "persistently challenged" by other "institutional forms," and "the exercise of authority within a given territory, generally regarded as a core attribute of sovereign states, has been problematic in practice and contested in theory."[2]

THE NEED FOR NEW MODELS OF GLOBAL POLITICS

With the end of the Cold War, it has become increasingly difficult to accept statist assumptions. Only a relatively few states continue to

dominate or successfully co-opt important groups within their boundaries and stave off serious competition from transnational forces. Norway is an excellent example, an exception that proves the rule: a country
that is proud of its hard-earned sovereign independent status, has a
strong sense of national identity and a popular monarchy, and enjoys a
remarkable prosperity that lessens social tensions and provides a buffer
against the external world. By contrast, most of the world's states find
it extremely difficult to cope; some are in a condition of outright civil
war or near-collapse; and a few have actually failed so badly that they
have virtually ceased to exist except on the maps of other states. The
1990s have witnessed a recrudescence of identities and ideologies that
clash with the obligations of individuals as citizens of sovereign states.
In some instances, this phenomenon constitutes a genuine reawakening
of earlier ideas and forms, in others a reinvention of the past, and
sometimes the appearance or at least recognition of a new identity or
ideology.

Our contention is, on the one hand, that the significance of the
existence of a world of sovereign states traditionally has been grossly
overrated and, on the other hand, that contemporary trends make such
a characterization of global politics even more misleading than it has
always been. The question is not whether sovereign states exist and
matter in some respects, for, of course, they do. Rather, the question is
what does the sovereign state model of global politics fail to tell us that
is important, or, worse, severely distort and obscure? Any casual survey
of the world's nearly two hundred sovereign states reveals that the
differences among them are far more numerous and significant than the
characteristics they share. Obviously, many states cannot even maintain
order domestically. Many national governments are widely seen as ille-
gitimate (some by nations within), and most of those whose legitimacy
is not at issue stand very low in the popularity polls. Many governments
are incapable of acting in anything like a unified fashion. There are vast
areas of economic and social life, with crucial impact on the welfare of
citizens, that most governments do not control or even influence to any
major degree. Political boundaries have not been immutable; rather they
have changed to a greater or lesser extent, sometimes quickly and more
often incrementally, throughout history. And so on. Why have most
observers and scholarly analysts of international relations failed to
understand such matters or accorded them only marginal significance?

There are several reasons. One is that most analysts have been
blinded by a profound Eurocentrism. Robert Kaplan writes: "[T]he map

of the world, with its 190 or so countries, each signified by a bold and uniform color: this map, with which all of us have grown up, is generally an invention of modernism, specifically of European colonialism."[3] We are too accustomed to looking at maps of neat state boxes, assuming that these provide an adequate picture of the primary units in global politics. When necessary, we redraw the boxes, less interested (strangely) in explaining how a supposedly sovereign unit could somehow be reduced or disappear than in reasserting that nothing really has changed because the new box is also sovereign.

A legalistic bias is another aspect of the European tradition. The only true authorities are supposedly those that are sanctified by law, and states are the only legal sovereigns. We forget that from the outset sovereignty, in practical terms, was never more than a claim to authority, which, to be sure, was (and continues to be) realized to a noteworthy degree in some countries. But it is a huge mistake to believe that sovereignty ever meant absolute control or, indeed, that sovereignty offers all that much to many states that possess it today. For many, it is like the fancy titles of dispossessed royalty from Tsarist Russia or Soviet Eastern Europe: it guarantees admission to the club but will not necessarily pay the dues or keep away creditors.

The Gulf War reaffirmed that sovereign boundaries may still count for something when a naked aggressor marshals an army and crosses them. However, oil-rich Kuwait may have been an exception, and in any event, especially during the last decade or so, monumental political changes have tended either to transcend state boundaries or to emanate from within them. Even where boundaries have remained the same, as in Hungary or Poland, the colors on the map really ought to change to reflect new political conditions. Before the Soviet collapse, the old Pentagon maps that showed all of Eastern Europe colored red—maps of empire (at least the Soviet one)—were far more accurate than anything based on sovereign states.

Historians and political scientists who have studied international relations have tended to perpetuate Eurocentric myths instead of engaging in (small-r) realistic analysis. Few scholars have been interested in history before Westphalia, and most have focused on the twentieth century and particularly the period since 1945. Many students of comparative politics have been specialists in one or two countries. Most political scientists embraced state-centric theories, such as Realism, neo-Realism, or Keohane-ian Institutionalism, and employed their own versions of state boxes for number-crunching purposes. Many insisted on maintaining a strict inside/outside divide, arguing that international relations is a state-to-state realm entirely separate from domestic politics. International lawyers actually did more than social scientists to highlight the growing importance of international organizations as well as emerging norms affecting matters like human rights.

Mesmerized by the state, almost everyone (except a few neo-Marxists, IPE, and business-oriented scholars) tended to neglect private sector economic actors like multinational/transnational corporations. Civil society was a matter for sociologists and specialists on domestic politics. Historians who discovered economic and cultural history genuinely thought they were offering an alternative to political history. A few scholars were concerned about changing technology but only as it affected nuclear deterrence, arms control, and the race for space. Ethnicity was seen as a quaint leftover from tribal times that modern governments were inexorably educating out of existence.

Now, after the events of the past few years, it appears that citizens and scholars alike were incredibly naive or caught in a Eurocentric intellectual time warp. Still today, unfortunately, not a few established international relations scholars and graduate programs remain flat-earthers, reluctant to set out beyond traditional shores. To mix metaphors, they have such an investment in familiar models that they are loath to declare bankruptcy. Accordingly, the proverbial person on the street who listens to the daily news may be better able to comprehend the (small-r) realities of global politics than many in the academy.

Why, it seems almost suddenly, are all of us required to do so much rethinking? The sovereign-state model has always been a distortion; however, to be fair, recent global trends—not least the end of the Cold War—make the need for better models much more evident. Ironically, what had appeared to be a post-World War II world of stable nation-state boundaries, that is, the ultimate triumph of a system of sovereign states, was, to the contrary, the triumph of two major empires. The Soviets and the West kept the lid on ethnic and other conflicts in their respective domains and competed only on the periphery. Under the shadow of the mushroom cloud, superpower security concerns tended to obscure everything else. The long peace among major powers is much easier to see in retrospect.

Future historians, it must be acknowledged, may look back on the post-Cold War period as a brief interlude before a return to security business as usual, that is, an intense and dangerous rivalry among major powers. Such a situation would tend to strengthen the governments of some states vis-a-vis their own peoples, again spotlight military preparation and alliances, and encourage us to dust off all our old Realist literature. More debatable is whether the sort of "political crack-up" sketched in sensational fashion by Kaplan—terrorists with nuclear weapons and so on—is, as he insists, "just beginning to occur worldwide" and what long-range effect that would have on states. Such a trend might either usher in an extended period of almost unimaginable chaos or perhaps raise popular anxiety, encourage authoritarian solutions, and thereby make for greater consolidation of state governments.

A WORLD OF FRAGMENTATION AND INTEGRATION

For the present, the threat of interstate conflict has receded, and remaining military security concerns focus on ethnic and tribal violence, civil war, nuclear nonproliferation, and combating terrorism. With the hands on the superpower nuclear clock shifted back from midnight, we are better able to recognize that security also includes grave problems of international political economy, environment, social welfare, and epidemic diseases.

The world has never been as anarchic as the Realists pictured it; rather, some issue areas have been much more Hobbesian than others. Various functional regimes and the European Community were well advanced before the Cold War ended. Nonetheless, the selfsame superpower rivalry that minimized great-power military conflict also politicized virtually every effort to create global regimes. Now the United Nations has been revitalized to such an extent that members have become acutely aware of its constitutional deficiencies, neglected infrastructure, costly budget, and outmoded procedures. International governmental organizations (IGOs) and regimes are proliferating at an unprecedented rate, as are nongovernmental organizations (NGOs) and their international counterparts (INGOs), and many of these are establishing complex webs of cross-border relationships and alliances. Peter Willetts estimates that there are ten thousand single-country NGOs, three hundred IGOs, and 4,700 INGOs. He points out: "Using people as a measure, many NGOs, particularly trade unions and campaigning groups in the fields of human rights, women's rights, and the environment, have their membership measured in millions, whereas 37 of the UN's members have populations of less than one million."[4]

Even as European Union member governments struggle to implement Maastricht, most notably a common currency, the EU, like NATO, is having to cope with demands for further expansion. Governments have transformed GATT into the WTO, a new NAFTA market has been created, and further trade cooperation is envisaged for the Western Hemisphere and the Asia/Pacific region. Yet despite their transnational institutional innovation, governments are no longer in the driver's seat in the world economy, and, for this very reason, they are less and less capable of managing their own national economies. The advance of capitalism, the current free-market ethos, and the increasingly global-ized character of business and finance emphasize as never before the fact that private sector resources far exceed those of governments. Corporations also seem much more able than governments to identify coherent interests, to think globally, and to act in a fast and flexible manner.

Paradoxically, political disintegration has accompanied political and economic integration. Russia and the former Soviet republics are all ex-periencing political and economic turmoil. China may or may not be next. Arthur Waldron comments: "Though the Chinese undoubtedly love their country, this does not translate smoothly into love of government, as rulers of this century have discovered. . . [N]o amount of solemn flag-raising ceremonies and patriotic education in the schools can ob-scure the need for genuine institutional change."[5] Although there has been significant progress in South Africa—and to a lesser extent in Ireland and the Arab-Israeli confrontation zone—civil wars, ethnic conflicts, and tribal violence have broken out with much greater fre-quency. Violence generates floods of refugees, and in Africa and else-where in the developing world it greatly exacerbates the terrible effects of poverty, famine, and other natural disasters.

The fact that international governmental and corporate integration have occurred along with widespread disintegration is paradoxical, but it is no coincidence. These processes are inextricably linked. Small political entities like the Baltic republics believe that the military threat to their security has greatly diminished and, in any event, that they can now rely on the umbrella provided by the western alliance. They also are confident they will have new associations with globalized business and regional markets to replace whatever economic relationships they choose to sever with the former dominant power. At the same time, smallness and redis-covery of ethnicity and religion provide a psychological refuge for indi-viduals and groups who are bewildered by the pace of change and who fear cultural homogenization. Arab fundamentalism, for example, has been at least partly a reaction against westernization.

The foregoing, then, are some of the broad features of our brave new world, or—we cannot emphasize too strongly—a world that is at once both new and also a living museum of past political forms, identities, and ideas. Francis Fukuyama could not have got it more wrong: 'history' certainly hasn't 'ended.'[6] His thesis, if anything, was more appropriate to the short Cold War era. Today history is being resurrected and reconstructed, in a somewhat new and rapidly changing context. We label the political form that emerged from medieval Europe and that was legitimated by the doctrine of sovereignty the 'Westphalian polity.' History is having its revenge on the Westphalian polity, and there are also shocks from a future that is as yet only partially perceived.

We urgently need better models to help us capture the complexities of global politics. The model we offer focuses on a world of many different types of polities that coexist, conflict, and cooperate and on their relationship to a wide range of human identities and loyalties.

OVERLAPPING IDENTITIES AND MULTIPLE POLITIES

Over several hundred years the Westphalian polity competed with others, such as universal empire, church, city, family, and tribe, and made considerable headway in becoming a major focus of citizens' identities and loyalties. The state, even in its European cradle, arguably never became the primary identity or loyalty, at least over family and self, for many individuals. The state succeeded to the degree that it did partly by coercion but mainly because it provided the psychological satisfaction of a broad group identity and a heightened measure of physical security and material satisfaction. Although persons were sometimes willing to fight for divine-right kings, the wedding in the late eighteenth and nineteenth centuries between state and nation as well as greater popular participation, gave them additional incentives. The state managed to convince a sufficient number of persons that putting their lives on the line for the fatherland was somehow a noble expression of self and a means of defending home and loved ones as well. Those whom it could not convince, it simply (or with difficulty) suppressed.

Equally important, the state enhanced its legitimacy by allowing individuals and nonstate collectivities considerable autonomy. This was a hallmark of the West but applied to many areas of social life almost everywhere. As long as one paid taxes and military service and did not deface public monuments, the state left one alone. One could have a family, practice a profession, drink at the social club, worship god, and so on, without any particular concern for the state. Henry VIII got rid of the Pope and made himself head of the church but posed no threat to other traditional religious practices. Over time, the state took on more and more functions, including in the late nineteenth and twentieth centuries, for example, substantial new responsibilities for economic regulation and social welfare. Doing so, however, met much resistance from the private sector, and in Russia it required nothing less than a full-fledged revolution and Communist ideology.

Now in the waning years of the twentieth century, citizens in western countries are less convinced of a need for military protection, impatient with high tax burdens and official corruption, and generally dubious as to whether government is any longer capable of delivering on its promises. There is a sense that problems have become too complex for public policy; that welfare beyond an uncertain minimum, for instance, can only depend on individual initiative and transnational economic cycles. As we have observed, especially but not exclusively in parts of the world where European forms never gained much of a hold, many states appear perilously close to collapse or have already failed. The Asian state model has performed far better economically, albeit with a high level of authoritarianism and corruption. Japan is currently in the doldrums, and the Asian emerging economies are experiencing severe growing pains. In any event, in the Asian model, it was always hard to distinguish public and private sectors from one another.

The Westphalian polity faces greater or lesser challenges from a host of other identities, ideologies, and polities—some old, some reconstructed, and some new. For example, although gender is as old as Adam and Eve, it has only recently arrived as a political identity and still offers the state very little competition.[7] By contrast, the familiar ideas of 'nation' and 'nationalism' have lately taken on a distinctly subversive, nonstate connotation. Yet another old identity, 'class,' has gone through several reformulations since the ancient world, when tensions between rich and poor threatened stasis in Greek *poleis*. Marxists in the nineteenth and twentieth centuries reconceived class as a product of capitalist exploitation, and proponents of the revolution of the proletariat earnestly believed that class would prove a more powerful basis of human identification than nation-states. Needless to say, they were deeply disappointed when European workers fought for their countries in 1914.[8] After the Bolshevik revolution, a Marxist-Leninist or Communist vision of class struggle provided an ideological foundation for Russia's totalitarian state and imperial expansion. Class reappeared in yet another transnational systemic structure guise during the 1970s when demands for a New International Economic Order highlighted the plight of Third World have-nots. With Marxism in retreat, class at least temporarily seems to have faded as an identity category.

The emergence, decline, and disappearance of political communities has been a key theme of political philosophy. Aristotle described the growth and contraction of political associations; Machiavelli concerned himself with princely realms; Hobbes and Rousseau employed the largely imaginary metaphors of 'state of nature' and 'contract.' The numerous identities that individuals have can and often do evolve into loyalties to a variety of politically active groups. What is far less clear is how identities are formed and why certain of them and associated political forms come to the fore at particular times and not at other times.

CHANGING IDENTITIES AND LOYALTIES

Common identities are forged only when individuals have access to information about others who, in one respect or another, appear to share a common fate. Thus the establishment of refugee camps in Jordan, Lebanon, and Gaza after Israel's war of independence played a major role in producing a Palestinian identity distinct from the Arab states that had failed the Palestinians. Communication also has to foster a sense of political efficacy and a belief that individuals can improve their lot or at least protect what they have if they organize politically. One significant result of the progress of global-village technology, of course, is that individuals no longer have to be concentrated in settings like refugee camps to communicate with others, perceive commonalities, and act conjointly.

What commonalities individuals will actually perceive is by no means predetermined, since identities are more a state of mind or social construction—identity assumed or imposed—than anything else. Consider the hoary nonsense of 'race.' Those who study these things assure us that any two individuals who happen to share skin color have many more attributes in common with other individuals who may or may not have the same or similar skin color. Undeniably, skin color has provided a highly visible basis for racial discrimination in many societies, yet it has also often been ignored when particular individuals have been sufficiently wealthy or influential. In fact, gender and caste have been equally powerful predictors of discrimination.

It is as hard to pinpoint what constitutes an ethnicity or a people or a nation as it is a race. For every common history, there are aspects of history that are not shared; for every language, dialects; for every religion, different versions of the one true faith. R. Brian Ferguson, for example, decries the "widespread tendency to identify ethnicity as a simple and primordial basis of conflict." In his view, we "must seek causes in the situations [of social stress] that give ethnicity salience," prompting "politicians to channel needs and anxieties into violent path-ways, and thereby to profit from the results," whereby "mythohistories are constructed, claiming timeless grudges, and placing blame on a demonized other."[9]

We-they perceptions frequently may seem to be insubstantial or even irrational, but they have been central to politics since time imme-morial. Such perceptions grow out of a belief that the fates of certain individuals are linked to and differentiated from the fates of others owing to some shared trait(s).[10] Thus until civil war erupted in the former Yugoslavia, Bosnian Muslims had rarely defined themselves in religious terms. "We never, until the war, thought of ourselves as Mus-lims," declared a school teacher. "We were Yugoslavs. But when we began to be murdered, because we were Muslims, things changed. The definition of who we are today has been determined by our killers."[11] Chechens had a similar experience after the Russia's invasion. Prior to that event: "Nobody talked about religion. But these days it seems that nobody can stop talking about it. Nearly every Chechen soldier swears allegiance to Allah, taking gazavat, the holy oath to die fighting the invaders."[12] In Algeria, Berbers have begun to arm themselves to resist non-Berber Muslim fundamentalists and the threat they seem to pose to Berber autonomy.[13] And, for black Christians and animists in the Sudan, the war waged against them by the Arab Islamic regime in Khartoum "is a war of identity."[14] The Sudanese government, guided by Hassan Turabi's National Islamic Front, has also sought to destabilize Eritrea, Ethiopia, and Uganda by aiding Islamic zealots.[15]

Neither sovereign states nor the loyalties that help to create and sustain them are necessary, unchanging, or permanent attributes of glo-bal politics. Increasingly, scholars (though rarely political scientists) are investigating "the role of memory and rhetorics of collective identity in constructing and maintaining the nation-state," and which may also be contributing to its decline.[16] Throughout history, identities and loyalties have continued to evolve, legitimating some forms of governance and delegitimating others. What is increasingly apparent today is that global politics is in the midst of one of those periodic eras of rapid and dramatic change that can neither be described nor explained in terms of conventional statist or power theories. As James N. Rosenau declares, "Given the profound transformations in the nature and location of authority, legitimacy, and compliance, and given the emergent roles and structures of the modern state, transnational organizations, social movements, common markets, and political parties, the basis for extensive re-examinations of government and governance in an increasingly interdependent world is surely compelling."[17] And many of these are, in his words, "boundary-spanning forms of control."[18]

When different polities adopt different policy stances, their followers may experience paralyzing dissonance as they try to decide which of their loyalties should prevail. Catholic women in Ireland and the United States must choose between church and gender when confronting reproductive issues. Bolsheviks after the October Revolution were at once the servants of a sovereign state and the vanguard of a worldwide movement. The tensions this produced were visible in the struggle between Trotsky and Stalin over the question of "socialism in one country." It was also apparent in what Theodore Von Laue calls "the tragedy of [Georgii] Chicherin, who assumed the post of People's Commissar for Foreign Affairs after Trotsky's resignation . . . and was placed at the center of the turbulent confluence of diplomacy and social revolution."[19] On the one hand, the Foreign Affairs Commissariat was supposed to pursue traditional diplomatic ends, especially the normalizing of relation between the new Soviet Union and the Westphalian states of Europe. On the other, it was supposed to aid the Comintern's effort to undermine these states and foment world revolution.[20]

Identity and political affiliation can be imposed. More often, they emerge whenever individuals come to believe that association will bring benefits. As the historian Polybius observed, "political societies" originate in the "natural weakness" of individuals.[21] Recognition, invention, or imposition of common identity is only the first step in the formation of a polity.[22] Also required are leadership, institutions, and the capacity to mobilize persons for political purposes, such as value satisfaction or relief from value deprivation. Each polity has its own domain, consisting of those individuals and other resources upon which it can draw and the particular issues in which it is engaged. Each polity is an authority within its domain to the extent that adherents recognize its effective control or influence. Effective control or influence need not be enshrined in law or even be considered legitimate, although polities that enjoy legal status and broad approval are obviously all that more secure. Loyalty can only be earned by producing sufficient satisfaction.[23]

Different polities (for example, Westphalian states, transnational corporations, kinship groups, and churches) are for the most part involved in different issues. Sometimes, however, different polities engage in the same issue(s) either as allies or as adversaries. Since it is common for more than one polity to attract and mobilize some of the same individuals, polities routinely compete for their loyalties and the resources (for example, votes, taxes, contributions, and skills) that they command. Competition may be minimized if such polities address different issues or stake out identical or compatible political positions on the same issue(s).

To the extent that polities share the loyalties and resources of the same pool of individuals and engage in the same issues, they also share political space. Conceptualizing space as an exclusive territorial domain and contemplating time as though it were distinct from space reflect, according to Jonathan Boyarin, "close genealogical links between the 'Cartesian coordinates' of space and time and the discrete, sovereign state, both associated with European society since the Renaissance. These links include relations of mapping, boundary setting, inclusion, and exclusion. . . ."[24] In the run-up to Augsburg and Westphalia, political, military, and economic power were tied to landed holdings. Today, however, 'land' remains only one of many ways to define the extent of a polity and the space that it occupies. In the present era, the technology of the Internet and satellite communication has virtually redefined space and time, or, as Boyarin expresses it, "our possible experiences of 'proximity' and 'simultaneity.' "[25]

Sovereign states claim to enjoy exclusive control over the space enclosed by their frontiers. In fact, to the contrary, all polities have a territorial reach of sorts, but it need not be exclusive in the sense connoted by traditional descriptions of the state system. The domains of polities extend wherever the persons, resources, and issues identified with them reside. Indeed, polities typically layer, overlap, or nest to a greater or lesser degree. This is one of many reasons why the traditional distinction between interstate and intrastate politics is so tenuous.

John Gerard Ruggie uses the example of the European Community and its "transnational microeconomic links" to illustrate the inadequacy of familiar statist definitions of territory. "Perhaps the best way to describe it . . . is that these links have created a nonterritorial 'region' in the world economy—a decentered yet integrated space-of-flows, operating in real time, which exists alongside the space-of-places that we call national economies. . . . In the nonterritorial global region . . . the conventional distinctions between internal and external . . . are exceedingly problematic, and any given state is but one constraint in corporate global strategic calculations."[26]

The picture that emerges from Michael Keating's and Liesbet Hooghe's work on regions in the EU is even more complex. They emphasize that no "homogeneous regional tier of government in the EU" has emerged: "There remain a variety of levels of territorial mobilization: historic nations; large provincial regions; units in federal or quasi-federal states; cities and city regions. . . . In some cases, the regions can be identified with a structure of government. In others, civil society or private groups are more important in defining and carrying forward a regional interest." Neither is there a "new regional hierarchy," nor can policy making "be explained simply by inter-state bargaining. . . . [N]ational politics are penetrated by European influences through law, bureaucratic contacts, political exchange, and the role of the commission in agenda-setting. Similarly, national politics are penetrated . . . by regional influences." In sum, what seems to be happening is "a Europeanization and a regionalization of national policy making" coupled with "a Europeanization of the regions and a regionalization of Europe."[27]

Europe is an obvious case of shared political space, but it is a worldwide condition. Michael Barnett's apt description of the overlapping identities and loyalties of Arabs is applicable in other contexts as well: "Until the late nineteenth century, inhabitants of the Fertile Crescent existed within a variety of overlapping authorities and political structures. The Ottoman Empire, Islam, and local tribal and village structures all contested for and held sway over various features of people's lives. With the Ottoman Empire's decline, imperialism, and new ideas of nationalism combined to challenge local political structures and identities, . . . [W]hile the great powers established a new geopolitical map, the political loyalties of the inhabitants enveloped these boundaries and challenged the very legitimacy of that map."[28]

NESTED IDENTITIES AND LOYALTIES

As new identities, loyalties, and accompanying symbols are forged and old ones are overcome, renewed, or diluted, some polities are partly or completely embedded within others.[29] We call this phenomenon nesting.

Old loyalties, identities, and political forms rarely disappear completely; rather they remain part of what we have described as a living museum, in which some exhibits are currently on special show, others are less prominently displayed, and still others are gathering dust in storage. Some polities find a comfortable niche in a more-inclusive polity and continue operating quite contentedly in their limited domain. Those that are outlawed and suppressed tend to become dormant or merge with new loyalties and identities in the manner that Christianity and Christian myths incorporated prior Jewish and pagan symbols.[30] Old loyalties, identities, and forms may then reappear with considerable vitality at a later (sometimes much later) date, especially when dominant polities appear to be vulnerable.

Indeed, in much of the developing world, the revival of nested precolonial identities such as the Maya of Chiapas and the Nahua of central Guerrero state in Mexico increasingly challenge the Westphalian structures imposed by conquering Europeans.[31] In the Mexican case, there was yet another revival in evidence, that of the Catholic Church, represented by the liberation theology preached by local priests. After the Revolution, the Mexican government seized the extensive property holdings of the Church and for many years banned the public practice of Catholicism. The Church from the outset of the Spanish conquest had found it necessary, mainly at the village level, to make some concessions to the beliefs and practices of indigenous Indian populations. Such grass-roots linkages inevitably increased when the Church had to go underground in the period following the Revolution. Once the Church was no longer persecuted, the fact that local priests tended to encourage and support Indian demands is therefore hardly surprising.[32]

Sometimes old identities, for example, cultural and religious categories, can be manipulated and wedded to later political forms to reinforce and intensify loyalties and to provide an additional measure of legitimacy. Thus the European Union is partly legitimated by the longstanding idea of 'Europe' with its supposedly shared history and cultural similarities, along with more recent symbols such as democracy and free markets. At the same time, traditional uncertainty as to the actual territorial bounds of Europe continues to be reflected (along with other considerations) in the "how wide" issue in EU debates. States with large Muslim communities frequently try to harness Islamic identities to state claims of sovereignty and thereby protect themselves from the challenge of loyalties to a broader transnational Islamic community. In this fashion, the rulers of Saudi Arabia clothe themselves in Islamic orthodoxy to guard against Islamic fundamentalists who seek to challenge the clan basis of the Saudi state.

As the Saudi example suggests, nested polities and the historical antecedents they symbolize help to explain why modern states—though all sovereign and descended from an ideal type that evolved out of medieval Europe—can differ dramatically from one another and sometimes seem to resemble other political forms. Any survey of contemporary states reveals that some are strong and others weak in terms of autonomy and capacity;[33] some are homogeneous and others heterogeneous in regards to ethnicity, language, and so on; some reflect tribal origins while others have imperial features. The differences are many, and these are rooted in the state's origins and historical evolution.

Even when old polities are digested, they continue to influence their successors, which often assume the characteristics of those embedded within them. The former Soviet Union was difficult to distinguish from the Communist Party of the Soviet Union that ruled for almost eight decades. The fiction that the union republics of the USSR were truly autonomous—and the status of the Ukraine and Belorussia as founding members of the United Nations—seemed more like a self-fulfilling prophecy when the collapse of the Soviet empire finally occurred. Now successor states must wrestle with the consequences of Moscow's having previously designated certain ethnic enclaves "autonomous regions" and "autonomous republics" (e.g., Chechnya). As Mark N. Katz observes, "the distinction between a union republic and an autonomous republic may have seemed clear to the Soviet inventors of the concepts, but it was never clear to the inhabitants of the latter."[34] Similarly, memories of a Russian empire dating back to Tsarist times encumber Moscow's efforts to establish a new Russian Federation identity as well as relationships with former republics and Eastern Europe, even as past glories inspire Russian radical-nationalist politicians to insist on reconstructing the empire.

Few of the sovereign entities in contemporary global politics resemble ideal Westphalian polities. States like Saudi Arabia and Jordan have a tribal flavor. Politics in a few Latin American countries still reflects the distinction between 'Europeans' and 'Indians' that was institutionalized after the Conquest. China continues to adapt its Confucian traditions to contemporary conditions and attempts to reconcile divisions between empire and regions—and various ethnicities—that is as old as the civilization itself. Waldron again: "China today is an amalgam of aspects of Chinese tradition, Stalinism, and the East Asian economic model as found in places like Taiwan and Singapore. This amalgam, created by revolution, is being tested by the forces unleashed by reform. . . . China, after all, is not the regime created by Mao and partly dismantled by Deng. It is a civilization, even a world."[35]

Like states as a whole, key statist institutions also echo the past. US aid and training bloated Latin American military establishments in the Cold War era. Left in most cases with no external enemies to fight, many instead found a vocation by meddling in domestic politics, sometimes to oust presumed incompetent, corrupt, or dangerously radical civilian politicians, but just as often to protect the institutional interests of the military themselves and to profit from the spoils of office.[36] African armies and mercenaries serve largely to maintain the dominance of one tribal group over others, although institutional loyalties and corruption are significant destabilizers on that continent too. Somalia, like Latin America, was affected by the Cold War, but there rival superpowers lingered only long enough to leave sophisticated weapons in the hands of warlord gangs.

When old identities resurface with explosive consequences, new political arrangements designed to re-establish peace, unfortunately, often merely guarantee that nesting will continue without a resolution of basic issues and thus sow the seeds of future conflict. An agreement reached in September 1995 among the warring parties in Bosnia and Herzegovina at American urging to create a single federal state with autonomous ethnic communities seems almost to assure the future revival of ethnic strife.[37] That proved to be the case with earlier communal arrangements in Lebanon and Cyprus. Similarly, the steps taken toward establishing a national Palestinian political entity in the West Bank and Gaza Strip under Yasser Arafat have at the same time revived loyalties to powerful clans. One observer declares that "[w]hile Mr. Arafat hopes ultimately to be the ruler of a nation-state, he may instead find himself consumed by holding together a group of rival clans without any allegiance to a single state—or to him."[38]

Once we take account of nesting, it is clear that the frontiers of Westphalian states never demarcated political life as theorists imagined but instead, like other polities, "regularly enclosed potentially rival authorities, divided others, and were themselves enclosed within the frontiers of still larger polities."[39]

THE COALESCENCE AND FRAGMENTATION OF POLITIES

Polities are always "becoming." Political evolution and devolution are constant, although sometimes so slow as to be almost imperceptible. In every historical epoch, some polities grow, either at the expense of others or when existing polities fully or partly merge. Other polities perforce contract, overlap, nest, or (rarely) disappear without a trace. These simultaneous processes of coalescence and fragmentation that Rosenau terms "fragmegration" are speeded up when it appears that existing institutions are unresponsive to the needs of adherents.[40] In such cases, old polities may reappear to meet those needs or new ones may emerge, like the Westphalian state itself during the Middle Ages or the confederal and federal unions in the United States of America. Coalescence may produce very different political forms, as did the Ch'in unification of China's city polities, the union of northern European cities to form the Hanseatic League, or the agreement of Europe's Westphalian states to form the European Union.

Ruggie suggests that "European leaders may be thought of as entrepreneurs of alternate political identities."[41] Perhaps it would be more accurate to say they are now offering an additional identity and polity, for purposes that can only be served conjointly, because for the foreseeable future, whether the EU's constituent Westphalian polities will ever become fully nested remains much in doubt. A United States of Europe is at least on hold, but there is no doubt that continued expansion of European integration, as in the past, can only mean further diminution of the domains of traditional state polities, along with the sort of mutual interpenetration that Keating and Hooghe describe. To the extent that the EU's various activities are decentralized, there might even be a growth of "government" under an EU logo in the UK, France, Spain, and so on.

When more and more authority was transferred to Washington in the US federal system, certainly bureaucracies at the state level continued to grow as well. Government at all levels was taking on more functions vis-a-vis civil society, partly because federal agencies like the FBI and the Social Security Administration needed local offices, and partly because states themselves had to administer numerous federally sponsored programs. At present, of course, more functions, from welfare to speed limits on highways, are being transferred back to the states. Like so many nested polities in human history, the states of the USA appear to be making a comeback of sorts.

Lately, the US Supreme Court has been wrestling with major constitutional issues affecting the very nature of federalism. In one case, the Court (barely) decided against the capacity of states to enact term limits on Congress; in another, against Washington's extending its power to regulate interstate commerce so far as to make it a federal crime to possess a gun near a school. Yale Law School professor Paul Gewirtz observed that Justice Clarence Thomas's dissent in the term-limits case actually embodied "the first principles of those who opposed ratification of the Constitution." Gewirtz recalled that American patriot ("Give me liberty or give me death!") Patrick Henry had declared in 1788, "I am not really an American, I am a Virginian," and complained that the authors of the Constitution had no authority "to speak the language of 'we the people' instead of 'we the states'." Justice John Paul Stevens, for the majority in the term-limits case, pointed out that the Preamble to the Constitution mentions the Founders' intention to create "a more perfect union." However, Justice Thomas countered that the original formulation of the Preamble was "We the people of the states of New Hampshire, Massachusetts," and so on, and that the phrase "the United States" is used consistently throughout the Constitution "as a plural noun."[42]

Our analysis elsewhere of several diverse historical epochs suggests that the expansion and contraction of polities are universal processes, exhibiting something of a dialectical relationship.[43] As we have noted in the post-Cold War period, the collapse of a major polity almost inevitably leads to regrouping within and beyond its bounds. Less often recognized is that the enlargement of a polity by conquest or coalescence tends to create, in a sense, its own nemesis: the conditions for later fragmentation. Other polities may be nested and sooner or later cause 'indigestion.' Moreover, the extension of central authority to additional territory or persons entails the growth of a bureaucracy that is not only harder to manage efficiently but may also perceive interests different from the center and even develop breakaway ambitions. Also, expansion or consolidation of a major polity often precipitates important economic and social changes that make society more complex and hence more difficult to govern. Lastly, expansion or consolidation may whet the appetite for further expansion, with risks of disastrous reversals or at least administrative overstretch. The process comes full circle when the large polity eventually fragments, and its successors prove too small to meet the demands of their constituents. Pressures build for selective or full-scale reunification or invite various forms of involvement by polities outside the original bounds.

Historical memories and myths sustain old identities and loyalties so that they may burn for generations, even centuries, awaiting either the emergence of issues and leaders that will activate their adherents or the enfeeblement of polities whose territory they share. Religion, literature, dialect, poetry, and ritual are only a few of the ways in which ancient identities are nourished. Any or all may be factors in the rediscovery of nation and demands for autonomy or national self-determination.

The hybrid concept of 'nation-state,' as we have noted, was born during the apparent fusion of the two ideas in Europe, especially in the late-eighteenth and nineteenth centuries. The evolution of states elsewhere was markedly different, and the territorial entities imposed by colonial masters rarely coincided with the frontiers of precolonial polities. The idea of nation-state is further muddled by the fact that nationalists frequently seek to disenfranchise others in existing states or to secede and create new ones for themselves. Even on the fringes of Europe and Canada, there are national groups that claim that their culture has been submerged by majorities within nation-states—Spanish Basques and Catalonians, French Bretons and Corsicans, Canadian Québécois, Ulster Catholics, Celtic Scots and Welsh, and others.

As Keating stresses in his examination of Québec, Catalonia, and Scotland, "minority nationalism" need not be "tribal" and may be willing to settle for some form of autonomy rather than full-fledged independence.[44] However, Québec, which is currently hovering on the brink between secession and new terms for autonomy, is an instructive case of how complex things can be. Parti Québécois premier Jacques Parizeau blamed his secession forces' loss of the 1995 referendum on "money and the ethnic vote," highlighting the presence of large number of non-Francophone English and other minorities ("allophones"). To complicate matters still further, indigenous Indian groups who claim half the territory of Québec were so alarmed by the referendum that they themselves threatened to secede. Moreover, were Canada ultimately to fall apart, Québec might well not be the only departure, because there are regional/provincial identities as well as ethnic ones, such as the Maritime provinces and British Columbia.

Ernest Gellner argues that for nationalists the "congruence between their own culture and that of the political, economic, and educational bureaucracies which surround them, becomes the most important single fact of their lives."[45] Nevertheless, whatever the preferences of nationalists, the frontiers of states and nations, especially outside Europe, usually diverge. Indeed, "national" frontiers themselves vary dramatically depending on which traits—religion, language, race, ethnicity, or whatever—define the common identity on which the "nation" is built.[46] Some current theorists are aware of the tension between Westphalian states and the nations of which they consist, and they are—at last!—beginning to abandon the term *nation-state*. Others continue to make the argument that nothing has really changed in the world because nationalists all want their own states. The argument is wrong or very misleading on three counts: It places the emphasis on the persistence of sovereign statehood as an idea, rather than as the struggle of secessionist movements precisely to break away from existing states. Also, many nationalist movements would be content with some form of autonomy. Lastly, many nationalist movements are obviously not going to succeed, but they will go on making life miserable for states anyway.

The processes of coalescence and fragmentation may be gradual and lengthy, as was the emergence of territorial states in Europe with the waning of the Middle Ages, when "the international system went through a dramatic transformation in which the crosscutting jurisdictions of feudal lords, emperors, kings, and popes started to give way to territorially defined authorities."[47] Or, the processes might be relatively rapid, as was the disintegration of Western Europeans' imperial polities after World War II, the development of regional integration in Europe and free-trade areas, the demise of the Soviet Union, and the virtual collapse of territorial states in extensive areas of Africa—all during a period of just under four decades.[48] However rapid or protracted the process is in different contexts, again, the key point is that it is ceaseless.

The emergence or reemergence of political forms competing with Westphalian states for the loyalties of citizens challenges, in Franke Wilmer's words, "the normative basis of international relations."[49] The triumph of European states over older political forms, encountered first in the Americas and later in Asia and Africa, enabled scholars and practitioners to speak of a "global state system" and to leave other polities off their maps of the world. States bestow sovereignty (and therefore whatever legitimacy derives from that status) on one another, while withholding it from entities located within or across their sovereign boundaries.

Because indigenous peoples like American Indian tribal groups were not regarded as sovereign in the sense that states were, Europeans in the nineteenth century had few qualms about renouncing treaties that had been concluded with them. Nonetheless, what treaties remained, and related autonomous arrangements like reservation lands and tribal councils have not proved inconsequential; indeed they have come into their own in the twentieth century. As in Québec, in the Pacific Northwest, upstate New York, and elsewhere, Indians have dusted off their old treaties and begun to interpret them to include the widest possible land claims. Discoveries of oil and other valuable mineral reserves on some reservations caused repeated wrangling among tribal councils, multinational firms, and the Bureau of Indian Affairs. Various tribes have also taken advantage of their peculiar legal status to establish booming tax-free shopping malls and fabulously successful gambling casinos, thereby undercutting potential government revenues from similar enterprises. Meanwhile, the current climate of political correctness, combined with the New Age nonsense that indigenous peoples are morally superior because they have always lived in harmony with their environment, makes it more difficult than previously for politicians to change the terms of the relationship.

In all events, at the global level, the claims of sovereignty to exclusive control over territory and freedom from external interference have been largely compromised in recent years. In the United Nations we hear less and less of Article 2, paragraph 7, of the Charter. The organization regularly intervenes in the domestic affairs of member states for humanitarian, peacekeeping, and human-rights purposes.[50]

TRANSITIONAL EPOCHS AND MYTHS AND MEMORIES OF THE PAST

Certain historical periods, which we term 'transitional epochs,' feature unusually dramatic shifts in identities, loyalties, and attendant political forms. Some of the many important transitional epochs in global history were the sixth century A.D. in the Near East, when an existing clan system and an aspiring universal religious community competed for loyalties; the sixteenth and seventeenth centuries in Europe and Latin America, when the Westphalian state was ratified by the international community, and Spain and (to a lesser extent) Portugal imposed European political forms on top of tribal ones in the Americas; the late eighteenth and nineteenth centuries, when modern nationalism added a newly explosive element to global politics, and the European empires consolidated their control over much of Africa and Asia; World War II and its aftermath, which saw the establishment of the two superpowers, the start of European integration, and the steady decline of Europe's former empires. The end of the Cold War and the increasing globalization of the economy appear to have ushered in yet another transitional epoch.

During transitional epochs, incompatible identities, loyalties, and political forms fiercely compete. One hallmark of transitional epochs is struggle over how history is written.[51] Determining the meaning of the past legitimizes one interpretation of the present and delegitimizes others, and such control affords political power. Did Christopher Columbus's discovery of the New World mark the first step in Europe's civilizing mission, was it the beginning of Europe's extermination of vibrant indigenous cultures, or was it a morally neutral clash or encounter of civilizations? Is Israel's occupation of the West Bank a fulfillment of a biblical promise, or is it a Zionist variation of Europe's penetration of the developing world? Does the relative absence of women from traditional accounts mean that men alone determine the course of history? The triumph of statist theory in Western history and political science reflects Europe's control over historical meaning and the related forgetting of rival forms of identity both in Europe and the areas Europe conquered.

With the end of the Cold War and the waning of the European epoch in global politics, the struggle for controlling the meaning of history and the memories it evokes has resumed, often with a vengeance. Boyarin has hypothesized that "identity and memory are virtually the same concept."[52] Be that as it may, it is difficult to overestimate the importance of the act of remembering, whether in national pageants, recollections of ancient wrongs, tribal ceremonies, religious convocations, or ethnic parades. Such rituals reinforce and renew collective myth and memory. Whether memorializing an idealized Battle of the Boyne on the part of Irish Protestants or the Battle of Kosovo on the part of Serb nationalists, almost any (sometimes fictionalized) historical event can be resurrected to mount a challenge to authority.

Currently, events in Islamic history, some dating back fourteen centuries, are being revived to reinforce the cleavage between one branch of Islam and another or to undermine existing state practices. The secular nation-state created by Mustafa Kemal in 1923 in Turkey to mimic the Westphalian polity is under siege. There, "an Islamic fundamentalist movement is spreading through the shantytowns that encircle Ankara and Istanbul" owing to the inability of the Kemalist secular state to cope either with economic crisis or the Kurdish revolt in eastern Anatolia.[53] The end of the Cold War and the refusal of Christian Europe to treat Turkey as one of its own have also contributed to the growth of Turkey's Islamic Welfare (Refah) Party. Similar tendencies are apparent in Algeria, Pakistan, Afghanistan, and Bosnia, where the fragmentation of Yugoslavia and the brutal aggression of Bosnian Serbs have promoted the revival of Islamic identities among a Muslim community previously noted for its secularism.[54] In a few cases, such as those of the Kurds who are dispersed in Turkey, Iran, Iraq, and Syria, or the Druse who live in Israel and Syria, religion and ethnicity support one another and foster transnational links.[55] In Malaysia, too, ethnicity and Islam combine to reinforce the majority's contrasting identity with the country's prosperous Chinese minority.

Various political movements have emerged that promote transnational Islamic identities and actions. For example, the Muslim Brotherhood, founded in Egypt in 1928, has leaders in Egypt, Saudi Arabia, Kuwait, and western Europe and, according to one report, has links with the Iranian and Sudanese regimes, the Islamic Group in Egypt, the Algerian Islamic Salvation Front, and Tunisia's Al Nahda. Controlling vast sums of money in banks around the world, the Brotherhood seeks "to advance the struggle to establish Islamic theocracies through wide infiltration of social structures, subsidized services, the control of mosques . . . and the establishment of secretive armed struggle."[56] In sum, as Bassam Tibi explains, "neither internal sovereignty, with its conception of citizenship and national identity and loyalty, nor external sovereignty, with its idea of mutual recognition of boundaries and authority over that territory, has a real counterpart in Arab-Islamic history."[57]

The outcome of growing tension between state and transnational Islam remains in doubt. Michael Barnett argues that Arab advocates of nationalism based on the division of the Arab world into sovereign territorial states initially triumphed over advocates of pan-Arabism. Today, however, he recognizes that "sovereignty is not permanently anchored": "Arab leaders must continually work to reproduce the state's sovereignty, its domestic and international authority, and the distinction between domestic and international space. The failure of statist ideologies has resurrected primordial, ethnic, and, most famously, religious identities, which in turn represent a potential threat to state sovereignty."[58]

GOD AND THE STATE

Tension between the Westphalian state—and the patriotic sentiments it encourages—and transnational or universal religious movements—and the strong loyalties they evoke—is hardly new. The struggle between church and state in Europe began in the Middle Ages and, in the case of modern states such as Ireland and Poland, has arguably not ended. The investiture controversy, the Reformation, the Thirty Years' War, and the Counterreformation were all part of the struggle between church and state in Europe, and the separation of church and state laid down in the US Constitution bears witness to the importance of the issue in American history.

Rulers as different as ancient Romans and Spanish Francistas recognized that religion, when harnessed to secular authority, could be a powerful asset. The very secular Machiavelli, in Chapter XI of *The Prince,* declares that "ecclesiastical principalities" can survive without ability or fortune because "they are sustained by ancient religious customs, which are so powerful and are of such quality, that they keep their princes in power in whatever manner they proceed and live."[59] In Chapter XI of *The Discourses* he praises Rome's official religion and describes religion as "the most necessary and assured support of any civil society . . . for where religion exists it is easy to introduce armies and discipline."[60] That same Rome, however, when confronted by those, like the Jews and early Christians, who refused to bow the knee to its gods and saw obedience to its officials as incompatible with loyalty to their church, had recourse to coercion. Many Jews chose death at Masada rather than accept Roman rule; in time, Christianity first penetrated, then conquered, and finally inherited Rome's empire.

Contemporary states, too, routinely seek to harness religion to promote their legitimacy or at least try to co-opt religious identities that might undermine the loyalty of citizens. Russia's postcommunist leaders, like the tsars of old, are investing themselves with the mantle of orthodoxy. Leaders of the Eastern Orthodox church in Greece "are convinced that Moscow is using its weight and power to regain its place at the center of the Orthodox world, at the expense of the Greek-led patriarchy in Istanbul."[61] And the extensive ruling family of Saudi Arabia has made *sharia* the law of the country.[62] In cases such as Calvin's Geneva and Khomeini's Iran, the state becomes almost indistinguishable from a religious movement, and in others religious values and beliefs pose a serious challenge to secular territorial rule.

Although we will shortly return to Islamic militancy, fundamentalist principles also inform some Christian movements in the United States, as well as Orthodox Judaism in Israel and Hindu nationalism in India.[63] Two Hindu nationalist parties, Shiv Sena and Bharatiya Janata, hold or share power in three Indian states that contain seventeen percent of the country's population: Maharashtra (including the city of Bombay), Gujarat, and Rajasthan. Shiv Sena was instrumental in the 1992 destruction of an ancient mosque at Ayodhya in Uttar Pradesh and the ensuing violence that swept Bombay. Shiv Sena means the "army of

Shiva" who was a seventeenth-century Hindu warrior-king, and the party seeks to transform India into a Hindu state in which Muslims would be relegated to second-class status.[64]

Militant Islamists believe they are acting on behalf of a universal Islamic community. No instance illustrates this more clearly than the Ayatollah Khomeini's 1989 fatwa (religious edict) that called for the murder of British writer Salman Rushdie for allegedly insulting Islam in his novel *The Satanic Verses*.[65] Khomeini was acting not as an official of the Iranian state but as a spiritual leader of Shiites everywhere. The Saudi royal house obtained a fatwa affirming Saudi Arabia's right to normalize relations with Israel, and this elicited a lively debate among Muslim clerics around the Arab world.[66] The career of Egyptian cleric Sheikh Abdel Rahman, who issued a fatwa authorizing the assassination of Anwar Sadat and who was convicted in the United States of plotting terrorist activities, also reflects a disdain for state claims of sovereign supremacy.[67] Islamic leaders like these argue that, in Judith Miller's words, "rule is a prerogative not of the people, but of God, who appointed the prophet, who, in turn, prescribed the general precepts of governance in God's own words, the Koran."[68]

Events from Afghanistan and Tajikistan to Bosnia have deepened Islamic identities and encouraged transnational Islamic loyalties.[69] Muslim veterans of the war in Afghanistan, calling themselves the Harkat-ul Ansar, have infiltrated Indian-occupied Kashmir and kidnapped and murdered Western hostages.[70] Others have joined Abu Sayyaf, the violent successor to the Moro Front in Mindanao in the Philippines.[71] Pakistan has instituted a mandatory death sentence for blasphemy and, according to one report, "is reckoned to have around five times as many Islamic militants as policemen."[72] Its northwest frontier province has become a center for militant Muslims, including Ramzi Ahmed Youssef, a suspect in the 1993 bombing of New York's World Trade Center, who was arrested in a joint US-Pakistani raid in Islamabad.[73] Islamic militants in Hezbollah may have been responsible for terrorist bombings against Israeli targets in London and Buenos Aires, as well as in Lebanon.[74] Militants in Hamas (Islamic Opposition Movement) and Islamic Holy War have repeatedly committed terrorism against Israelis in order to undermine the fragile Palestinian-Israeli peace agreement and to replace Yasser Arafat and the PLO.[75] In order to bring pressure on France, home to five million Muslims, to abandon its opposition to a fundamentalist government in Algeria, Islamists hijacked a French plane, assassinated French residents in Algeria, and carried out a bombing campaign in France itself.[76]

Whether fairly or unfairly, strident Islam appears to Western observers, in "images of car bombs, murder, and young, bearded holy warriors bent on historic revenge," and as a major challenge to the sovereign state and its ideology of modernity.[77] "Islam," declares Samuel Huntington in a particularly terse and colorful phrase, "has bloody borders."[78] Some western officials, such as Newt Gingrich and Willy Claes, former NATO secretary-general, speak of Islamic fundamentalists in terms once reserved for communists.[79] Of course, there is no single transnational Islamic movement, and militants in different countries sometimes do battle with one another. Sunni-Shiite animosity continues to divide Islam as it has since the murder of the Prophet's cousin and son-in-law, the fourth caliph, Ali ibn Abi Talib, in 661 A.D.[80] Shiites believe that political legitimacy depends upon direct descent from the Prophet, and they consider all subsequent Sunni rulers to be usurpers. Divisions between the two communities play an important role in the political life of several Arabic states, including Iraq, Saudi Arabia, and Lebanon.

BLOOD AND POLITICS: THE CHALLENGE OF FAMILY, CLAN, AND TRIBE

Kinship memories (real or invented) and loyalties to tribal and clan polities are reemerging, not least in Africa and the Middle East, to challenge the autonomy of states or in some cases to make them appear to be little more than family property. Examples of the latter include Haiti under the Duvaliers, Nicaragua under the Somozas, Jordan under the Hashemites, and Saudi Arabia under the Sauds.

The effort to build a territorial state for Palestinians in the Middle East runs up against the tribal traditions of powerful clans. Considerable political power in the town of Jericho resides in the Council of Jericho Families, consisting of members of the town's six most powerful clans, which enforces its decisions with traditional punishments such as ostracism. In the words of one Muhammad Jalaytta, a member of the Council of Jericho Families, "People are used to the traditional way of resolving problems. Even the police come to us, asking us to use our family connections to get someone to cooperate with their investigations. Family is stronger than the Palestinian Authority."[81] Arafat "has been criticized for making key appointments to his government with an eye more to winning the loyalties of the most important clans than to choosing the most qualified candidate."[82]

In Africa, the existence of governments that are extensions of tribal power, along with the failure of authorities to cope effectively with explosive socioeconomic problems, weakens loyalties to the state while intensifying older tribal identities. Rwanda and Burundi exist only in atlases; the real organizing entities are Hutu and Tutsi. The Nigerian government and armed forces are largely instruments to perpetuate Hausa political power. National politics in Kenya is mainly a reflection of relations among the Luo, the Kikuyu, and other tribal groups. In Liberia, the overthrow of the country's Americo elite in 1980 transformed the political scene into conflicts among tribal groups such as the Krahn, Mende, and Gbandi. In many other parts of Africa, the situation is much the same.

MARKETS: FIRMS, BANKS, AND CRIMINAL ENTERPRISE

State-centric theorists are wont to regard the private sector as somehow existing at the sufferance of government. In capitalist countries, the argument goes, the state levies taxes upon companies and carefully regulates their activities at home and relationships with the external world. In socialist countries the state actually owns all or most of the national economy and provides for social welfare. The traditional view is accurate enough for socialist regimes, nearly all of which, however, have been privatizing to a greater or lesser extent in recent years. As for capitalist systems, the state-centric position offers only a partial and somewhat misleading description of the actual situation in a few strong-state Western countries, fits not at all the situation in most of the developing countries, and seems less and less (small-r) realistic everywhere, given current trends in the globalization of business and finance.

Today global and regional patterns of trade, investment, and financial speculation largely transcend state boundaries. Historically, too, political boundaries rarely coincided with economic zones. For thousands of years, merchant traders have been important actors and usually have enjoyed special privileges in both home and host societies. As early as the ninth century, Baghdad banks had branches with checking accounts in key cities throughout the Islamic Empire. Until about the end of the thirteenth century, what R. H. C. Davis calls "the central clearing-house of European trade and finance" were the Fairs of Champagne. There were six of them; each lasted six weeks and was truly transnational. "Italian bankers sent agents who issued letters of credit which could be cashed in almost any stated currency and in any part of Europe." Davis speaks of an "essential unity of the European economy" before 1250: "there were no national customs-systems, no 'tariff walls,' and no restriction on the movement of merchants, ecclesiastics, scholars, or labourers from one country to another."[83] Trading companies and banks like those of the Bardi and Peruzzi became increasingly powerful. Some Italian traders settled in foreign trading centers, where they formed local associations or "nations" for mutual advancement and protection. Firms thus created their own "permanent diplomatic missions" paralleling those pioneered by the Venetian empire. Large banks established such a symbiotic relationship with local and foreign governments, as well as the popes, that it was often difficult to tell who was more dependent upon whom.

Italian communes and German trading leagues like the medieval Hanseatic League were imaginative organizational efforts on the part of small city polities to reduce the interference of feudal rulers in economic and political transactions and to replicate the benefits of scale associated with the internal markets of large territorial states such as France and England. The League provided physical protection to traders, extracted economic concessions from trading partners, afforded some standardization of weights and measures, and shielded its members from external economic competitors.[84]

Trading and plantation companies also accompanied or facilitated the growth of European empires throughout the world. Companies such as the Dutch East Indian, the English East India, and Hudson Bay extended the economic reach of states and merchants well beyond existing sovereign frontiers. Dutch companies tended to be private, while French companies were state enterprises.[85] Such companies, argues Janice Thomson, "were, as a rule, granted full sovereign powers. In addition to their economic privileges of a monopoly on trade with a given region or in a particular commodity and the right to export bullion, they could raise an army or a navy, build forts, make treaties, make war, govern their fellow nationals, and coin their own money."[86]

During their heyday, Westphalian states regularly augmented their military and political clout by following mercantilist policies that impeded natural markets. In some cases where sovereign frontiers reflected a market-based logic, such as the Austro-Hungarian Empire, political and national strains ultimately produced disintegration that ignored such logic. The result was economically crippled nation-states that quickly became economic dependencies of Germany. Germany itself consolidated in the late nineteenth century under Bismarck's leadership, combining Prussian military might with a *zollverein* to undermine hundreds of local principalities. In Italy, cities incorporated various smaller jurisdictions in their *contados*; and then some cities began incorporating other cities to a point where a few, like Venice, Florence, and Milan, were actually regional polities (Venice, in fact, was an empire).

Political authorities have used a variety of expedients in cases where political and economic frontiers are incompatible. Extension of political frontiers by conquest to incorporate markets and sources of raw materials in the manner of ancient Rome or Japan in the 1930s, is one approach; the creation of closed overseas empires, in the manner of eighteenth and nineteenth-century Europeans, is another. To some extent, the modern-day creation of regional free-trade areas is a successor to empires and imperial preference.

However, it is also important to recognize that, even within the boundaries of states, the line between private-sector activities and various manifestations of public authority is constantly evolving. In the United States, the federal power to regulate interstate commerce was a major step in the shift from a confederal to federal system and, nevertheless, has been subject to strikingly different interpretations over the years. Public authorities tax and regulate corporations but cannot do so beyond the bounds allowed by traditional safeguards for private property and a political process heavily influenced by large campaign contributions and lobbyists. In fact, as deregulation of some industries has lately shown, much former regulation was little more than government protection of private sector price fixing. Moreover, from the outset government has been expected to provide the private sector with appropriate infrastructure and services. Complex political coalitions arise in policy making that often deflect conceptions of the national interest into more parochial channels. For instance, levels of US defense spending reflect, as much or more than objective readings of threats to security, the reluctance of the military establishment, defense industries, and local communities with affected bases or factories to endure substantial cuts. Likewise, corporations able to take advantage of open markets provided most of the support required to push through the NAFTA agreement.[87]

The United States Government is still more able than most to maintain at least some limited measure of autonomy from, and control over, the private sector. How many governments in the world have a reasonable grasp of what is happening in their own national economy, who is producing what, and what taxes are owed, let alone the capacity to collect them and keep the national treasury from being plundered by corrupt officials with numbered accounts abroad? In Italy, the most dynamic part of the private sector (apart from the Mafia) is composed of smaller enterprises which are largely undocumented and virtually untaxed. One of the results is that it is almost impossible accurately to rank the productivity of leading European economies.

Some private-sector entities have enormous resources that make those available to most governments seem paltry by comparison, and such resources are being wielded across state boundaries with increasing impunity and almost unimaginable rapidity. The fifty largest transnational companies each has an annual sales revenue greater than the GNP of 131 members of the United Nations.[88] Initially, most business expansion was multinational, that is, corporations establishing production facilities abroad to take advantage of local cheap labor and raw materials— or to get in under tariff walls. Since the 1980s, direct investment abroad has grown explosively, yet for all that and full mergers, much of the action has been shifting to alliances such as joint ventures, partnerships, knowledge agreements, and outsourcing arrangements. Some of these arrangements involve substantial investment; more often it is through mutually supporting production, development, or knowledge sharing. When there is mutual investment, it is often only a minority share, sort of a symbolic bonding of the allied parties.

One of the results of alliances is the growing difficulty of determining the country of origin of particular products, which (along with other factors) challenges traditional foundations of trade policy. Intergovernmental efforts to liberalize tariff and nontariff barriers to trade now, in fact, seem rather to be opening the door after most of the horses have already left the stable. Governments can concentrate their efforts on a few remaining troublesome sectors and highly publicized disputes. Meanwhile, in the developing world and former Soviet countries, the main action has shifted to IMF and World Bank preferences for austerity and free-market policies. Peter F. Drucker writes that "[corporate] alliances, formal and informal, are becoming the dominant form of integration in the world economy." Drucker adds: "Some major companies, such as Toshiba, the Japanese electronic giant, and Corning Glass, the world's leading maker of high-engineered glass, may each have more than one hundred alliances all over the world. Integration in the [EU] is proceeding far more through alliances than through mergers and acquisitions, especially among the middle-sized companies that dominate European economies. . . . Businesses make little distinction between domestic and foreign partners in their alliances."[89]

Alliances are only part of the overall globalization picture. In US accounts, about half of all trade in goods and services is intrafirm. More and more trade is not in goods but in services, which, of course, is one of the reasons intergovernmental talks have given so much attention to services in recent years. Government statisticians readily acknowledge that services are so hard to track that they may well be underestimating the actual flow by as much as 50 percent. The United States has the largest share of services trade among the developed countries, followed by the United Kingdom. Japan is at the bottom of the list. Hence the much-ballyhooed trade deficit between the US and Japan may not be a real deficit at all.

Improved communications and especially the information revolution have practically made possible the globalization of business and finance. Financial markets grew up in the aftermath of the collapse of the international monetary system in the 1970s and the liberalization of national controls on transnational currency transactions. Now globalized finance has become something of a Frankenstein's monster—arguably the single most formidable obstacle to the reconstruction of any sort of international monetary system and even to regional currency standardization as envisaged in the EU. Real stabilization or a single currency would put too many speculators out of work.

By the end of the 1970s, the foreign-exchange market was globalized, and between 1983 and 1992, foreign-exchange trading exploded from about $60 billion to $900 billion a day. That figure has continued to rise and is now estimated at $1.3 trillion a day. By contrast, the total foreign-currency reserves of the major industrial countries is a mere $640 billion. "The foreign-exchange market," argues Jeffrey Frankel, "is a 1,000-pound gorilla, and intervention is a flimsy leash. When the gorilla has a good idea where it wants to go, there is no point in trying to restrain him. But sometimes the gorilla is willing to be led."[90] In the 1980s, the bond market also was globalized. Between 1983 and 1993, transnational sales of US Treasury bonds grew from $30 billion to $500 billion; between 1982 and 1994, the volume of international bonds soared from $259 billion to over $2 trillion.[91]

Consider the case of Mexico. President Salinas took office in 1988, renegotiated his country's enormous foreign debt, undertook various market reforms and privatizations that boosted foreign investor confidence, and joined NAFTA. Between 1990 and 1994, Mexico received more foreign investment than any other country except China. The government hoped that the country's continuing attractiveness to foreign investment would help keep Mexican money invested at home, and that dependence on foreign capital would lessen as the large gap between imports and exports gradually closed. Salinas, not illogically, believed that Mexican exports would soar once NAFTA reduced trade barriers. Unfortunately, all that foreign investment helped sustain the peso at a greatly overvalued level, led to a surge of imports, and encouraged Mexicans to use their overvalued money to invest in the US and elsewhere outside the country. The US Federal Reserve raised interest rates, the revolt flared in Chiapas, and the Mexican bubble burst. There was the equivalent of a run on the Mexican bank, which threatened to spread to other countries, when the Clinton administration moved to plug the dike with highly controversial loan guarantees.

Another dimension of commercial activity that offers a major challenge at least to many states is, of course, organized crime. Governments have been battling the likes of freebooters, pirates, smugglers, and illicit arms dealers since ancient times. Some governments or parts thereof have combated crime by establishing their own market shares. Indeed, it is not far wrong to conceive of the problem of large-scale crime as a market phenomenon, that is, another form of alliance between criminal enterprises and their employees, consumers, and corrupt officials. For example, dictator President Rafael Trujillo, his family, and immediate cronies controlled something like two thirds of the entire economy of the Dominican Republic, and the national military in many developing countries have profited similarly in legal and illegal pursuits. Drug cartels in Colombia and the Mafia in Italy have made such inroads that the state itself has at times seemed almost congruent with criminal networks. Although the situation is not quite that bad in places like Japan and Mexico, official corruption has been so pervasive that it has contributed to serious political instability. The Russian Mafia has set up what is effectively a parallel economy to that of the state and has also established itself transnationally.

Criminal activity like drug cartels may rightly be seen as a macrolevel phenomenon in global politics, but organized crime is also an integral part of social life at every level. Not only in Colombia, but also in Peru, Bolivia, Mexico, and drug-trade countries elsewhere in the world, peasants have no alternative but to depend on drug lords for a livelihood, and parts of the national territory are literally off-limits to central authority. The developed world, too, is far from immune. In the New York metropolitan area, for example, police corruption has been a perennial issue, and (prior to the Guiliani administration) news reports highlighted criminal control of New York's Fulton Fish Market, the Javits Convention Center, and garbage collection in New Jersey. The Russian Mafia is making inroads in various New York neighborhoods; Chinese gangs control many businesses in Chinatown and illegal immigration from the Far East.

CONCLUSION: MANIPULATING MYTHS AND MAPS

The pressures placed on Westphalian polities by citizens' loyalties to potentially rival polities places a premium on manipulation of ancient symbols or their invention by contemporary elites seeking to gain or retain political power. Even revolutionary elites recognize the legitimating power of foundation myths that imply that they are part of a continuous historical stream, especially if mythical origins include some type of divine sanction. Indeed, reconstructing old myths and refining them for contemporary political purposes is an ancient and honorable practice. Chinese dynasties routinely depicted themselves as heirs to China's mythical sage kings of antiquity who were divinely mandated by heaven to create and sustain the empire. Shinto, which proclaimed Japanese emperors to be divine, served a similar function until Japan's defeat in World War II. One of the most successful foundation myths was that of Augustan Rome. The Emperor Augustus commissioned Virgil to write the Aeneid both to legitimize imperial Rome (and Augustus as emperor) and, by inventing Trojan ancestry, to emphasize continuity and differentiate Romans from Greeks.

Manipulating myths and symbols has continued to play an important legitimating and mobilizing role into the twentieth century. Stalin invented national roots for the Soviet Union's nomadic Muslim communities in order to dilute the more threatening Turkic and Islamic identities. "Soviet policy," argues James Rupert, "firmly established the 'nationalities' into which Central Asia is now divided. In pre-Soviet Turkistan, people had defined themselves primarily as Turkic or Tajik Muslims, identities that could have permitted the evolution of a unified polity across the region. The Soviets sought to prevent that by establishing five Central Asian republics, forcing on each a distinct 'national' language and culture."[92] However, national roots are not deep in the steppeland of Central Asia, and the post-Soviet states of the region have reached into their mythic pasts to find appropriate national symbols. In the case of Kirgizistan, this has led to a revival of an epic poem about a hero called Manas who is said to have resisted the Chinese. In Kazakhstan, the government has revived interest in the nineteenth-century poet and novelist Abai Kunanbaev, and in neighboring Uzbekistan, the fourteenth-century conqueror Tamerlane has been trundled out as a symbol of Uzbek nationalism.[93]

"[W]hat better way," asks Anthony D. Smith, "of suggesting and inducing that sense of belonging than by 'rediscovering' submerged or lost ethnic roots in the mists of immemorial time?"[94] Writing of the Middle East, Barnett argues: "Manufacturing consent through the reconstruction of political identity can prove to be a cost-effective method of creating support. . . . For instance, even Mu'ammar al-Kaddafi . . . attempted to create a 'Libyan Arab' national identity through historical texts, holidays, and monuments. In Iraq the Ba'athist party, which stresses pan-Arabism and the singularity of the Arab people, established an ongoing project to demonstrate the existence of an Iraqi identity that had roots in Mesopotamia."[95] And if nonstate identities and loyalties cannot be co-opted or modified by state authorities, they may seek, however unsuccessfully, to suppress them. Thus, in France, authorities banned the wearing of Muslim head scarves in school as a challenge to the secularism of the French state.[96]

Unfortunately for them, state officials must confront new challenges to the primacy of the Westphalian state as an object of citizens' identities and loyalties at the very time when their repertoire of potential responses has been further limited by future shock trends. The Westphalian polity is as legally sovereign as ever, but being so seems to guarantee less and less in terms of effective control over persons, resources, and issues. Modern weaponry and not least trends in communications and related technology—the instantaneous transmission of information, images, and money across vast distances—have altered the very nature of space and time as factors in global politics. Individuals and collectivities are increasingly unable to insulate themselves from the actions of others whom they do not know and probably will never meet. Their lives are touched not only by wars, terrorists, and microbes traveling on jetliners but also by the decisions of investors, consumers, and voters who go about their daily business unconscious of the full consequences of their actions. In a real sense, the promise of a global system is finally being realized, and the emergence of enormous forms, ranging from transnational corporations that span the globe to continental free trade areas, reflects that fact. Paradoxically, as we have stressed, centralization of authority encourages a search for greater personal control and reinforces loyalties to local authorities. One manifestation of this is the tidal wave of secessionist and autonomy movements that, in the name of self-determination, has eroded the cohesion of many states.

As we near the end of the second millennium (by one calendar), the shape of post-Westphalian global politics (what Rosenau terms "postinternational politics") is becoming more and more obscure. Maps that portray the world divided into exclusive sovereign states tell only part of the tale and, for many issues, not the most important part. The classic distinction between domestic and international events means less and less; the role of state frontiers as walls between 'us' and 'them' continues to erode. This by no means signals the end of we-they cleavages; instead, it means that the criteria for such cleavages are changing, sometimes issue by issue.

What sort of map are we going to need? Kaplan, in his own flamboyant style, maintains that "the last map" will be "an ever-mutating representation of chaos."[97] His apocalyptic vision captures some of the sheer uncertainty of the present but falls short of depicting how much governance would exist even if Westphalian polities were to disappear tomorrow (which they are unlikely to do). There are a host of international functional regimes. The European experiment and other regional schemes, by fits and starts, continue to evolve; nongovernmental organizations are proliferating; corporations and markets have their own shifting structures; most religions have church hierarchies of one form or another; some tribes still have chiefs and elders; more autonomy arrangements for certain minorities are almost certain to emerge; for that matter, already existing within many present Westphalian polities are numerous other public entities like the fifty states of the USA, counties, parishes, cities, local school districts, and so on. There is plenty of room for maneuver, for greater or lesser modifications of authority and responsibilities in response to changing circumstances.

The political forms they used to teach in school—unitary, federal, or confederal—now seem hopelessly inadequate to describe all the possible variations on these models, not to mention the sort of complexity that is developing in places like Europe and in global politics generally from layered, overlapping, and interacting polities. But contemplate other forms of governance than the Westphalian polity is what we must do, because we already have a wide range of them, and past and future, converging in the present, are certain to require and bring us many more.

NOTES

1. The first version of this chapter was prepared for the Research Seminar at the Norwegian Nobel Institute, Oslo, Norway, 30 January, 1996, when Professor Ferguson was Senior Fellow at the Institute. He gratefully acknowledges the Institute's generous financial support and warm hospitality.

2. Stephen D. Krasner, "Westphalia and All That," in Judith Goldstein and Robert O. Keohane, eds., *Ideas and Foreign Policy* (Ithaca, NY: Cornell University Press, 1993), pp. 235, 237.

3. Robert D. Kaplan, "The Coming Anarchy," *The Atlantic Monthly* (Feb. 1994), p. 69.

4. Peter Willetts, "The Role of 'Non-State Actors': Transnational Actors and International Organizations in Global Politics," in John Bayliss and Steve Smith, eds., *The Globalization of World Politics* (Oxford: Oxford University Press, 1997).

5. Arthur Waldron, "After Deng the Deluge: China's Next Leap Forward," *Foreign Affairs* 74, no. 5 (Sept./Oct. 1995), p. 149.

6. Francis Fukuyama, *The End of History and the Last Man* (New York, Free Press, 1992).

7. In Anne Tickner's words, "Including previously hidden gender inequalities in the analysis of global insecurity allows us to see how so many of the insecurities affecting us all . . . are gendered in their historical origins, their conventional definitions, and their contemporary manifestations." J. Ann Tickner, *Gender in International Relations* (New York: Columbia University Press, 1992), p. 129. The present authors have been (correctly) described as advocating "studying authority patterns 'out there' while not recognizing the gender-eclipsing authority 'in here.' " Christine Sylvester, *Feminist Theory and International Relations in a Postmodern Era* (New York: Cambridge University Press, 1994), p. 218.

8. With a few exceptions, such as Rosa Luxemburg and Karl Liebknecht, German social democrats were caught up in the militarist spirit that pervaded Europe's states after the Sarajevo assassination. See Carl E. Schorske, *German Social Democracy, 1905-1917* (Cambridge, MA: Harvard University Press, 1955). To be sure, some Communist Party organizers in Germany and elsewhere saw support for the war strictly as a tactical maneuver to protect and strengthen the party so that it could make the revolution at a later, more favorable time.

9. R. Brian Ferguson, "(Mis)understanding Resource Scarcity and Cultural Difference," *Anthropology Newsletter* (Nov. 1995), p. 37.

10. See Richard W. Mansbach and John A. Vasquez, *In Search of Theory: A New Paradigm for Global Politics* (New York: Columbia University Press, 1981), pp. 143–85.

11. Cited in Chris Hedges, "War Turns Sarajevo Away From Europe," *The New York Times*, July 28, 1995, p. A4. See also Roger Thurow, "Muslims

From Bosnia Find Refuge in Islam While Adrift in Europe," *The Wall Street Journal*, Sept. 6, 1994, pp. A1, A5.

12. Michael Specter, "Faith Reinforces Hate in the Caucasus," *The New York Times*, Jan. 15, 1995, Section 4, p. 5.

13. Youssef M. Ibrahim, "Violence Drives a Minority in Algeria to Take Up Arms," *The New York Times*, Oct. 1, 1994, p. 3.

14. Donatella Lorch, "Sudan's Long Civil War Threatening to Spread," *The New York Times*, Nov. 22, 1994, p. A3.

15. "The Orwellian State of Sudan," *The Economist*, June 24–30, 1995, pp. 21–22, 24.

16. Jonathan Boyarin, "Introduction," in Jonathan Boyarin, ed., *Remapping Memory: The Politics of TimeSpace* (Minneapolis: University of Minnesota Press, 1994), p. viii.

17. James N. Rosenau, "Governance, Order, and Change in World Politics," in James N. Rosenau and Ernst-Otto Czempiel, eds., *Governance Without Government: Order and Change in World Politics* (New York: Cambridge University Press, 1992), p. 4.

18. James N. Rosenau, "Governance in the Twenty-First Century," *Global Governance* 1:1 (Winter 1995), p. 20.

19. Theodore H. Von Laue, "Soviet Diplomacy: G. V. Chicherin, Peoples Commissar for Foreign Affairs, 1918–1930," in Gordon A. Craig and Felix Gilbert, eds., *The Diplomats 1919–1939*, Vol. 1: *The Twenties* (New York: Atheneum, 1965), p. 235.

20. Von Laue, p. 259.

21. Polybius, "The Histories," in William Ebenstein, edition *Great Political Thinkers*, 4th ed. (New York: Holt, Rinehart & Winston, 1969), p. 116.

22. James N. Rosenau defines such a group as a "movement"—"a loosely knit aggregate of like-minded individuals and organizations who seek to have influence on one or more aspects of human affairs. . . ." *Turbulence in World Politics: A Theory of Change and Continuity* (Princeton: Princeton University Press, 1990), pp. 125–126. Rosenau's concept of 'movement' may shade into what we call 'polities' when he suggests that movements "may have informally recognized leaders or spokespersons." (p. 126).

23. For a more complete discussion of the concepts of polity, domain, and authority and their relationship to identities, loyalties, ideology, and political change, see Yale H. Ferguson and Richard W. Mansbach, *Polities: Authority, Identities, and Change* (Columbia, SC: University of South Carolina Press, 1996), especially chapter 2.

24. Jonathan Boyarin, "Space, Time, and the Politics of Memory," in Boyarin, ed., *Remapping Memory*, p. 4.

25. Boyarin, p. 13.

26. John Gerard Ruggie, "Territoriality and Beyond: Problematizing Modernity in International Relations," *International Organization* 47, no. 1 (Winter 1993), p. 172.

27. Michael Keating and Liesbet Hooghe, "By-Passing the Nation State? Regions and the EU Policy Process," in Jeremy J. Richardson, ed., *European Union: Power and Policy-Making* (London: Routledge, 1996).

28. Michael N. Barnett, "Sovereignty, Nationalism, and Regional Order in the Arab States System," *International Organization* 49, no. 3 (Summer 1995), p. 492.

29. Partial nesting refers to the fact that the boundaries of newer polities may cut an existing polity apart; some adherents live within the newer polity, separated from their brethren by new frontiers. The Kurds and the Palestinians in contemporary global politics reflect identities that were separated by state frontiers.

30. Such as the Isis myth.

31. See, for example, Anthony DePalma, "For Mexico's Indians, Promises Not Kept," *The New York Times*, June 15, 1994, pp. A1, A6.

32. However, it must be said that the liberation theology message owes as much to Marxist thought as it does to the less radical strategies for achieving social reform advocated by recent popes in Rome.

33. See, for example, Peter B. Evans, Dietrich Rueschemeyer, and Theda Skocpol, eds., *Bringing the State Back In* (New York: Cambridge University Press, 1985).

34. Mark N. Katz, "Nationalism and the Legacy of Empire," *Current History* (October 1994), p. 328.

35. Waldon, "After Deng the Deluge," p. 153.

36. Only perhaps in Peru during the 1960s can we credit the military with intervening to engineer genuine social reform.

37. "A Framework for Bosnia: Text of an Accord by 3 Governments," *The New York Times*, Sept. 27, 1995, p. A8.

38. Amy Dockser Marcus, "Big Palestinian Clans Enjoy a Resurgence That May Hurt Arafat," *The Wall Street Journal*, Sept. 13, 1995, p. A1.

39. Yale H. Ferguson and Richard W. Mansbach, "Beyond Inside/Outside: Political Space and Westphalian States in a World Of 'Polities,' " *Global Governance* 2, no. 2 (May-Aug. 1996), pp. 261–87.

40. James N. Rosenau, "New Dimensions of Security: The Interaction of Globalizing and Localizing Dynamics," *Security Dialogue* 25 (Sept. 1994), p. 256.

41. Ruggie, "Territoriality and Beyond: Problematizing Modernity in International Relations," p. 172.

42. *The New York Times*, May 29, 1995, p. A19.

43. Ferguson and Mansbach, *Polities: Authority, Identities, and Change.*

44. Michael Keating, "Must Minority Nationalism Be Tribal? A Study of Quebec, Catalonia, and Scotland," in Kenneth Christie, ed., *Tribalism and Ethnic Conflict: A Global Perspective* (forthcoming). By contrast with Quebec, Keating notes, "In Catalonia, nationalism has always had a strong civic dimension, and since the 1960s this has been dominant. Nationalists repeatedly stress that anyone who lives in Catalonia and wishes to belong is Catalan."

45. Ernest Gellner, *Encounters with Nationalism* (Oxford, UK: Blackwell, 1994), p. viii.

46. See, for example, E. J. Hobsbawm, *Nations and Nationalism Since 1780* (New York: Cambridge University Press, 1990), pp. 46–79.

47. Hendrik Spruyt, *The Sovereign States and Its Competitors* (Princeton: Princeton University Press, 1994), p. 3; also Stephen Krasner, "Westphalia and All That."

48. See Mansbach and Vasquez, *In Search of Theory*, p. 166, for the points along the continuum of coalescence and fragmentation—unitary actor, coalition, faction, and competing actors—and the characteristics of these several points.

49. Franke Wilmer, *The Indigenous Voice in World Politics* (Newbury Park, CA: Sage Publications, 1993), p. 42.

50. Jarat Chopra and Thomas G. Weiss, "Sovereignty Is No Longer Sacrosanct: Codifying Humanitarian Intervention," in Steven L. Spiegel and David J. Pervin, eds., *At Issue: Politics in the World Arena*, 7th edition (New York: St. Martin's Press, 1994), p. 408.

51. See, for example, Joanne Rappaport, *The Politics of Memory* (New York: Cambridge University Press, 1990).

52. Rappaport, p. 23.

53. John Darnton, "Discontent Seethes in Once-Stable Turkey," *The New York Times*, Mar. 2, 1995, pp. A1, A6. See also Alan Cowell, "Muslim Party's Growth Posing Challenge to Turkey's Secular Heritage," *The New York Times*, Nov. 30, 1994, p. A8. For a more sanguine view, see "What's the Difference between Algeria and Turkey," *The Economist*, Mar. 18–24, 1995, pp. 49–50.

54. In Israel, as well, there is conflict between those who wish to promote the secular values of a modern territorial state and those who memorialize the biblical history of a chosen people.

55. See, for example, Youssef M. Ibrahim, "When Nations Draw Lines, the Druse Find a Way," *The New York Times*, Apr. 20, 1995, p. A4.

56. Youssef M. Ibrahim, "Palestinian Religious Militants: Why Their Ranks Are Growing," *The New York Times*, Nov. 8, 1994, p. A7.

57. Bassam Tibi, "The Simultaneity of the Unsimultaneous: Old Tribes and Imposed Nation-States in the Modern Middle East," in Philip Khoury and Joseph Kostiner, eds., *Tribes and State Formation in the Middle East* (Berkeley: University of California Press, 1990), p. 127.

58. Barnett, "Sovereignty, Nationalism" p. 509.

59. Niccolo Machiavelli, *The Prince and The Discourses*, Modern Library College Editions (New York: Random House, 1950), p. 41.

60. Machiavelli, pp. 146, 147.

61. Marlise Simons, "At a Crossroads, Rifts Pull at Orthodox Churches," *The New York Times*, Nov. 5, 1995, Section 1, p. 3.

62. For the status of the Islamic movement in Saudi Arabia, see Youssef M. Ibrahim, "Saudi Arabia Cracks Down on Islamic Militants, Seizing Many," *The New York Times*, Sept. 22, 1994, p. A4; Youssef M. Ibrahim, "Saudi King Sets Up Commission in Move to Curb Islamic Radicals," *The New York Times*, October 6, 1994, p. A4; "Challenge to the House of Saud," *The Economist*, Oct. 8–14, 1994, p. 41.

63. The assassin of Israeli Prime Minister Yitzhak Rabin was an Orthodox Jew and believer in "Greater Israel" who, according to an acquaintance, "was imbued with a sense of divine mission and believed that God's decrees were above everything else." Cited in Joel Greenberg, "Investigators Describe a Deliberate, Determined Killer Who Also Stalked Peres," *The New York Times*, Nov. 6, 1995, p. A7.

64. John F. Burns, "Bombay's Bleak Nationalism: 'Hindustan' for Hindus Only," *The New York Times*, Nov. 2, 1995, pp. A1, A6.

65. Secular intellectuals such as Egyptian author Naguib Mahfouz and the Bangladesh feminist writer Taslima Nasrin are commonly targeted by Islamic militants. In Algeria hundreds of "teachers, feminists, intellectuals, artists and government officials have been assassinated since 1992." Youssef M. Ibrahim, "Algerians Hope for Better Life and War's End," *The New York Times*, June 6, 1995, p. A6.

66. Youssef M. Ibrahim, "Muslims Argue Theology of Peace with Israel," *The New York Times*, Jan. 31, 1995, p. A4.

67. Youssef M. Ibrahim, "Muslim Edicts Take on New Force," *The New York Times*, Feb. 12, 1995, Section 1, no. 4.

68. Judith Miller, "Faces of Fundamentalism," *Foreign Affairs* 73, no. 6 (Nov./Dec. 1994), p. 137.

69. "For the Russian troops stationed in Tajikistan, the river [Pyandzh] represents the thin line between Russian-backed security and the wild forces of Islamic extremism." "Russian confusion," *The Economist*, Sept. 24–30, 1994, p. 39.

70. "Schadenfreude," *The Economist*, Aug. 19–25, 1995, pp. 31–32.

71. Keith B. Richburg, "Peace Is Not on Their Agenda," *The Washington Post National Weekly Edition*, May 29–June 4, 1995, p. 19.

72. "Holy War," *The Economist*, January 28–February 3, 1995, p. 37. Also John F. Burns, "Pakistan Asks U.S. to Help in Crackdown on Militants," *The New York Times*, March 22, 1995, p. A4. In late 1995, rumors surfaced

of a coup plot by Islamic officers to overthrow the government of Benazir Bhutto. "The Plot Thickens," *The Economist*, Oct. 27-Nov. 2, 1995, pp. 38-39.

73. John F. Burns, "Network of Islamic Terrorism Traced to a Pakistan University," *The New York Times*, Mar. 20, 1995, pp. A1, A4.

74. Tim Weiner, "Iran and Allies Are Suspected in Bomb Wave," *The New York Times*, July 29, 1994, pp. A1, A2.

75. Hamas was founded in December 1987, when the *intifada* began in Gaza and the West Bank. Alan Cowell, "Militant Once Seen as Useful to Israel," *The New York Times*, Oct. 20, 1994, p. A7.

76. Youssef M. Ibrahim, "Violence Affects Algeria-France Ties," *The New York Times*, Mar. 12, 1995, Section 1, p. 9; Youssef M. Ibrahim, "A Wary France Cracks Down on Its Muslims," *The New York Times*, Sept. 7, 1995, p. A3.

77. Miller, p. 126.

78. Samuel P. Huntington, "The Clash of Civilizations?" Foreign Affairs 72, no. 3 (Summer 1993), p. 35. See also "Islam and the West," special survey, *The Economist*, August 6–12, 1994.

79. Steven A. Holmes, "Fundamentalism Alters the Mideast's Power Relationships," *The New York Times*, August 22, 1993, Section 4, p. 1; "Why Islam Is Turning Violent in Pakistan," *The Economist*, March 4–10, 1995, p. 35.

80. See, for example, "Karachi Shiites Vow Revenge For 20 Slain at Two Mosques," *The New York Times*, Feb. 26, 1995, p. 8.

81. Cited in Amy Dockser Marcus, "Big Palestinian Clans Enjoy a Resurgence That May Hurt Arafat," *The Wall Street Journal*, Sept. 13, 1995, A1.

82. Cited in Marcus.

83. R. H. C. Davis, *A History of Medieval Europe: From Constantine to Saint Louis*, 2nd edition (New York: Longman, 1988), pp. 377–79.

84. Spruyt, pp. 109–29.

85. Janice E. Thomson, *Mercenaries, Pirates, and Sovereigns* (Princeton: Princeton University Press, 1994), p. 33.

86. Thompson, p. 35.

87. There were other arguments, too, including the need to enhance political stability in neighboring Mexico and stem the tide of illegal immigration.

88. The smallest of the fifty had sales of $32.5 billion in 1994 (statistics from Willetts).

89. Peter F. Drucker, "Trade Lessons from the World Economy," *Foreign Affairs* 73, no. 1 (Jan./Feb. 1994), pp. 103-104.

90. Cited in "Who's in the Driving Seat?" special report, *The Economist*, Oct. 7–13, 1995, p. 30.

91. Ibid., pp. 9–10.

92. James Rupert, "Dateline Tashkent: Post-Soviet Central Asia," in Spiegel and Pervin, eds., *At Issue*, p. 316.

93. "A Time of Heroes," *The Economist*, September 23–29, 1995, p. 28.

94. Smith, *The Ethnic Origins of Nations*, p. 2.

95. Barnett, "Sovereignty, Nationalism, and Regional Order in the Arab States System," p. 498. For discussion of how archeology is used in the Middle East to forge a national identity, see Asher Silberman, *Between Past and Present: Archeology, Ideology, and Nationalism in the Modern Middle East* (New York: Henry Holt, 1989); also Samir al-Khalil, *The Monument: Art, Vulgarity, and Responsibility in Iraq* (Berkeley: University of California Press, 1991).

96. Youssef M. Ibrahim, "France Bans Muslim Scarf in Its Schools," *The New York Times*, Sept. 11, 1994, Section 1, p. 5.

97. Kaplan, p. 75.

CHAPTER 11

Our Global Neighborhood

Pushing Problem-Solving Theory to Its Limits and the Limits of Problem-Solving Theory

MICHAEL G. SCHECHTER

The widely publicized and proclaimed Report of The Commission on Global Governance[1] is taken as the starting point of this inquiry into the strengths and limits of problem-solving theory (i.e., midlevel theory aimed at making contemporary global relations and institutions " . . . work smoothly by dealing effectively with particular sources of trouble . . . ").[2] It will be argued that this synthetic, farsighted, and, in its own way, radical Report illuminates the limits to problem-solving theory and the need for an alternative way to conceptualize (and effectuate) multilateralism at the end of the twentieth century.[3] This chapter will propose critical theory[4] as that alternative mode of inquiry,[5] contending that it is possible to conceive of critical theory as policy-relevant. Even though few think of it in those terms,[6] there are studies that no one would dispute exemplify this approach.[7] For the purposes of this study, I will be using Robert W. Cox's classic distinctions between problem-solving and critical theory:

> [P]roblem-solving theory. It takes the world as it finds it, with the prevailing social and power relationships and the institutions into which they are organized, as the given framework for action. The general aim of problem solving is to make these relationships and institutions work smoothly by dealing effectively with particular sources of trouble . . .

[C]ritical theory. It is critical in the sense that it stands apart from the prevailing order of the world and asks how that order came about. Critical theory, unlike problem-solving theory, does not take institutions and social and power relations for granted but calls them into question by concerning itself with their origins and how and whether they might be in the process of changing. It is directed toward an appraisal of the very framework for action, or problematic, which problem-solving theory accepts as its parameters. Critical theory is directed to the social and political complex as a whole rather than to the separate parts.[8]

OUR GLOBAL NEIGHBORHOOD: THE REPORT OF THE COMMISSION ON GLOBAL GOVERNANCE

It is probably fair to conclude that there is "... very little in the way of original thought" in the Commission Report: it reads, in large part, "... more like an accumulation of ideas and proposals presented before an organization ..."[9] than a reflective essay building on earlier literature on global governance, especially the academic, theoretical, and epistemological. But it does provide a trenchant analysis of the current state of world order, one which, for instance, draws attention to the "feminization" of poverty, the role of the global media in strengthening the consumerist ethos in societies in the early stages of development, and the rising "culture of violence." Moreover, its analysis is not limited to a narrow focus on the United Nations and other top-down forms of multilateralism. This is particularly evident in the Report's calls for an annual Forum of Civil Society and a Council of Petitions.

The Report's importance is magnified by the fact that its authors, the members of the Commission, are bright, thoughtful, and well connected.[10] As such, its readership has been wide and influential. Its ideas, some of which other problem solvers find quite radical (like a global taxation system, a phasing out by the year 2005 of the veto for the Permanent Five of the UN Security Council, the establishment of a UN Volunteer Force of up to ten thousand troops), are likely to comprise much of the reformist agenda and debate of the next decade. Given the recent call to concentrate on the power of discourse and ideas, the words of this potentially influential work also merit some detailed attention. Many of its passing remarks are sufficiently insightful, original, and provocative to warrant further reflection, such as the need to: 1) reach out to elements in civil society;[11] 2) redefine security to focus on a broad-based security of individuals rather than military security of countries; 3) increase the "transparency" of the Bretton Woods institutions (and the Security Council); and 4) empower the currently voiceless, especially women.

Unfortunately, one of the frustrating elements of the Report is its format, which involves few well-developed and no documented arguments.[12] Still, as would be expected given the nature and authorship of the Report, some of this language appears to have been adopted already. For example, the World Bank now leads the chorus of those chanting the themes of transparency.[13]

PROBLEM SOLVING AND CRITICAL THEORY

As suggested at the outset, the goals of this chapter include using the Commission's Report as a basis of an inquiry into the strengths and limits of problem-solving theory and the potential of policy-relevant critical theory as an alternative mode of analysis and policy prescription. While Cox is clearly a partisan of critical theory and employs it in his work, in part to open up the possibility of choosing a different valid perspective, he identifies some strengths in the problem-solving approach.[14] "The *ceteris paribus* assumption upon which such theorizing is based makes it possible to arrive at statements of law or regulations which appear to have general validity."[15] That, in turn, allows for cumulative research and for developing ". . . law-like explanations of 'reality' which can serve as guides to action."[16] Cox follows with his critique of problem solving. Such studies ". . . can be represented . . . as serving particular national, sectional, or class interest which are comfortable within the given order. Indeed, the purpose served by problem-solving theory is conservative, since it aims to solve the problems arising in various parts of a complex whole in order to smooth the functioning of the whole."[17] For problem-solving theorists, then, the key focus is on reform of the world as given, for on the whole it is taken to be good.[18] The purpose for Cox, on the other hand, is to study (especially international political economy) transformations and particularly the place, autonomy, and direction of diverse social forces in those transformations. His focus is on the emancipatory potentials of social forces (and new social movements) that might emerge with changes in global production processes.[19] In sum, the goal for the critical theorist is to explore ". . . the potential for structural change and the construction of strategies of change."[20] This is in keeping with the contention that one's scholarship and perspective derive out of the context in which one lives and thinks. For us, Cox takes that to mean, as for Ibn Khaldun who lived six centuries ago, "living and acting in a period of historical change, a period of decline and disintegration of the social and political structures that had been the underpinnings of past glory and stability . . ."[21] This is what has led Cox to see his approach as a "bottom-up" one, as contrasted to the typical problem solvers' "top-down" one, where change is seen to depend on the preferences of the currently powerful major states, sometimes effectuated through international organization.[22]

The Commission is sensitive to changes within the post-Cold War international system, including those related to the evolution of global civil society. Their remedial proposals follow logically from this, including the call for greater adherence to the rule of international law and increased roles for a variety of state and nonstate actors as forces of systemic changes.[23] Still, the Commission clearly casts its lot with those committed to problem-solving theory:

> The international system that the UN Charter put in place needs to be renewed. The flaws and inadequacies of existing institutions have to be overcome. There is a need to weave a tighter fabric of international norms, expanding the rule of law world-wide and enabling citizens to exert their democratic influence on global processes. . . . We also believe that the world's arrangements for the conduct of its affairs must be underpinned by certain common values[24]

This focus on problem solving seems to fit with Cox's notion of the traditional approach and an effective way to produce policy-relevant work. It speaks to other policy participants and, related, works within the given international system. Even so, the Commission seems concerned that more tradition-bound policymakers who think about feasibility first and desirability only later might reject their proposals out of hand. Thus the Commissioners stress that their purpose is not to be concerned with the "technical considerations" of how a particular proposal might be implemented—what some think of as "tinkering"[25]—but rather to think big about the key problems of the contemporary international system, the inadequate response by extant international institutions, and to propose ways to solve those problems.[26] Implicit in the Report, however, is an understanding that Gill suggests typifies that of "neo-realist" thinking. Reform, even very significant reform, when suggested by problem solvers simply reflects ". . . a series of inter-state bargains between states, rather than a series of structural changes which generate new conditions and promote changing conceptions of interest and identity . . ."[27]

Thus the Report allows us to further the debate as to the nature, strengths, and limits of problem-solving theory. It allows us to see whether such theory—even when it focuses on desirable, nontechnical changes—is capable of addressing change in an era of rapid political, economic, and technological transformations and whether such theory is the only theory that can be policy-relevant. It should also help us assess the degree to which it, like all theories as seen from a critical perspective, is imbued with a particular ideology (i.e., written for someone and for some purpose).[28] And, if so, who that someone is and what that purpose might be:

> All theories have a perspective. Perspectives derive from a position in time and space, specifically social and political time and space. The world is seen from a standpoint definable in terms of nation or social class, of dominance or subordination, of rising or declining power, of a sense of immobility or of present crisis, of past experience, and of hopes and expectations for the future. The more sophisticated a theory is, the more it reflects upon and transcends its own perspective; but the initial perspective is always contained within a theory and is relevant to its explication. There is, accordingly, no such thing as theory in itself, divorced from a standpoint in time and space.[29]

OUR GLOBAL NEIGHBORHOOD: PUSHING PROBLEM-SOLVING THEORY TO ITS LIMITS AND THE LIMITS OF PROBLEM-SOLVING THEORY

The Commission's Report contends that governance at the global level ". . . must now be understood as also involving nongovernmental organizations (NGOs), citizens' movements, multinational corporations, and the global capital market" along with transgovernmental relationships and the global mass media.[30] But it also reached the "firm conclusion that the United Nations must continue to play a central role in global governance," owing to its universality and role as the ". . . only forum where the governments of the world come together on an equal footing and on a regular basis to try to resolve the world's most pressing problems."[31] Even more pointedly, it contends that ". . . it is not the Charter that has failed but the policies and practices of its members . . . ,"[32] a Charter which reflects a statecentric, pre-atomic, colonial, and still largely Eurocentric world.[33] It reaches these conclusions in spite of the Report's own recognition that the UN currently lacks sufficient credibility and resources to fulfil its responsibilities,[34] its belief that NGOs provide hope for a future with the sort of more democratic and participatory decisionmaking which it thinks is necessary for the future of legitimate global governance,[35] and the existence of a large number of studies that suggest that the possibilities for significantly reforming the organization are close to nil, and thus other means for multilateralism need to be pursued.[36] Such conclusions are in keeping with the problem solvers' conservatism.

But such conclusions are at odds with the perspectives of critical theorists who see us as living through an era of significant global structural transformation, of which the end of the Cold War is only a minor episode. Such theorists posit that the UN will continue to exist long after the structural conditions that gave rise to and sustained it have perished, but as a consequence it will continue to lose global legitimacy and effectiveness. The critical theorist can, however, conceive of a (potentially important) role for the UN as an agent of systemic change.[37] But that requires that it dislodge itself from the residual power base which initially supported and sustained it, something that problem solvers do not contemplate or recommend. Even though the Commission is "pushing the envelope" within the context in which it and the UN are operating, it can be seen, as can all problem-solvers, ". . . as serving . . . particular national, sectional, or class interests, which are comfortable within the given order."[38] Many instances can be cited to reinforce this point.

For example, the Commission tries to square the circle in terms of state sovereignty. "Double standards must be eliminated: states should not be free to seek the protection that sovereignty affords at one moment and then ignore the limits it imposes at another." The Commission's conclusion on this point resonates with statements made by the UN Secretary-General in his famous *Agenda for Peace*, namely that " . . . the principle of sovereignty and the norms that derive from it must be further adapted to recognize changing realities."[39] The serious debate, however, is what those changing realities are and what that implies for the notion of state sovereignty. In practical terms, this asks when Article 2(7), the Charter's domestic sovereignty provision, can be bridged and who decides that. The Commission responds that it can and has been bridged when gross violations of individual rights are involved. A slightly reformed UN Security Council is in charge of administering the litmus test. Scholars with a more critical viewpoint, such as Camilleri and Falk and Scholte, however, emphasize the political implication of using the sovereignty discourse, even one that is "further adapted to recognize changing realities."[40] It privileges the already privileged, running counter to the explicit goals of many critical theorists with a "bottom-up" normative perspective and seemingly at odds with the Commission's own ideological predilections. By not building on the theoretical, epistemological, and ontological foundations available to them, the Commission's recommendations are not simply unoriginal but seem to run counter to some of their own normative preferences. A similar point, of course, can be made by their meliorist approach to Security Council reform.

One of the places where the Report most explicitly dissents from the traditional statecentric approach to world politics is in its discussion of an "early warning" system to cope with impending crises. There the authors look to unspecified nongovernmental organizations to assist in the process. Not simply does this seem to avoid the necessity of drawing distinctions amongst NGOs (in terms of their goals, funding bases, and the forms of their decision-making processes), but it seems to assume that NGOs will have easy access to the sites where the seeds of crises are likely to be planted.[41] While that is true for some NGOs, it is arguably true precisely because those NGOs have been loathe to share publicly the sort of information, often quite detrimental to host governments, that an early warning process of necessity would require.[42] Again, we find that the Commissioners have failed to raise the necessary structural questions that might make their proposal feasible or at least would allow one to identify the obstacles to their achievement. Thus they miss an opportunity to point in the direction of the structural transformation that would be necessary to achieve the goals that they have in mind.

One of the Report's more striking recommendations focuses on the need for "neighborhood values," i.e., ". . . a common commitment to a set of core values that can unite people of all cultural, political, religious, or philosophical backgrounds."[43] Those values, not surprisingly, include traditional, largely first- and second-generation human rights: ". . . respect for life, liberty, justice, and equity, mutual respect, caring, and integrity," but also include third generation rights, exemplified by the right to a sustainable environment.[44] But this is done in a context in which the world is not envisaged now or in the future in terms of ". . . alternative intersubjective worlds coexisting without losing, each of them, their internal conviction and dynamism; and without coming to dominate and absorb the others . . .", that is, ". . . distinct, thriving macrosocieties, each with its own solidarity, each pursuing a distinct *telos*, which could coexist through a supra-intersubjectivity . . . [which] would have to embody principles of coexistence without necessarily reconciling differences in goals."[45] Had the Commission done so, it would, of necessity, have wrestled with issues related to cultural relativism and questions relating to the adequacy of any currently extant international organization to meet the task.

It might also have confronted the notion of the biosphere (or nature) as an autonomous actor in world politics with the capacity for vetoing economic growth, expansion, and development—one that calls into question the validity of the notion of sustainable development, for that depends upon the market system effectively signaling environmental hazards and scarcities in time for individuals to respond.[46] Again, albeit implicitly, the Commission's Report takes the world (and the market) as it is. And thus its recommendations—endorsement of the Commission on Sustainable Development[47] and the reconfiguring of the Trusteeship Council into a Trusteeship of the Global Commons—seem forward-looking within the context in which the authors are operating, but possibly out of synch with the needs for the world of the twenty-first century that they are trying to address.

The Commission's calls for a code for transnational corporations and increased powers of multilateral surveillance by the IMF are quite similar. The Commission is right in noting that now might be the apt moment for resurrecting such notions. What was filibustered to death in the 1970s and 1980s may now be ripe for discussion if not passage. Countries may have learned the lessons of corporate corruption and a debt problem exacerbated by the lack of IMF oversight. But that begs some of the most important questions relating to multinational corporations and especially international financial markets. A code of good transnational corporate behavior that might have been appropriate, even desirable from the perspective of the less advantaged in the 1960s, may be less appropriate, feasible, or even desirable as post-Fordism (i.e., the era in which short-run production for a greater variety of more specialized, niche markets replaces large-plant, mass production of standardized goods) takes hold.[48] Whereas there is certainly reason to debate the merits of increasingly centralized management of relations between national currencies, exchange rates, and related matters, much more important issues relating to international financial markets would hardly be affected by any of the Commission's suggestions.[49] The importance of this is underscored by the fact that while the Commission is arguing for greater participation, openness, and shared decision making in the World Bank and the Fund, virtually no attention is paid to the non-democratic financial structures which are "inseparable from capitalism on a world scale." "Central banks, for example, are secret, élitist, and authoritarian institutions . . . ," yet they are ignored in the Commission's analysis, which speaks the rhetoric of globalization. However, it often falls back into old habits of differentiating domestic from international, private from public. In a similar vein, the Commission pays little to no attention to the ". . . shift in power from governments (democratic or not) to markets [which] is a derogation of popular power."[50] It is possible that at the end of the day Strange is right, effective *international* regulation is not possible, and only the US government can do the regulating by actions taken regarding the US financial market.[51] Even if that was true, it would hardly justify, much less make desirable, the Commission's predictable and explicable omissions.

POLICY-RELEVANT CRITICAL THEORY AS A POSSIBLE ALTERNATIVE

The brief discussion above of the Report's proposed NGO Early Warning System exemplifies the way in which a critical theory approach can be seen as having policy relevance. By assisting in identifying the structural preconditions for a successful NGO Early Warning System—conditions which do not presently exist—it allows scholars to point in the direction for policy makers and advocates to pursue. In this instance it points to the need to break down the discourse and barriers of state sovereignty, with states making intelligence information available to nonstate actors and nongovernmental actors able and willing to speak out loudly without fear of state retribution. Identifying such structural necessities could contribute to the mobilization of social movements favoring the sorts of structural transformations required to achieve the Commission's goals.[52]

The Report's discussion of NGOs underscores another advantage of a critical perspective. The focus on NGOs to the exclusion of social movements, not to mention social forces, is both conventional and unfortunate.[53] A much less conventional but potentially more fruitful perspective is one which conceives of the UN as ". . . *an element* in a wider social movement for the realization of world order values. In this regard, the United Nations is looked upon less as the outcome of governmental policy at the state level than as one expression of social movements committed to promoting drastic global reforms." Such a perspective would allow for the consideration of the UN as a "nexus between systemic and antisystemic [or hegemonic and counterhegemonic] politics."[54] Such a perspective would also avoid overlooking the pervasive, yet largely

latent, opposition of the oppressed in hierarchical social systems. While
". . . the oppressed are too weak—politically, economically, and ideologically—to manifest their opposition constantly, . . . we know, when
oppression becomes particularly acute, or expectations particularly de-
ceived, or the power of the ruling stratum falters, people have risen up
in an almost spontaneous manner to cry halt. This has taken the form
of revolts, of riots, of flight."[55] Thus the critical theorists' inclusion of
social movements not only increases the complexity of one's vision of
the global system, but it provides policy-relevant insights as to potential
sources of conflict and structural transformation, *and* new tasks, possibly legitimizing tasks, for the UN.[56]

In many ways the same point is evident in the Commission's frustration with international economic institutional reform. While the Commission suggests that the IMF has been wrongfully maligned in terms of
its programs of conditionality, noting that they have been successful in
turning some countries' economies around, and that the WTO is a step
in the right direction, they recognize that their own suggested Economic
Security Council is neither novel nor a panacea. They do not believe it
will solve all of the globe's economic problems or even be quickly implemented, although they are hopeful in the last regard. What this chapter
suggests is that the reasons for their frustration, and ultimately for the
inadequacy of their policy recommendations, comes from their approach.
That approach accepts the international political economy, including the
global distribution of power that it implies, as givens and tries to torque
institutions in ways to make them responsive to the needs identified by
those in powerful positions in that current system. Had they been able to
think beyond the current system, which they knew was undergoing massive structural transformations as they were meeting, and tried to envisage what institutional remedies might be most desirable from the vantage
point of currently disadvantaged and largely silenced voices, they might
actually have come up with a widely different set of proposals, including
some that point in the direction of remedies around which large numbers
might mobilize. In other words, the Commission's Report would have
read quite differently had the Commissioners tried to follow the critical
theorists' lead by accepting that ". . . there is nothing determinate about
the real world 'out there' . . . it can be examined and understood from a
perspective other than the dominant hegemonic perspectives."[57] A commission report making proposals from such a perspective would undoubtedly have sounded much different and likely much less defensive than
does *Our Global Neighbourhood*.[58]

Sinclair's creative work on credit rating agencies is suggestive. He argues that

> ... nonstate institutions exist in the global political economy which condition the thoughts and actions that comprise the investment process. Because these structure investment, such institutions can be understood as private makers of global public policy ... [even though] ... rating institutions create pressures for fundamental analysis of investment, for a particular view of appropriate management forms and policy lines ... and contribute to a more abstract investment process which is likely to have the effect of transforming social relationships within the dominant alliances of social forces.[59]

Sinclair contends that identification of "private makers of global public policy," of which credit rating agencies are but one example, is essential to understanding the structure of global capital flows, yet they are undiscussed and largely unregulated by international institutions. They are private. The Commission's Report, by starting with the public sector and with a focus on extant international institutions, seems oblivious to the impact of such "private makers of global public policy." Thus they have "no reason" to propose their reform.[60]

In what might be a relevant point, given the authorship of the Commission's Report, Sinclair also suggests that policy-makers, especially those "infused with neoliberal business ethics," might not be aroused by the lack of regulation of such phenomena. They lack the hostility that they have to unregulated interstate interactions.[61] Stephen Gill's detailed studies of the transnational managerial class, which could be seen to include the Commission, make a similar point as to the expected (self-serving?) limits to conventional analyses which privilege actors in the so-called public sphere. It also further evidences the policy-relevant insights of critical theory.[62] Gill argues persuasively that focusing on the sources and impact of the ideas of groups like the Trilateral Commission (and The Commission on Global Governance?) are essential if one hopes to analyze the direction, timing, and challenges to global structural transformation, including the role that the UN and other (reformed or not) international institutions play and can play in fostering and blocking such change.[63] Whether or not Sinclair's or Gill's observations begin to answer the question of why the Report is written from the perspective it is, the point of this essay remains: students of international public policy would do well to take a critical perspective that draws their attention beyond traditional actors and interactions.

The issue of migration ties the Commission's Report to these insights, the strengths and limits of problem-solving theory, and the value of a policy-relevant critical theory alternative. The Commission's Report is to be admired for underscoring that "migration is likely to be a subject of growing difficulty" and making explicit the fears of those in rich countries about the ongoing and impending mass migration from low-income countries. The Commission's suggestion for dealing with this key dilemma is, in its own language, "farsighted," that is, endorsing what it calls the NAFTA approach, ". . . trying to assist the labor-exporting country through a widening of trade opportunities."[64] But, as a recent structural account concludes:

> Contrary to the view that economic growth will itself remove the need for migration, it must be recognized that the emerging global economic and social system is one in which population movements will continue to increase rather than decline. A comprehensive, nonexodus approach . . . will be self-defeating. Global apartheid will collapse as surely as the South African version has done. In the postmodern world, we must learn to live with ethnocultural diversity, rapid social change, *and* mass migration. There is no peaceful alternative.[65]

The point is not that Richmond is right and the Commission is wrong, but rather that there are significant policy advantages from adopting a critical perspective that does not begin with the world as it is and seek remediable action but focuses on the agents and consequences of inevitable global, structural transformations. Such an approach would, of necessity, focus on the "intersection between globalized production and migration," conceptualized through a variety of different levels of analysis, only one of which need look like a state-dominated world, with a reformed United Nations.[66] It might, for example, have pointed to the need to cope with conflicting intersubjectivities.

The Commission on this issue, as on so many others, would have served its own interests better had it started at a different point. That is, if it had been critical in its approach, it could have had more valuable policy insights to offer. It would have, of necessity, considered the views and means accessible to actors other than those currently vested with power in the international system and offered some suggestions as to how to empower those potential solvers of this essential problem. In doing so, they could have contributed to building the coalition of systems transformers needed to confront the dilemmas they have identified. But as Gill and others continually remind us, the Commission's inability to provide such guidance is both predictable and a part of the paradox. Those with the power today to make the changes needed to confront the problems besetting the world of the twenty-first century are precisely those least likely to make them, even when those changes seem to be their expressly stated goal.

NOTES

1. The Commission on Global Governance, *Our Global Neighborhood* (New York: Oxford University Press, 1995).

2. Robert W. Cox, "Social Forces, States, and World Orders: Beyond International Relations Theory," in *Neorealism and Its Critics*, Robert O. Keohane, ed. (New York: Columbia University Press, 1986), pp. 208–9.

3. For the purposes of this paper, *multilateralism* shall be broadly defined as it was for the MUNS (Multilateralism and the United Nations System) project, "... i.e., a commitment to maximum participation in dialogue among political, social, economic, and cultural forces as a means of resolving conflicts and designing institutional processes." Robert W. Cox, *Programme on Multilateralism and the United Nations System, 1990–1995* ([Tokyo]: The United Nations University, April 1991), p. 4.

4. For a discussion of a variety of critical approaches, see Hoffman's review article: Mark Hoffman, "Restructuring, Reconstruction, Reinscription, Rearticulation: Four Voices in Critical International Theory," *Millennium: Journal of International Studies* 20 (Summer 1991), pp. 169–85.

5. Although related, the contention here is different from Knight's, which seems to posit the possibility, if not actually the desirability, of works that synthesize problem-solving and critical theory approaches. His examples of this include Oran Young's work. Young's work, however, is positivist in nature, and to begin to try and synthesize positivist and post-positivist, critical approaches seems problematic. See, e.g., Oran R. Young, *International Governance: Protecting the Environment in a Stateless Society* (Ithaca: Cornell University Press, 1994). W. Andy Knight, "Beyond the UN System? Critical Perspectives on Global Governance and Multilateral Evolution," *Global Governance: A Review of Multilateralism and International Organization* 1 (May–August 1995), pp. 208–9.

6. This may, in part, be because few clearly distinguish critical approaches to international relations from postmodern ones. Cox, however, is an important exception here. He also has little time "... for theoretical discussion unrelated to real-world problems." This seems to flow logically from what he identifies as the key influences in his work: Antonio Gramsci, Karl Polanyi, and Fernand Braudel, all of whom were concerned with strategy as well as analysis. "As someone once said, the purpose of understanding the world is to be better able

to change it." Robert W. Cox, "Critical Political Economy," in *International Political Economy: Understanding Global Disorder*, Björn Hettne, ed. (Atlantic Highlands, NJ: Zed Books, 1995), p. 35.

7. See, for example, Robert W. Cox, "Debt, Time, and Capitalism," *Studies in Political Economy: A Socialist Review* 48 (Autumn 1995), pp. 165–70.

8. Cox, "Social Forces," pp. 208–9.

9. Knight, p. 236.

10. The Commission co-chairs were Ingvar Carlsson (Swedish Prime Minister, 1986–1991) and Shidrath Ramphal (Secretary-General of the Commonwealth, 1975–1990). Other prominent members included global leaders such as Oscar Arias (Nobel Prize winning President of Costa Rica), Allan Boesak (leading figure in South African's struggle against Apartheid), Barber Conable (President of the World Bank Group, 1986–1991), Jacques Delors (President of the European Commission, 1985–1994), Enrique Iglesias (President of the Inter-American Development Bank from 1988), Sadako Ogata (UN High Commissioner for Refugees from 1991), Jan Pronk (Dutch Minister for Development Co-operation), Maurice Strong (Secretary-General of the UN Environmental Conferences in Stockholm and Rio) and Brian Urquhart (Under Secretary-General for Political Affairs at the UN, 1972–1986).

11. The Report speaks of " . . . the emergence of a vigorous global civil society . . . " including a " . . . multitude of institutions, voluntary associations, and networks—women's groups, trade unions, chambers of commerce, farming or housing co-operatives, neighbourhood watch associations, religion-based organizations, and so on." Commission, p. 32. On the tendency to use the term *global civil society* loosely, a critique that is also applicable to the Commission's Report, see R. B. J. Walker, "Social Movements/World Politics," *Millennium: Journal of International Studies* 23 (Winter 1994), pp. 690-99, and Robert W. Cox, *UNU Program on Multilateralism and the UN System: Final Report by the Programme Coordinator* (Toronto, 1996, Photocopy), p. 10. See also Roger A. Coate, Chadwick F. Alger, and Ronnie D. Lipschutz, "The United Nations and Civil Society: Creative Partnerships and Sustainable Development," *Alternatives* 21 (January–March, 1996), p. 99.

12. This is less true of the background papers written in conjunction with the Commission's work. See *Issues in Global Governance: Papers Written for The Commission on Global Governance* (Boston: Kluwer Law International, 1995).

13. International Bank for Reconstruction and Development, *Governance: The World Bank's Experience* (Washington: The World Bank, 1994), pp. 29–36.

14. Cox, "Social Forces," pp. 207–8. This point is most theoretically developed in his work on Ibn Khaldun and clearly underlies the MUNS (Multilateralism and the United Nations System) program, whose perspective is inclusive, i.e., one which " . . . implies empowerment of the less powerful social groups through enabling them to articulate their perspectives into the process of international organization." Robert W, Cox, "Towards a Post-Hegemonic

Conceptualization of World Order: Reflections on the Relevancy of Ibn Khaldun," in *Governance Without Government: Order and Change in World Politics*, James N. Rosenau and Ernst-Otto Czempiel, eds. (Cambridge: Cambridge University Press, 1992); Cox, *Programme on Multilateralism*, p. 4. This "foundationalist" approach is one of the bases upon which Cox is criticized by postmodernists. Neufeld summarizes: the very basis on which Cox criticizes problem-solving theory (i.e., that it rests on a false premise, since the social and political order is not fixed, but rather is changing) ". . . is a clear foundationalist appeal to the 'true nature' of reality—an appeal which is arguably in contradiction to a reflexive stance." Mark Neufeld, *The Restructuring of International Relations Theory* (Cambridge: Cambridge University Press, 1995), p. 144, n104. See also Richard K. Ashley, "Living on Border Lines: Man, Poststructuralism, and War," in *International/Intertextual Relations: Postmodern Readings of World Politics*, James Der Derian and Michael J. Shapiro, eds. (Lexington: DC Heath and Company, 1989), p. 275.

15. Cox, "Social Forces," p. 208.

16. Neufeld, p. 143, n81. Obviously one should worry about that cumulative research, given the problem-solving theory's basic conservatism, expectation of limited structural change, and inability to explain significant structural changes. I appreciate Tim Sinclair's bringing this particular point to my attention.

17. Cox, "Social Forces," p. 209.

18. Cox, "International Political Economy," p. 31.

19. "At the base [of the emerging structure] are social forces. Whether they are self-conscious and articulated into what Gramsci called an historical bloc, or are depoliticized and manipulable, is the key in making the future . . . The old social movements—trade unions and peasant movements—have suffered setbacks under the impact of globalization; but the labour movement, in particular, has a background of experience in organization and ideology that can still be a strength in shaping the future." Robert W. Cox, "Global Restructuring: Making Sense of the Changing International Political Economy," in Richard Stubbs and Geoffrey R. D. Underhill, eds., *Political Economy and the Global Order* (London: The Macmillan Press, Ltd., 1994), pp. 52–53.

20. Cox, "Critical Political Economy," p. 32.

21. Cox, "Towards a Post-Hegemonic," p. 136.

22. Cox, "Social Forces." Robert W. Cox, "Gramsci, Hegemony, and International Relations: An Essay on Method," *Millennium: Journal of International Studies* 12 (Summer, 1983), pp. 162-75. Falk makes a related point by contrasting the project of those in the dominant position in the world today with those—and their fellow-travelers—who are not. "This perspective can be summarized as follows: the main statist/market project of the North is to sustain geopolitical stability, which in turn calls for the continuous expansion of world trade, economic growth, and the suppression of nationalist and regionalist challenges emanating from the South, by force if necessary. This project of

the North is more or less challenged by several oppositional tendencies in international society, including a variety of fundamentalisms that refuse to collaborate and a range of democratizing processes that conceive of human rights and justice, not stability, as the end of politics. One major uncertainty is whether those forces supporting the strengthening of global civil society can gain sufficient influence to qualify as a genuine 'counter-project,' rather than merely a societal tendency, confined to the margins of policy in the North and of little relevance to the South." Richard A. Falk, "Democratizing, Internationalizing, and Globalizing," in Yoshikazu Sakamoto, ed., *Global Transformation: Challenges to the State System* (New York: United Nations University Press, 1995), p. 477.

23. Commission, p. xiv.

24. Commission, p. xiv.

25. J. Martin Rochester, "Global Policy and the Future of the United Nations," *Journal of Peace Research* 27 (No. 2, 1990), p. 150.

26. Commission, p. 159.

27. Stephen Gill, "Gramsci and Global Politics: Towards a Post-Hegemonic Research Agenda," in Stephen Gill, ed., *Gramsci, Historical Materialism, and International Relations* (Cambridge: Cambridge University Press, 1993), p. 6.

28. Neufeld contends that it is within the *non*-Gramscian theoretical traditions that the insight is most fully developed, (p. 60).

29. Cox, "Social Forces," p. 207.

30. Commission, pp. 2–3.

31. Commission, p. 6.

32. Commission, p. 233.

33. Richard A. Falk, "The Pathways of Global Constitutionalism," in Richard A. Falk, Robert C. Johansen, and Samuel S. Kim, eds., *The Constitutional Foundations of World Peace* (Albany: SUNY Press, 1993), pp. 15–17.

34. Commission, p. 6.

35. Commission, p. 34. It might be added that it falls into the frequent trap of seeing Rio as the high-water mark of NGO participation and influence in global decision making, hoping that the NGO experience at Rio would be replicated in Cairo, Beijing, and Copenhagen (and presumably Istanbul). For a somewhat more sanguine assessment of the roles of NGOs in Rio, see Peter Willetts, "From Stockholm to Rio and Beyond: The Impact of the Environmental Movement on the United Nations Consultative Arrangements for NGOs," *Review of International Studies* 22 (January 1966), pp. 57–80.

36. See, e.g., Marie-Claude Smouts, "United Nations Reform: A Strategy of Avoidance," in Michael G. Schechter, ed., *Innovation in Multilateralism* (London: Macmillan for the United Nations University Press, 1998); Takeo Uchida, "Northern Perspectives for Peace and Security Functions of the United Nations," in *Innovation in Multilateralism*, Michael G. Schechter, ed. (London:

Macmillan for the United Nations University Press, 1998); Maurice Bertrand, "Can the United Nations Be Reformed?" in Adam Roberts and Benedict Kingsbury, eds., *United Nations, Divided World: The UN's Roles in International Relations* (Oxford: Clarendon Press, 1988), pp. 203–4.

37. Cox speaks of the UN system as acting as *interlocuteurs valables*. Cox, *UNU Program*, p. 22.

38. Cox, "Social Forces," p. 209.

39. Commission, pp. 69, 71.

40. Joseph A. Camilleri and Jim Falk, *The End of Sovereignty? The Politics of a Shrinking and Fragmenting World* (Aldershot, England: Edward Elgar, 1992); Jan Aart Scholte, *International Relations of Social Change* (Buckingham: Open University Press, 1993).

41. Cox has noted the value of viewing the NGO phenomenon "critically." Robert W. Cox, "MUNS Program: Final Symposium, San Jose, Costa Rica, December 1995, Guide for Paper Writers," August 1995, mimeographed.

42. Such seems to be the case with the International Red Cross and Red Crescent societies.

43. Commission, p. 48.

44. Commission, pp. 49, 57. The notion of three generations of rights is usually credited to the French jurist Karel Vasak, whose inspiration was the normative themes of the French Revolution: first generation of civil and political rights (liberté); second generation of economic, social, and cultural rights (égalité); and the third generation of so-called solidarity rights, such as development, self-determination, and clean air (fraternité).

45. Cox, "Towards a Post-Hegemonic," p. 159.

46. This provocative idea is developed in Peter Harries-Jones, Abraham Rotstein, and Peter Timmerman, "A Signal Failure: Ecology and Economy After the Earth Summit," in Michael G. Schechter, ed., *Future Multilateralism: The Political and Social Framework* (London: Macmillan for the United Nations University Press, 1998).

47. Whose problems with representation—one of the Commission's own clearly articulated, high priority goals—has already been widely noted. See, e.g., Coate, Alger, and Lipschultz, "United Nations," p. 111.

48. "Production and Hegemony," p. 47. For a contrast of Fordism and post-Fordism, see Robert W. Cox, "Production and Security," in David Dewitt, David Haglund, and John Kirton, eds., *Building a New Global Order: Emerging Trends in International Security* (New York: Oxford University Press, 1993), pp. 141-144.

49. Strange does a good job of discussing international financial structures, which she defines as ". . . the sum of all the arrangements and institutions governing the availability of credit *plus* all the arrangements and factors determining the terms on which currencies—units of account—are exchanged for one

another." As she notes, "On the whole, it is the latter which has dominated the literature of international political economy." The Commission's Report is no exception to Strange's more general observation. Susan Strange, "The Structure of Finance in the World System," in Yoshikazu Sakamoto, ed., *Global Transformation: Challenges to the State System* (New York: United Nations University Press, 1994), p. 230.

50. Strange, "Structure," p. 247.

51. Susan Strange, *Casino Capitalism* (New York: Basil Blackwell, 1986), pp. 165–68.

52. In this context, it should be noted that one of the reasons that Cox is not persuaded as to the utility of most postmodernism is that it serves to undermine any attempt to mobilize a broad basis for social and political action, one of the explicit goals of many critical theorists, Cox among them.

53. Rosenau, who contends that social movements are "much less structured but no less important" in terms of global governance than NGOs, characterizes them as having "...no definite memberships or authority structures." James N. Rosenau, "Governance in the Twenty-First Century," *Global Governance: A Review of Multilateralism and International Organizations* 1 (Winter 1995), p. 24.

54. Richard A. Falk, Samuel S. Kim, and Saul H. Mendlovitz, "The Role of Social Movements," in Richard A. Falk, Samuel S. Kim, and Saul H. Mendlovitz, eds., *The United Nations and a Just World Order,* Studies on a Just World Order, Number 3 (Boulder: Westview Press, 1993), p. 14.

55. Giovanni Arrighi, Terence K. Hopkins, and Immanuel Wallerstein, "Dilemmas of Antisystemic Movements," in Richard A. Falk, Samuel S. Kim, and Saul H. Mendlovitz, eds., *The United Nations and a Just World Order*, Studies on a Just World Order, Number 3 (Boulder: Westview Press, 1993), p. 16.

56. An obvious example relates to the movement that organized a seven-year international boycott of Nestlé products. To focus simply on the WHO's actions, and propose ways to reform the WHO to cope with contentious issues, would be a significant lost opportunity for policy reform.

57. Jim George, *Discourses of Global Politics: A Critical (Re)Introduction to International Relations* (Boulder: Lynne Rienner, 1994), p. 181.

58. Writing of the proposed Economic Security Council (ESC), "The idea is not original—others have made similar proposals—but we have formulated it in terms we believe have the best prospect of early implementation and successful outcome." Commission, pp. 155–56.

59. Timothy J. Sinclair, "Between State and Market: Hegemony and Institutions of Collective Action Under Conditions of International Capital Mobility," *Policy Sciences* 27 (1994), p. 447. See also Timothy J. Sinclair, "Passing Judgement: Credit Rating Processes as Regulatory Mechanisms of Governance in the Emerging World Order," *Review of International Political Economy* 1 (Spring 1994), pp. 132–59.

60. To use the language of Gill, Law, and Cox, the Commission has focused on the international economy to the exclusion of the global economy, i.e., an economic space transcending all country borders, which co-exists with the international economy. Stephen Gill and David Law, *The Global Political Economy: Perspectives, Problems, and Policies* (Baltimore: The Johns Hopkins University Press, 1988), p. xxiii; Robert W. Cox, "Structural Issues of Global Governance: Implications for Europe," in Stephen Gill, ed., *Gramsci, Historical Materialism, and International Relations*, (Cambridge: Cambridge University Press, 1993), p. 260.

61. Sinclair goes on to hypothesize as to the possible consequences of such lack of concern and regulation. On the one hand, it means that some issues are removed from domestic political debate, presumably allowing those with greater technical experience and interest to make the crucial decisions. On the other hand, the lack of governmental or intergovernmental oversight might reduce the dynamics that one would expect with an active political executive involved, whereby adaptations to changes in the global system might be more forthcoming and creative. Sinclair, "Passing Judgement," p. 153.

62. *American Hegemony and the Trilateral Commission* (Cambridge: Cambridge University Press, 1990). See also Kees van der Pijl, "The Second Glorious Revolution: Globalizing Elites and Historical Change" in Björn Hettne, ed., *International Political Economy: Understanding Global Disorder* (Atlantic Highlands, NJ: Zed Books, 1995).

63. Gill suggests that for counterhegemonic ". . . challenges to be meaningful, there needs to be a synergy between progressive movements and political parties," taking advantage of whatever political space may be opened up as a consequence of structural transformations. "Gramsci and Global Politics," p. 25.

64. Commission, pp. 206–7.

65. Anthony H. Richmond, *Global Apartheid: Refugees, Racism, and the New World Order* (New York: Oxford University Press, 1994), 217.

66. See, for example: James N. Mittelman, "The Global Restructuring of Production and Migration," in Yoshikazu Sakamoto, ed., *Global Transformation: Challenges to the State System* (New York: United Nations University Press, 1994).

CHAPTER 12

From Local Knowledge and Practice to Global Environmental Governance

RONNIE D. LIPSCHUTZ

> Even though there is desperate need for worldwide change, limited by
> the knowledge my place makes possible, I hesitate to legislate the law
> of other places. . . . To act in the world and make it better you have
> to be someone, be somewhere, tied to institutions, related to people.
> And be limited by that body, place, and time. You have to have a
> place, a home.[1]

One of the central issues facing human civilization at the end of the
twentieth century is governance: Who rules? Whose rules? What rules?
What kind of rules? At what level? In what form? Who decides? On
what basis? Many of the problems that give rise to questions such as
these are transnational and transboundary in nature, with the result
that the notion of global 'management' has acquired increasing currency in some circles. This is especially true given that economic globalization seems to point toward a single integrated world economy in
which the sovereign state appears to be losing much of its authority and
control over domestic and foreign affairs.[2] Contrary to the expectations
of neofunctionalists and others, however, economic integration is not
generating a parallel process in the political realm. Rather, what we see
is political fragmentation and the emergence of a multilevel and very
diffuse system of governance, within which local management, knowledge, and rule are of growing importance to coordination within domestic and international political hierarchies and amongst regions and

countries. The issue of environmental protection and restoration, in which these contrary trends are evident, illustrates this proposition. In this chapter, I examine the relationship between local knowledge and global environmental governance, and the role of what I call "global civil society" in fostering such governance.[3] I propose that, to a growing degree, it is in functional areas such as these that we must look in order to see the emerging outlines of twenty-first century global politics.

Knowledge is defined here as a system of conceptual relationships—both scientific and social—that explains cause and effect and offers the possibility of human intervention and manipulation in order to influence or direct the outcomes of certain processes. *Local knowledge* encompasses such knowledge, as well as the specific and sui generis social and cultural elements of bounded social units. *Civil society* includes those political, cultural, and social organizations of modern societies that are autonomous of the state but part of the mutually constitutive relationship between state and society. *Global civil society* extends this concept into the transnational realm, where it constitutes something along the lines of a "regime" composed of local, national, and global nongovernmental organizations. Finally, governance is, in Ernst-Otto Czempiel's words, the "capacity to get things done without the legal competence to command that they be done."[4] In this sense, it is a form of authority rather than jurisdiction.[5]

I begin the chapter with a discussion of the much-noted phenomenon of economic integration accompanied by political fragmentation, and its political and social implications. Although at first glance this might not seem relevant to the question of environmental governance, it is central. If there is a causal, or even dialectical, relation between the two processes, global governance becomes a quite different proposition than "global management."[6] I propose that such governance is as likely to rest with management functions centered in civil society, both local and global, as it is with states and governments.

Next, I consider what global civil society can and cannot do where environmental protection and restoration are concerned. It cannot, in the near-term, at least, change the big structures or systems that drive much of the destruction and degradation of nature of which we are increasingly aware. At the same time, however, agency and action are not impossible, and alternatives are not foreclosed. I then consider a central question implied in this analysis: where must people act, and under what conditions, in order to begin a process of changing practices on a larger scale? Here I consider the ways in which the menu of possibilities in any given place is constrained by those big structures, but not fully determined by them. To paraphrase others, women and men can make history, as long as they are aware of the conditions established by those who have come before.

Finally, I conclude with a discussion of governance and the problem of, as one author has put it, "coordination without hierarchy." I argue that we must look to the growing number of alliances, coalitions, networks, and projects that link together more local environmental protection and management efforts and work within a wide range of transnational and international organizations. The emerging system of global governance is functionalist rather than comprehensive; it does not presage a world government with black helicopters, but it does add up to more than an international community.

W(H)ITHER THE GLOBAL POLITY: GROWING TOGETHER OR COMING APART?

Back in 1990—in what now seems like ancient times—the Public Broadcasting System televised a miniseries entitled *After the Warming*. With James Burke as writer/commentator/guide, the program provided graphic illustrations of an imagined future in 2050, looking back upon a chaotic past disrupted by global warming. The impacts were, of course, widespread and horrific: how else to illustrate the premise of the show? But the proffered solution was somewhat hubristic: a Planetary Management Authority run, "of course" (as Burke put it), by Japan. The PMA, housed in a futuristic building that, even today, looks garish and anachronistic, would consist of a formidable system of computers and sensing devices that, utilizing a complex climatic model, could assess the impacts on global climate of human activities all over the planet. As necessary, the PMA would then issue appropriate directives to mitigate or ameliorate the climatic consequences—A global panopticon, in other words (in a prison in which the inmates would be free to run riot), not a *World State* but a *World Manager*, with complete authority and power.

Such a centralized management system is quite improbable. It flies in the face not only of logic but also a contemporary global politics that is characterized as much by fragmentation within existing polities as global economic integration among them.[7] But why are economic integration and political fragmentation linked, and what is the relevance of this process to the arguments advanced in this chapter? The relationship between the two suggests that the global management problem will be even more difficult than has been so far imagined, inasmuch as the number of sovereign or semisovereign entities participating in world politics and subject to transboundary effects could well increase over the coming decades from the fewer than two hundred we now have to many more. That is not the only complication; many of these entities may not even exercise effective political control over their own juridical territories, much as is presently the case in various "failed" states and ethnic-torn polities around the world.[8] Environmental protection and the governance it entails might well require different political arrangements than the international cooperation among states we now take for granted, a point to which I will return.

Global economic integration is a condition whose origins are to be found in the nineteenth century with the Industrial Revolution, the rise of English liberalism, and the institutionalization of free trade as propagated by the Manchester School. With fits, starts, and retreats, such integration has spread into virtually all corners of the world, creating myriad webs of material linkages and changing even the lives of those who, at first glance, seem quite remote from the global economy.[9] The fact that such integration has become so widespread does not, of course, mean that all places in the world share in the resulting benefits, as growing domestic and global gaps between rich and poor indicate.[10] But the global economy requires such disparities if it is to operate most efficiently. Indeed, it is uneven development that makes capitalism so dynamic, and it is the constant search for new combinations of factors of comparative advantage that drives innovation; the fact that there are multiple economic "systems" present in any one location simply adds to the dynamism of that process.[11] Today's comparative advantage may, consequently, be tomorrow's competitive drag.[12]

The political implications of such a process have not been given much serious thought. Contrary to the arguments of much of neoclassical trade theory and political advocates of free trade, comparative advantage no longer appears to be a feature of states as a whole—it has never really been, although the loosening of state control over national economies has made this more visible in recent years—but of region and locale, where the combination of technological and intellectual material is, perhaps only momentarily, fortuitous.[13] The specific comparative advantages of a place such as Silicon Valley—in many ways, an historical accident as much an outgrowth of deliberate policy—may in the future have only limited spillover in terms of the country as a whole.[14]

These conditions, moreover, seem not to be easily reproduced in the short term.[15] The competition among places to attract investment and jobs thus becomes more of a zero-sum than a positive-sum game, and this point is not lost, for example, on US states and cities who have established foreign trade offices in various global cities and regularly send trade missions abroad, as well.[16]

Capital has its choice of locations in which to invest and can pick and choose among them. Cities, communities, places, and to a certain degree, labor are much more constrained and have a limited menu of factors of production that can be flaunted to attract capital. As an article in the *San Francisco Examiner* describing the activities of a consulting firm providing city and regional marketing programs for economic development put it, these programs resemble those "of an international arms dealer—selling weapons to one ruler and then making a pitch to the neighboring potentate based on the new threat. Part of the pitch for these [economic development] programs is that a region needs its own program to survive against the rival programs of other areas."[17] Such competition may become the cause of considerable political antagonism, against both the neighbors who win and the authorities who have contributed to these conditions of competitive struggle in the first place.[18]

How such antagonisms play themselves out is contextual and contingent, of course, and often depends on pre-existing social and political fault lines that fracture under the pressures of real, potential, or imagined competition. In some places, these fault lines were intended to be administrative but were drawn up in ethnic or national terms; in other places, the fault lines are linguistic, religious, clan-based, tribal, or even vaguely cultural.[19] It goes without saying that those places in which people have fallen to killing each other have nothing to offer global capital—they have, quite literally, fallen out of history—whereas those places able to break away from the political grip of larger polities, as Slovenia escaped the competitive drag of Serbia, could find themselves well placed to participate in the global economy.[20] Inevitably, this process of political fracturing and fragmentation will lead to a much more complex "neofederalized" global system, which our modern concepts of international system, nation-state, and power will hardly begin to describe.[21]

Some have suggested that we confront a "new mediaevalism"; others have proposed as organizing principles "heteronomy" or "heterarchy."[22] Ole Wæver argues that

For some four centuries, political space was organized through the principle of territorially defined units with exclusive rights inside, and a special kind of relations on the outside: international relations, foreign policy, without any superior authority. There is no longer one level that is clearly the most important to refer to but, rather, a set of overlapping authorities.[23]

What is important here is the concept of 'authority,' in the sense of the ability to get things done because of one's legitimacy as opposed to one's ability to apply force or coerce, rather than 'law' or 'power.' As John Ruggie points out, "who has the right to act as a power" (or possesses authority) in even a relatively unsocialized political system is at least as important as the *capability* of actors to force others to do their bidding.[24]

In the emerging heteronomy, authority will be fragmented among many centers, often on the basis of specific issues rather than territories. In a way, this will generate a form of functionalism (really, functional differentiation) rather than federalism, inasmuch as different authorities will deal with different problems—some spatial, others not: toxic wastes moving through a neighborhood here, protection of a marsh there. And because these problems are embedded within a global economic system, such functionalism will inevitably reach beyond localities into and through that global system.[25]

This is not the same as the functionalism of the 1960s. Whereas older theories of functionalism envisioned political integration as the outcome of international functional coordination, it appears that contemporary functionalism may lead to something quite different as a consequence of the marriage of local knowledge and governance at multiple levels.[26] In the present instance, functionalism can be understood as a consequence of rapid innovation, of the generation of new scientific-technical and social knowledge(s) required to address different types of issues and problems.[27] Inasmuch as there is too much scientific and social knowledge for any one actor, whether individual or collective, to assimilate, it becomes necessary to establish knowledge-based alliances and coalitions whose logic is only partly based on space or, for that matter, hierarchy. "Local" knowledge is spatially situated, while "organizational" knowledge—how to put knowledge together and use it—is spaceless; together, the two become instrumental to technical and social innovation.[28]

Acquisition of such knowledges and practices also leads to new forms and venues of authority, in that only those with access to such capabilities can act successfully. In some sense, the management function finds itself located at that level of social organization at which the appropriate combination of local and global knowledges come together.[29] This level is more likely to be local—in the lab, the research group, the neighborhood, the watershed—than global. Or, as Richard Gordon puts it,

> Regions and networks . . . constitute interdependent poles within the new spatial mosaic of global innovation. Globalization in this context involves not the leavening impact of universal processes but, on the contrary, the calculated synthesis of cultural diversity in the form of differentiated regional innovation logics and capabilities. . . . The effectiveness of local resources and the ability to achieve genuine forms of cooperation with global networks must be developed from within the region itself. . . . [30]

Such functionalist regionalization points back toward the political fragmentation discussed above: lines must be drawn somewhere, whether by reference to nature, power, authority, or knowledge. From a constructivist perspective, such lines may be as fictional as those which currently separate one country, or one county, from another. Still, they are unlikely to be wholly disconnected form the material world, inasmuch as they will have to map onto already existing patterns and structures of social and economic activity.

THE AGENCY-STRUCTURE QUESTION REDUX—HISTORY COUNTS

Where in this emergent structure is there a space for agency, for organized political action? At its core, the agent-structure debate is more than just an obscure discussion among academics; it is really about the possibilities of political action in a world where, as John Agnew, a geographer, puts it, "[People] are *located* according to the demands of a spatially extensive division of labour, the global system of material production and distribution, and variable patterns of political authority and control."[31] In citing Agnew, however, I do not mean to say that people's lives are determined by these patterns, only that their choices must be made within the constraints imposed by them (and the histories of the places where they are located). Large-scale opportunities to engineer genuine ideational and material change are rare; the "stickiness" of structures and the institutions that accompany these patterns can defy all efforts to change them.[32]

What and where, then, are the possibilities for action, if they are not to be found at the macrolevel? To discover these, we must look to the history of social, economic, and political entities; history does count. Any social situation in which people, both individually and collectively, find themselves is a product of history, as Marx pointed out; to this we might add that it is both the history of people and the history of places, made by people. To understand how one has arrived at a particular time and place, therefore, one has to know, first, what has come before and, second, how our conventional histories of the past may have been misleading or misinformed (whether intentionally or not). In the language of economics, the present is a product of path dependency;[33] in the language of cultural studies, it is a consequence of how we have acted on what was thought to have happened.[34] This history, in turn, says something about the menu of choices for the future available at any given time.[35]

While such statements might seem self-evident and perhaps even simplistic, they are neither, most of our routine behaviors are the result of habit, of repetition, of unquestioned circumstances, of institutions and associated practices.[36] This is the context in which we make ordinary choices; indeed, it is the realm of the microeconomists' rational actor.[37] But, as the discussion above suggests, there are constraints on choices; they must be imagined to be realized, and, although many might be possible in theory, not all that might be imagined are necessarily feasible in political terms.[38] As John Thompson has put it, "As constellations of social relations and reservoirs of natural resources, specific institutions form a relatively stable framework for action and interaction; they do not determine action but *generate* it in the sense of establishing, loosely and tentatively, the parameters of permissible conduct."[39] Sometimes, however, social constraints make what is a necessary choice difficult, if not almost impossible. It is at this point that human agency becomes important, as the individual actor struggles to move away from habit-driven action, which simply reproduces the status quo.

The patterns, or "historical structures," described by Agnew (and others such as Robert Cox and Stephen Gill) do put people in their place, but this does not mean that they are then left without choices.[40] John Walton argues that

> The constitution of local society . . . is far more than an imposition or small-scale reflection of the national state. On the contrary, it is the evolving product of multiple influences—the people, the economy, natural resources, intermediate levels of state authority, local accommodation to some broader designs, determined resistance to others

and, perhaps above all, collective action founded on cultural meaning. Action takes place within social structures that forcibly shape experience, yet people live in local societies where particular customs, exigencies, and choices mediate structural constraints. On the ground people construct their lives in consciously meaningful ways that cannot be read from state-centered directives any more than they can be deduced from modes of economic production.[41]

Beyond this, there are historical junctures at which the menu of choices expands, so to speak, offering alternative paths that might not at other times be available.[42] Agency is thus a matter of being aware of alternatives and helping to foster conditions under which meaningful choices can be made.

Such agency should be distinguished from the form more common to contemporary or modernizing societies: consumer preference, choice or autonomy, sometimes called "green consumerism" when it involves choosing "environmentally friendly" products, which is not agency at all. Rather, it is a response to particular profit-seeking strategies pursued by capital.[43] It is not my intention to dismiss environmentally driven consumer behavior as irrelevant—it does have real impacts—but rather to point out that it is subject to very real constraints imposed by others. And, although environmental protection mediated via markets can improve various types of environmental quality, these do not (and cannot) alter fundamental institutional structures and practices.[44]

MAKING CHOICES, TAKING ACTION

If individualistic choice and action are not sufficient to effect changes in the habit-driven behaviors characteristic of people in particular social and political contexts, what is? Norman Long points out that

> Effective agency...requires organizing capacities; it is not simply the result of possessing certain persuasive powers or forms of charisma. . . . *[A]gency (and power) depend crucially upon the emergence of a network of actors who become partially, though hardly ever completely, enrolled in the "project" of some other person or persons.* . . . It becomes essential, therefore, for social actors to win the struggles that take place over the attribution of specific social meanings to particular events, actions, and ideas.[45]

These struggles over the "attribution of specific social meanings" are not about science or data or cost-benefit ratios or, indeed, about any of

the things that are quantifiable; they are about ontologies and epistemologies of place, life, and history, within which the methods and
findings of science and economics are tools or means to an end.[46]
Again, not all social meanings are available—the repertoire is limited
by history, political economy, and culture—but successful agency is
possible when a context can be explained in terms of one or more of
the meanings in the repertoire. What is central, therefore, to effective
social action is the ability to recognize the relationship between choices
and meanings; indeed such an ability is central to politics, inasmuch
as the articulation of the relationship is essential for successfully "en-
rolling" people in a "project."[47]

It now begins to become apparent how and why, at the international level, "projects" are so difficult to effect. While power and wealth
are important, they do not include all sources of social authority, especially those that may play central roles, akin to Gramscian hegemony,
in the domestic politics of culturally different societies. Consider the
question of climate change, which is ordinarily described in terms of
impacts that are difficult to quantify with great precision, especially in
regional or local terms (e.g., a two to three degree centigrade average
rise in global temperature as a result of a doubling of carbon dioxide
levels in the atmosphere). Implicit in these numbers is the notion that
everyone will be affected to his or her detriment. Consequently, echoing
Dr. Pangloss, the present—the status quo ante of the future—is the
"best of possible worlds." The intended result of such an assumption
is, as Deborah Stone points out, the creation of a "natural community"—inhabitants of the Blue Planet, whether animal, vegetable or
mineral—with a shared interest.[48] In this case, that interest in preventing or minimizing global environmental change requires the construction of a shared, albeit artificial, history and culture around the process,
which allows a group of actors to negotiate a text on which they can
all agree. The text, in turn, tells a story with a specific social meaning.

Thus, for example, in the Preamble to the Framework Convention
on Climate Change, signatories "acknowledge that the global nature of
climate change calls for the widest possible cooperation by all countries
and their participation in an effective and appropriate international
response, in accordance with their common but differentiated responsibilities and respective capabilities and their social and economic conditions . . . "[49] As posed in the document, this is a story about a problem
and the conditions deemed necessary, by the signatories, to its resolution. What is not told here, or, for that matter, anywhere in the conven-

tion itself, are the actual social meanings that the parties and their societies bring to the negotiations. These meanings can be read in the controversies that litter the growing literature and debates on the potential political, economic, and social impacts of climate change.[50] Conversely, the collective social meaning embedded in the convention by the delegates may have little or no meaning to the members of the societies that ultimately must implement the terms of the document.[51] It is unlikely, therefore, that these individuals will enroll in this project in the absence of such an accepted meaning. In other words, to be successfully implemented, the Framework Convention on Climate Change must have many different social meanings, each of which is context-dependent, but each of which may be "essentially contested" by other parties to the convention.[52] The result is that a textual resolution mostly depends on how a particular story is told, on whose social meaning is more compelling and able to garner more votes.[53]

In the midst of struggles over meaning, then, history counts not only in terms of explaining how one has arrived at a particular place, but also in terms of how convincingly the story is to be told. This, in turn, has much to do with being able to make choices under constrained conditions, inasmuch as the ways in which a story is told will generate different projects and programs. The politics of meanings, as described here, explains why crises offer the greatest opportunities for agency and social change. It is during these times that conditions become "underdetermined," that people are ready and willing to seek and follow new solutions to their immediate dilemma, and that political entrepreneurs are most able to mobilize followers around specific projects.[54] Another example can be found in the campaign to save the Amazon rainforest. Here we find, on one side, indigenous groups, rubber tappers, and, in some instances, *garimpieros*, regional research organizations, social movements in Brazilian cities, international environmental organizations based in the United States and Europe, industrialized country governments, and international organizations. Arrayed somewhat in opposition to this coalition are the Brazilian government and military, organizations of ranchers and landowners, Brazilian state governments, other industrialized country governments, and, in all likelihood, national and international corporate actors.[55]

This, then, is the basis for the possibilities open to agency: the ability to place historically a given context—making strategic decisions about how that history is to be told—and understanding how the confluence of structures provides openings for different futures. Of course, no choices are final, although they can and do foreclose other choices, both in the present and in the future. But, final or not, such choices are best made at the most localized level at which they make practical and political sense, especially if we acknowledge that decisions made at the supralocal level cannot be very sensitive to local conditions and might, in fact, engender local resistance that undermines such decisions.[56] It is also clear from this argument that somehow localized agency becomes a necessary, albeit not a sufficient, element of environmental governance.[57] The key question, which I address in the following section, is whether it is possible to nurture a governance system that privileges local choice and, at the same time, takes into account global complexities, connections, and justice.

WHO RULES? WHOSE RULES? FROM GLOBAL ENVIRONMENTAL MANAGEMENT TO GLOBAL ENVIRONMENTAL GOVERNANCE

In order to understand the relationship between locally based civil society, knowledge, and global governance, much can be learned by examining the histories of environmental projects at the local and regional level. For example, in his study of the century-long struggle against the city of Los Angeles by the residents of the Owens Valley in eastern California, John Walton discusses that local groups engaged in resistance to the state of California were only successful when they were able to draw on the expanding federal authority and the legitimation of various environmental strategies as a means of putting pressure on the city to alter its patterns of water removal from the valley.[58] In a broader sense, this coalition took advantage of local knowledge and a nationally redefined ideology of ecology legitimated by the US government to recast social meanings for political purposes. Whereas Los Angeles tapped the Owens Valley water resources for industrial and urban growth, both the local residents and Washington, DC sought to conserve water and restore the landscape by framing the conflict in terms of an increasingly accepted story of environmental protection and restoration. This is not to suggest that self-interest was absent from the scenario, only to point out that collective action required collective meanings.

Beyond this, the insight provided by Walton's story is that our conventional concepts of 'the state' and 'governance' are too limited. The state—even a federal one—is not restricted to discrete levels of government; it is more than that. As Theda Skocpol points out:

On the one hand, states may be viewed as organizations through which official collectivities may pursue collective goals, realizing them more or less effectively given available state resources in relation to social settings. On the other hand, states may be viewed more macroscopically as configurations of organizations and action that influence the meanings and methods of politics for all groups and classes in society.[59]

Skocpol perhaps offers a conception of the state that is too broad in encompassing society, but her point is, in my view, an important one. The state is more than just its constitution, agencies, rules, and roles, and it is embedded, as well, in a system of governance. James Rosenau argues that

Governance . . . is a more encompassing phenomenon than government. It embraces governmental institutions, but it also subsumes informal, nongovernmental mechanisms whereby those persons and organizations within its purview move ahead, satisfy their needs, and fulfil their wants. . . . Governance is thus a system of rule that is as dependent on intersubjective meanings as on formally sanctioned constitutions and charters. . . . [I]t is possible to conceive of governance without government—of regulatory mechanisms in a sphere of activity which function effectively even though they are not endowed with formal authority.[60]

From this view state and civil society are mutually constitutive, and, where the state engages in *government*, civil society often plays a role in *governance*. What is striking, especially in terms of relationships between environmental organizations and institutionalized mechanisms of government, is the growth of institutions of governance at and across all levels of analysis.

What this implies is that, even though we recognize that there is no world government, as such, there is an emerging system of global governance. Subsumed within this system of governance are both institutionalized regulatory arrangements, some of which we call 'regimes,' and less formalized norms, rules, and procedures that pattern behavior without the presence of written constitutions or material power.[61] This system is not the state, as we commonly understand the term, but it is statelike, in Skocpol's second sense. Indeed, we can see emerging patterns of behavior in global politics very much like those described by Walton in the case of the Owens Valley: alliances between coalitions in global civil society and the international governance arrangements associated with the UN system.[62] In the Amazon case mentioned above, too, each of the actors at one time or another acquired a certain amount of governance authority within a poorly specified political, economic, or social realm. Each of these actors at one time or another finds it useful to ally with others at other levels, so as to put pressure on yet other actors at still other levels. The result might look more like a battlefield than a negotiation, and indeed violence is an all-too-real component of this particular campaign; but, while there is no definitive ruler, the process is not entirely without rules or structure.[63]

To push this argument further, let us return for a moment to what scholars of international environmental policy and politics regard as the sine qua non of their research: the fact that, as it is often put, environmental degradation respects no borders. This feature automatically thrusts many environmental problems into the international realm where, we are reminded, there is no government and no way to regulate the activities of sovereign states. From this follows the need for international cooperation to internalize transboundary effects, a need that leads logically to the creation of international environmental regimes. Such regimes, it is often noted, are the creation of states, and scholars continue to argue about the conditions necessary for their establishment and maintenance.[64] Whether they undermine the sovereignty of states or are, in themselves, a form of state-building is as yet unclear.[65] What is less well recognized or acknowledged is that some regimes are merely the "tip of the iceberg," so to speak, or they will be if they reach fruition.

Much of the implementation and regulation inherent in regimes such as the emerging one addressing climate change must, as I suggested above, take place at the regional and local levels, in the places where people live, not where their laws are made. If this climate regime is successful—whatever 'success' means in such a context—it will, for all practical purposes, function as a global institution of governance with elements at the local, regional, provincial, national, and international levels.[66] It will, in effect, transfer some of the jurisdictional responsibilities of the state both upwards and downwards, enhancing political authority at the global as well as the local level. But the politics of this and other similar regimes will make domestic politics simple by comparison. Rather than two- or even three-level games, what we see, and will see more of, are n-level games, in which intermediate levels are squeezed or strong-armed by those above and below.[67] This is commonly discussed in terms of coalitional strategies between grassroots social movement organizations and international institutions, but in fact these coalitions are much more complex, often link together multiple levels as well as multi-level actors, and may also shift and change as a situation demands.[68] What should we call such a process? Clearly, it is governance but not government (although it contains elements of government); at the same time, it does not mark the end or disintegration of the state as an institutionalized form of politics (although it might, of course, mark the end of particular states).

Perhaps these arrangements are best understood as a dialectical relationship between two mutually constitutive structures: states and global civil society. This can be seen more clearly by considering the relationship of domestic civil societies to the state in which they are located.[69] Within many states, civil society and state are mutually constitutive. Each is necessary for the functioning of the other, and each serves to legitimate the other. At times, moreover, civil society fulfils a regulatory function in place of the state, as is the case with the medical and legal professional associations in the United States and other countries.[70] These associations not only provide credentials to practitioners through certification of practitioners' knowledge, they also provide a set of rules and norms that a practitioner must adhere to, at the risk of losing her or his license to practice.

While these rules and norms have a moral quality, as, for example, in the Hippocratic Oath, there is clearly an element of self-interest about them, too. And this is true of most, if not all, of the associations of civil society. Not everyone observes all of the norms and rules to which they have subscribed all of the time, but the adherence rate is generally pretty good.[71] More to the point, the members of these associations internalize these rules and norms and follow them, whether the element of self-interest is evident or not.[72] Rules, in other words, take the place of explicit rule; governance replaces government; informal networks of coordination replace formal structures of command. Governance is effected.

ONE EARTH, MANY WORLDS

How, then, are we to proceed? I would argue that, rather than through global hierarchy or markets, governance through social relations of the type discussed above, in which shared norms, cooperation, trust, and mutual obligation play central roles, is most likely to protect nature. Such governance seems increasingly characteristic of the emerging global political economy characterized by economic integration and political fragmentation. The fundamental units of governance are, in this system, defined by both function and social meanings anchored to particular places but linked globally through networks of knowledge-based relations. Coordination occurs because each unit plays a functional role where it is located, but also because the functional units share goals with other functional units. Relations such as these develop when the costs of acquiring information through normal channels becomes too great; they bear a remarkable resemblance to transactions and economies oriented around kinship relations, in which trust and membership replace formal hierarchies and markets.[73] The phenomenon of networking also resembles the form of organization described above, a form that is characteristic of relations within global civil society. It is a form that best lends itself to collaboration without centralization, without global management.

Such a system need not necessarily be a second-best one, either. There is reason to think that a governance system composed of collective actors at multiple levels, with overlapping authority, linked together through various kinds of networks, might be as functionally efficient as a highly centralized one.[74] Such a decentralized system of governance has a number of advantages over a real or imagined hierarchical counterpart. As Donald Chisholm points out,

> [F]ormal systems often create a gap between the formal authority to make decisions and the capacity to make them, owing to a failure to recognize the necessity for a great deal of technical information for effective coordination. Ad hoc coordinating committees staffed by personnel with the requisite professional skills appear far more effective than permanent central coordinating committees run by professional coordinators.[75]

Chisholm goes on to argue that formal systems work so long as appropriate information, necessary to the system's function and achievement of its goals, is available. The problem is that

> Strict reliance on formal channels compounds the problem [of trying to prevent public awareness of bureaucratic failure]: reliable information will not be supplied, and the failure will not be uncovered until it is too late to compensate for it. Informal channels, by their typically clandestine nature and foundation on *reciprocity and mutual trust*, provide appropriate means for surmounting problems associated with formal channels of communication.[76]

Compare this observation with Richard Gordon's discussion of the organizational logic of innovation:

> While strategic alliances involve agreements between autonomous firms, and are oriented towards strengthening the competitive position of the network and its members, interfirm relations *within* the alliance itself tend to push beyond traditional market relations. Permanently contingent relationships mediated by strict organizational independence and market transactions—the arms-length exchange structure of traditional short-term linkages—are replaced by long-term relations intended to endure and which are mediated by highly personalized and detailed interaction.... *Cooperative trust, shared norms and mutual advocacy overcome antagonistic independence and isolation.*[77]

In policy terms, this is not a very satisfying or parsimonious framework. It does not provide an entry for either easy explanation or manipulation. It relies on the possibly heroic assumption that people can and will help to create "social choice mechanisms" in their collective self-interest that will also help to protect nature.[78] But it offers more than global management of a passive or resistant population. It suggests that people acting locally can have real and significant global impacts. Such social and political change will not occur quickly, nor will it come easily, and it will never encompass the entire world. But, at the very least, by illuminating and examining change where it is underway, we can offer to others a model of action based on local knowledge that might, over the longer term, make a meaningful difference.

NOTES

This chapter is based upon Ronnie D. Lipschutz, with Judith Mayer, *Global Civil Society and Global Environmental Governance: The Politics of Nature from Place to Planet* (Albany: SUNY Press, 1996). A similar version appeared as "From Place to Planet: Local Knowledge and Global Environmental Governance," *Global Governance* 3 (1997) pp. 83–102 (copyright 1997, Lynne Rienner Publishers, reprinted by permission).

1. Wade Sikorski, "Building Wilderness," pp. 24–43, in Jane Bennett and William Chaloupka, eds., *In the Nature of Things—Language, Politics, and the Environment* (Minneapolis: University of Minnesota Press, 1993), p. 28.

2. The literature on this point is vast and growing; see, for example, Kenichi Ohmae, *The Borderless World—Power and Strategy in the Interlinked Economy* (New York: HarperCollins, 1990).

3. The term *governance* is defined below; suffice it here to say that it is about rules and power. See Nicholas G. Onuf, *World of Our Making—Rules and Rule in Social Theory and International Relations* (Columbia, SC: University of South Carolina Press, 1989).

4. Ernst-Otto Czempiel, "Governance and Democratization," pp. 250-71, in James N. Rosenau and Ernst-Otto Czempiel, eds., *Governance without Government: Order and Change in World Politics* (Cambridge: Cambridge University Press, 1992), p. 250.

5. All of these concepts are defined in greater detail in Lipschutz, *Global Civil Society and Global Environmental Governance*, ch. 3, and the references cited therein.

6. Already, in a world of 185 states, the prospect of getting all to act together is problematic; how much more difficult will this be in a world of two hundred or five states? See Bob Davis, "Global Paradox: Growth of Trade Binds Nations, but It Also Can Spur Separatism," *Wall Street Journal*, June 20, 1994 (Western ed.), p. A1. Another report on the multiplication of nations is a report on the recent conference in the Hague of the Unrepresented Nations and Peoples Organization; see Frank Viviano, "World's Wannabee Nations Sound Off," *San Francisco Chronicle*, Jan. 31, 1995, p. A1.

7. This literature is also growing. See especially the work of Stephen Gill and the collection of essays in Yoshikazu Sakamoto, ed., *Global Transformation—Challenges to the State System* (Tokyo: United Nations University Press, 1994).

8. A graphic, if sometimes inconsistent, description of such places can be found in Robert D. Kaplan, "The Coming Anarchy," *The Atlantic Monthly*, February 1994, pp. 44–76, and his subsequent book, *The Ends of the Earth: A Journey at the Dawn of the Twentieth Century* (New York: Random House, 1996).

9. See, for example, David J. Kyle, "The Transnational Peasant: The Social Construction of International Economic Migration and Transcommunities from the Ecuadorean Andes," Ph.D. dissertation, Dept. of Sociology, The Johns Hopkins University, 1995.

10. UN Development Program, *Human Development Report* (New York: UNDP, 1996).

11. By this I mean that, in any one location, there are economic systems of local, regional, national, transnational, and global extent. These are linked but not all of a single piece. Thus, for example, Silicon Valley is tightly integrated into the global economy, but some of its inhabitants are also participants in a service-based economy that, although coupled into global systems is largely directed toward meeting local demand. For further discussion of the notion of "multiple" economies, see Richard Gordon, "Globalizaton, New Production Systems, and the Spatial Division of Labor," pp. 161–207, in Wolfgang Litek and Tony Charles, eds., *The Division of Labour—Emerging Forms of World Organization in International Perspective* (Berlin: Walter de Gruyter, 1995).

12. See the letter, responding to a review in *The New York Review of Books*, Oct. 20, 1994, by Benjamin Friedman, of Paul Krugmann, *Peddling Prosperity—Economic Sense and Nonsense in the Age of Diminished Expectations* (New York: Norton, 1994). The writers suggest that, as with evolution,

economic success may be highly contingent (Marshall E. Blume, Jeremy J. Siegel, and Dan Rottenberg, "Technology's Lesson," *New York Review of Books*, Jan. 12, 1995, p. 53).

13. See, e.g., Heizi Noponen, Julie Graham, and Ann R. Markusen, *Trading Industries, Trading Regions—International Trade, American Industry, and Regional Economic Development* (New York: Guilford, 1993).

14. The term for such historical contingency is *path dependency*. See the discussion of this point in Krugman, *Peddling Prosperity*, ch. 9.

15. How intentional or fortuitous is, of course, the key question. Silicon Valley was hardly the product of chance; rather, it was the result of intentional mobilization of resources by the state in its pursuit of national security. The difficulty of maintaining such a development pole is illustrated by the relative collapse of the high-tech center on Route 128 around Boston. Some of the difficulties facing policymakers who might like to replicate such mobilization are discussed in Beverly Crawford, "Hawks, Doves, but No Owls: International Economic Interdependence and the Construction of the New Security Dilemma," pp. 149–86, in Ronnie D. Lipschutz, ed., *On Security* (New York: Columbia University Press, 1995).

16. Michael H. Shuman, "Dateline Main Street: Courts versus Local Foreign Policies," *Foreign Policy* 86 (Spring 1992): 158–77; Michael Shuman, *Towards a Global Village: International Community Development Initiatives* (London & Boulder: Pluto Press, 1994). See also Ivo D. Duchacek, *The Territorial Dimension of Politics—Within, Among, and Across Nations* (Boulder: Westview, 1986), ch. 9.

17. Louis Trager, "All's Fair in Selling Growth to Cities," *San Francisco Examiner*, Jan. 22, 1995, p. C-1.

18. In California, for example, such antagonisms have led Governor Pete Wilson, to declare that "California is a proud and sovereign state, not a colony of the federal government." See Steven A. Capps, "Wilson Sworn in with a Blast at Feds," *San Francisco Examiner*, Jan. 8, 1995, p. A-1.

19. Georgi M. Derlugian, "The Tale of Two Resorts—Abkhazia and Ajaria before and since the Soviet Collapse," in Beverly Crawford and Ronnie D. Lipschutz, eds., *The Political Economy of Cultural Conflict* (forthcoming).

20. Clearly, individuals are deeply implicated in this process of "choosingpaths." For a discussion of the agency-structure question relevant to this point, see below.

21. The point I am making here is not that 'states' will disappear, but that power and legitimacy will become much more complex and problematic than they seem to have been for the past fifty to one hundred years. Just to take an example from one such event, on February 2, 1995, the US Federal Reserve Board has raised its basic interest rate by one half of a percentage point in order to moderate domestic economic growth and thereby stifle incipient inflation. This move pleases investors and distresses producers and consumers. What are the impacts of this move on US power? Some would argue little or nothing, but

President Clinton is reputed to have said upon taking office, "You mean to tell me that the success of my [economic] program and my re-election hinges on the Federal Research and a bunch of [expletive] bond traders?" Quoted in Tom Hayden, "Orange County Could Use Some Role Models," *San Francisco Chronicle*, Dec. 21, 1994, p. A23.

22. The best-known discussion of the "new mediaevalism" is to be found in Hedley Bull, *The Anarchical Society—A Study of Order in World Politics* (New York: Columbia University Press, 1977), pp. 254–55, 264–76, 285–86, 291–94. The notion of 'heteronomy' is found, among other places, in John G. Ruggie, "Continuity and Transformation in the World Polity: Toward a Neorealist Synthesis," *World Politics* 35, 2 (Jan. 1983), p. 274, n30. The term *heterarchy* comes from C. Bartlett and S. Ghoshal, "Managing Innovation in the Transnational Corporation," pp. 215-55, in C. Y. Doz and G. Hedlund, eds., *Managing the Global Firm* (London: Routledge, 1990), quoted in Gordon, "Globalization . . . ," p. 181.

23. Ole Wæver, "Securitization and Desecuritization," pp. 46-86, in Lipschutz, *On Security*, n59.

24. John G. Ruggie, "International Structure and International Transformation: Space, Time, and Method," pp. 21–35, in Ernst-Otto Czempiel and James N. Rosenau, eds., *Global Changes and Theoretical Challenges* (Lexington, MA: Lexington Books, 1989), p. 28.

25. One example of this is the growing environmental justice movement, which is becoming globalized and addressing not only the local disposition of toxic waste but its export and disposal in other places around the world; see, e.g., Jennifer Clapp, "The Toxic Waste Trade with Less-Industrialized Countries: Economic Linkages and Political Alliances," *Third World Quarterly* 15, 3 (1994).

26. David Mitrany, *A Working Peace System* (Chicago: Quadrangle Books, 1966); Ernst B. Haas, *Beyond the Nation-State* (Stanford: Stanford University Pres, 1964).

27. The following paragraphs are based on Gordon, "Globalization."

28. Judith Mayer has pointed out that even organizational knowledge is, to a large degree, also contextual, inasmuch as successful organization aimed at solving a localized functional problem must be based on a solid understanding of local social relations. Personal communication, Jan. 26, 1995.

29. Lipschutz, *Global Civil Society and Global Environmental Governance*, ch. 2.

30. Gordon, "Globalization," pp. 196, 199.

31. John Agnew, "Representing Space—Space, Scale and Culture in Social Science," pp. 251–71, in James Duncan and David Ley, eds., *Place/Culture/Representation* (London: Routledge, 1993), p. 262.

32. James N. Rosenau, "Before Cooperation: Hegemons, Regimes, and Habit-Driven Actors in World Politics," *International Organization* 40, 4 (Autumn 1986): 849–94.

33. Krugman, *Peddling Prosperity*, ch. 9.

34. This is a social constructivist argument, but social constructions have real material consequences. We act not on the basis of how events actually happened, but on how we understand them to have taken place and the significance and meanings we collectively put on them.

35. Such a menu is nicely illustrated in Maria Todarova, "Identity (Trans)Formation among Bulgarian Muslims," in Crawford and Lipschutz, eds., *The Political Economy of Cultural Conflict*. Todarova shows how the collapse of the communist regime in Bulgaria left an underdetermined situation in which Muslims (not Turkish but Bulgarian) have been presented with a choice of "identities," ranging from demands for economic improvement within Bulgaria to fusion with Turkey to conversion to Christianity to American patronage. Which will ultimately be chosen depends on the extent to which the agents of each choice are able to mobilize these people. Derlugian, "A Tale of Two Resorts," makes similar points with respect to Abkhazia and Ajaria.

36. Rosenau, "Before Cooperation." See also the discussion of institutions in Ronnie D. Lipschutz and Judith Mayer, "Not Seeing the Forest for the Trees: Property Rights, Constitutive Rules, and the Renegotiation of Resource Management Regimes, "pp. 246–73, in Ronnie D. Lipschutz and Ken Conca, eds., *The State and Social Power in Global Environmental Politics* (New York: Columbia University Press, 1993), which draws, in part, on Oran Young's discussion of institutions in *Resource Regimes—Natural Resources and Social Institutions* (Berkeley: University of California Press, 1982).

37. For an illuminating critique of rational choice epistemologies, see Deborah A. Stone, *Policy Paradox and Political Reason* (Glenview, IL: Scott, Foresman and Company, 1988).

38. Norman Long, "From Paradigm Lost to Paradigm Regained? The Case for an Actor-Oriented Sociology of Development," pp. 16-43, in Norman Long and Ann Long, eds., *Battlefields of Knowledge—The Interlocking of Theory and Practice in Social Research and Development* (London: Routledge, 1992), pp. 24-25.

39. John Thompson, *Studies in the Theory of Ideology* (Berkeley: University of California Press, 1984), p. 135. Emphasis in original.

40. Robert W. Cox, *Production, Power, and World Order* (New York: Columbia University Press, 1987); Stephen Gill, ed., *Gramsci, Historical Materialism, and International Relations* (Cambridge: Cambridge University Press, 1993).

41. John Walton, *Western Times and Water Wars—State, Culture, and Rebellion in California* (Berkeley: University of California Press, 1992).

42. Path dependency, in other words, proceeds from specifiable choice points; the trick is to recognize such points when they present themselves. This should not be confused with the chaos theory equivalent of the "butterfly's wings" creating hurricanes. This notion of a 'menu of choices' is akin to the *bricolage* of Levi-Strauss.

43. Lipschutz, *Global Civil Society and Global Environmental Governance,* pp. 243–44.

44. See, e.g., Peter Passell, "For Utilities, New Clean-Air Plan," *New York Times,* Nov. 18, 1994 (national ed.), p. C1, which describes a swap of carbon dioxide credits for sulfur dioxide allowances.

45. Long, "From Paradigm Lost," pp. 23–24. My emphasis.

46. This point is elaborated in Lipschutz, *Global Civil Society and Global Environmental Governance,* ch. 7.

47. On this point, albeit in a different framing, see Stone, *Policy Paradox,* "Conclusion," esp. p. 309. It is also discussed with respect to the Presidency in Franz Schurmann, *The Logic of World Power—An Inquiry into the Origins, Currents, and Contradictions of World Politics* (New York: Pantheon, 1974), pp. 33–39.

48. Stone, *Policy Paradox,* p. 135.

49. International Negotiating Committee for a Framework Convention on Climate Change, *United Nations Framework Convention on Climate Change* (Geneva: UNEP/WMO Information Unit on Climate Change, n.d.), p. 2.

50. Compare, for example, Richard E. Benedick, *Ozone Diplomacy—New Directions in Safeguarding the Planet* (Cambridge, MA: Harvard University Press, 1991); Stephen H. Schneider, "The Changing Climate," pp. 25–36, in *Scientific American, Managing Planet Earth* (New York: W. H. Freeman, 1990); Jeremy Leggett, ed., *Global Warming—The Greenpeace Report* (Oxford: Oxford University Press, 1990); Ann Hawkins, "Contested Ground: International Environmentalism and Global Climate Change," pp. 221-45, in Lipschutz and Conca, *The State and Social Power* (New York: Columbia University Press, 1993); Vandana Shiva, *The Violence of the Green Revolution* (London: Zed/Third World Network, 1991); Joni Seager, *Earth Follies: Coming to Feminist Terms with the Global Environmental Crisis* (New York: Routledge, 1993).

51. Or, as T. H. Marshall once put it, "[W]e find that legislation, instead of being the decisive step that puts policy into immediate effect, acquires more and more the character of a declaration of policy that it is hoped to put into effect some day." *Citizenship and Social Class* (Cambridge: Cambridge University Press, 1950), p. 59.

52. Perusal of the issues of *ECO* and the *Earth Negotiations Bulletin,* both of which report on meetings of the FCCC's Conference of the Parties and subgroups, should convince anyone of this point.

53. It is for this reason that recorded votes are rarely held in such negotiations; the ideal is consensus, which means that the contestation over social meaning occurs mostly in small, informal groups that meet in hallways or over coffee. An American perspctive on the entire voting process in such fora can be found in Michael Lind, "One Nation One Vote? That's Not Fair," *New York Times,* Nov. 23, 1994 (national. ed.), p. A15.

54. Lipschutz and Crawford, "Economic Globalization," pp. 7–8.

55. Susanna B. Hecht and Alexander Cockburn, *The Fate of the Forest—Developers, Destroyers and Defenders of the Amazon* (New York, HarperPerennial, 1990); Schmink and Wood, *Contested Frontiers*; João Pacheco de Oliveira Filho, "Frontier Security and the New Indigenism: Nature and Origins of the Calha Norte Project," pp. 155–78, in David Goodman and Anthony Hall, eds., *The Future of Amazonia—Destruction or Sustainable Development?* (New York: St. Martin's Press, 1988); David Cleary, "After the Frontier: Problems with Political Economy in the Modern Brazilian Amazon," *Journal of Latin American Studies* 25, 2 (May, 1993): 331–50; Susanna B. Hecht, "The Logic of Livestock and Deforestation in Amazonia," *BioScience* 43, 10 (Nov. 1993): 687–96.

56. See *Global Civil Society and Global Environmental Governance*, ch. 2, 7; Ronnie D. Lipschutz, "Bioregional Politics and Local Organization in Policy Responses to Global Climate Change," in David L. Feldman, ed., *Global Climate Change and Public Policy* (Chicago: Nelson-Hall, 1994).

57. This is, at the moment, the core of an argument against the revival of states' rights. More to the point, just as there was great resistance in the American South to the implementation of civil rights for blacks during the 1960s, there is no reason to think that local governance will, by its very nature, necessarily be environmentally-friendly. Pursuing this parallel further, however, it is difficult to imagine governments sending national troops into communities in order to enforce the letter of environmental law.

58. John Walton *Western Times and Water Wars* (Berkeley: University of California Press, 1992).

59. Theda Skocpol, "Bringing the State Back In: Strategies of Analysis in Current Research," pp. 3-37, in Peter B. Evans, Dietrich Reuschemeyer, and Theda Skocpol, eds., *Bringing the State Back In* (Cambridge: Cambridge University Press, 1985).

60. James N. Rosenau, "Governance, Order, and Change in World Politics," pp. 1-29, in James N. Rosenau and Ernst-Otto Czempiel, eds., *Governance without Government: Order and Change in World Politics* (Cambridge: Cambridge University Press, 1992).

61. This point is a heavily disputed one: To wit, is the international system so undersocialized as to make institutions only weakly constraining on behavior, as John Mearsheimer or Stephen Krasner might argue, or are the fetters of institutionalized practices sufficiently strong to modify behavior away from chaos and even anarchy, as Nicholas Onuf might put it? See Stephen D. Krasner, "Westphalia and All That," in Judith Goldstein and Robert O. Keohane, eds., *Ideas and Foreign Policy* (Ithaca: Cornell University Press, 1993); Onuf, *World of Our Making*.

62. A good illustration of this process can be found in Franke Wilmer, *The Indigenous Voice in World Politics* (Newbury Park: Sage, 1993).

63. One might ask why these should not be treated as simple interest groups lobbying various institutions of governance at different levels? This

perspective is correct, to some degree, but some nongovernmental groups exercise governance jurisdiction in some arenas, while some governmental agencies find themselves lobbying in other arenas.

64. Two of the best-known works addressing regimes and the conditions of creation and maintenance are Stephen D. Krasner, ed., *International Regimes* (Ithaca: Cornell University Press, 1983), and Robert O. Keohane, *After Hegemony: Cooperation and Discord in the World Political Economy* (Princeton, NJ: Princeton University Press, 1984). More recent works on environmental regimes include: Peter M. Haas, Robert O. Keohane, and Marc A. Levy, eds., *Institutions for the Earth—Sources of Effective International Environmental Protection* (Cambridge, MA: MIT Press, 1993); Oran R. Young and Gail Osherenko, eds., *Polar Politics—Creating International Environmental Regimes* (Ithaca: Cornell University Press, 1993); Oran R. Young, *International Governance—Protecting the Environment in a Stateless Society* (Ithaca: Cornell University Press, 1994); and Karen T. Litfin, *Ozone Discourses—Science and Politics in Global Environmental Cooperation* (New York: Columbia University Press, 1994).

65. On this point, see Daniel Deudney, "Global Environmental Rescue and the Emergence of World Domestic Politics," pp. 280–305, in Lipschutz and Conca, *The State and Social Power*, pp. 286–89; Janice E. Thompson, "Explaining the Regulation of Transnational Practices: A State-Building Approach," pp. 195–218, in Rosenau and Czempiel, *Governance Without Government*.

66. For some thoughts on this matter, see Oran R. Young, "The Effectiveness of International Governance Systems," pp. 140–60, in Young, *International Governance*; Peter Sand, *The Effectiveness of International Environmental Agreements* (Cambridge: Cambridge University Press, 1994).

67. The notion of 'two-level games' was originally developed by Robert D. Putnam, "Diplomacy and Domestic Politics—The Logic of Two Level Games," *International Organization* 42, 3 (Summer 1988): 427–60; See also Peter B. Evans, Harold K. Jacobson, and Robert D. Putnam, eds., *Double-Edged Diplomacy—International Bargaining and Domestic Politics* (Berkeley: University of California Press, 1993). A brief discussion of 'three-level' games can be found in Janie Leatherman, Ron Pagnucco, and Jacki Smith, "International Institutions and Transnational Social Movement Organizations: Transforming Sovereignty, Anarchy, and Global Governance," Kroc Institute for International Peace Studies, University of Notre Dame, August 1994, working paper 5:WP:3, esp. pp. 23–28.

68. See Leatherman, et al, "International Institutions."

69. As Brian Ford puts it, if we look at the "functional system of governance associated with the particular level of civil society in question, whether it be on a global or regional level . . . [it is important to recognize that] this system of governance is a political formation that not only transcends both geographical borders and state jurisdictions, but as a matter of practice includes elements of the institutional machinery of various states." ("Trade, Transnational

Civil Society, and the Formation of Ethical Content in World and Regional Systems: Transcending the Posted Borders of the Modern System," paper presented at the American Political Science Association Conference, New York, 1–4 Sept., 1994, p. 1.)

70. Personal communication from Robert Meister.

71. Which is why we are so shocked when the rules of such professions are violated in a major way. Such associations provide a setting in which social constraints operate more strongly than in society at large. To violate the rules is to violate a trust, and this could lead to being thrown out into the cold, cruel world.

72. Fred Hirsch, *Social Limits to Growth* (Cambridge: Harvard University Press, 1976), pp. 120–121, 137–40, 146.

73. Another example of this phenomenon is the wholesale diamond trade in New York, Antwerp, and Israel, which historically has been based on trust in one's ethnic or religious "kin." See, e.g., Mats Alvesson and Lars Lindkvist, "Transaction Costs, Clans, and Corporate Culture," *Journal of Management Studies* 30, 3 (May 1993): 427–52; William G. Ouchi, "Markets, Bureaucracies, and Clans," *Administrative Science Quarterly* 25 (March 1980): 129–41.

74. Much of the following discussion is based on Donald Chisholm, *Coordination Without Hierarchy—Informal Structures in Multiorganizational Systems* (Berkeley: University of California Press, 1989).

75. Chisholm, *Coordination Without Hierarchy*, p. 11.

76. Chisholm, *Coordination Without Hierarchy*, p. 32. My emphasis.

77. Gordon, "Globalization . . . ," pp. 30-31. Emphasis in original.

78. The term 'social choice mechanisms' comes from John S. Dryzek, *Rational Ecology—Environment and Political Economy* (Oxford: Basil Blackwell, 1987).

PART FIVE

CONCLUSION

CHAPTER 13

Toward an Ontology for Global Governance

JAMES N. ROSENAU

In an era marked by shifting boundaries, relocated authorities, weakened states, and proliferating nongovernmental organizations (NGOs) at local, provincial, national, transnational, international, and global levels of community, the time has come to confront the insufficiency of our ways of thinking, talking, and writing about government. And this imperative is all the greater because the dynamics of change, the shrinking of social, economic, and political distances, and the focus on the inherent weaknesses of the United Nations on the occasion of its fiftieth birthday—to mention only the more conspicuous sources—have led to a surge of concern for a still amorphous entity called "global governance." Welcome as this new focus is, however, it suffers from a reliance on artifacts of the very past beyond which it seeks to move. While myriad books, journals, and study commissions have debated what such an entity involves and whether there are any prospects for its realization, such inquiries are plagued by a lack of conceptual tools appropriate to the task of sorting out the underpinnings of political processes sustained by altered borders, redirected legitimacy sentiments, impaired or paralyzed governments, and new identities.[1]

A depleted toolshed suggests that understanding is no longer served by clinging to the notion that states and national governments are the essential underpinnings of the world's organization. We have become so accustomed to treating these entities as the foundations of politics that we fall back on them when contemplating the prospects for governance on a global scale, thereby relegating the shifting boundaries, relocated authorities, and proliferating NGOs to the status of new but secondary dimensions of the processes through which communities allocate values and frame policies. To be sure, these dimensions are regarded as important, and few observers would dismiss their impact as peripheral. Nonetheless, the predominant tendency is to cling to old ways of thought that accord primacy to states and national governments. Even an otherwise praiseworthy attempt to clarify and define the nature of global governance proved unable to break free of the conventional conception which posits states and governments as the organizing focus of analysis: while acknowledging the enormous changes at work in the world, the transformation of boundaries, the erosion of state authority, and the proliferation of NGOs, in the end this definitional undertaking falls back on old ways of thought and specifies that global governance involves "doing internationally what governments do at home."[2] Such a formulation amply demonstrates the large extent to which we remain imprisoned by the idea that the line dividing domestic and foreign affairs still serves as the cutting edge of analysis.

How, then, to update our perspectives so that they can more fully and accurately account for a world in which the dynamics of governance are undergoing profound and enduring transformations? How to render political inquiry more incisive, more able to treat seemingly anomalous developments as part and parcel of modern-day governance? How to equip ourselves so that we are not surprised by a Soviet Union that peacefully collapses overnight, by a Canada that borders on fragmentation, by a Yugoslavia that seeks membership in the European Union even as it comes apart, by a currency crisis that surfaces simultaneously around the world, by a South Africa that manages to bridge a long standing and huge racial divide, by the splintering of a long-unified Israel, or by international institutions that intrude deeply into the domestic affairs of states (to mention only a few of the surprising developments of recent years)?

The answers to these questions lie, I believe, in the need to develop a new ontology for understanding the deepest foundations of governance. Such an ontology—and the paradigms that flow from it—should recast the relevance of territoriality, treat the temporal dimensions of govenance as no less significant than the spatial dimensions, posit as normal shifts of authority to subnational, transnational, and nongovernmental levels, and highlight the porosity of boundaries at all levels of governance. Awesome as this task surely is, what follows offers some initial thoughts on what the outlines of a new ontology should encompass. The goal is not to specify in detail the key ontological premises (the details can be developed only as the ontology is used in empirical inquiries); rather it is to briefly indicate the substantive shifts that people are likely to undergo as they think about the purposes, processes, structures, and loci of governance. By focusing on these prospective shifts, hopefully we can accelerate the pace at which they unfold.

ONTOLOGIES AND PARADIGMS

Let us start by drawing some conceptual distinctions. The concept of an 'ontology' originates in the field of philosophy. It refers to the broad assumptions that people make about the nature of reality. Here the concept is adapted to the field of world politics and is conceived to involve the broad assumptions people make about the realities of global affairs. A 'paradigm,' on the other hand, is conceived here as an empirical specification of what follows from the assumptions encompassed by an ontology. Stated differently, ontologies are foundational in that they highlight what basic elements are regarded as comprising the existing order, whereas paradigms are seen as referring to the ways in which the elements are interactively organized and order is thus imposed upon them. Put in still another way, ontologies are static in that they identify the essential components of the whole they comprise, but paradigms allow for movement on the part of the components and thus focus on the changes as well as the stabilities that comprise the whole. It follows that while one's ontology identifies what actors engage in what forms of behavior to sustain a particular form of global governance, one's paradigm focuses on how and when the actors are likely to maintain or vary their behavior.[3] Viewed from the more encompassing perspective in which people perceive and talk about reality, of course, ontologies and paradigms cannot be clearly delineated from each other. We separate them only for analytical purposes (together they constitute what is often referred to as the "social construction of reality").

The need for ontologies and paradigms derives from the fact that people can never grasp reality in its entirety and are thus forced to select some features of the ongoing scene as important and dismiss the rest as trivial. So as to achieve a modicum of order out of the welter of phenomena they select as important, people need to link the various phenomena to each other coherently; that is, they need to render the world orderly so that they can understand and adapt to it. The ways in which the important features are arranged in relation to each other form the bases of the ontologies and paradigms through which the course of events is interpreted and order imposed upon them. The end result for either individuals or collectivities is an intersubjective—and not an objective—understanding. As Cox puts it, "Reality is made by the collective responses of people to the conditions of their existence. Intersubjectively shared experience reproduces reality in the form of continuing institutions and practices."[4] In short, "Ontologies tell us what is significant in the particular world we delve into—what are the basic entities and key relationships. Ontologies are not arbitrary constructions; they are the specification of the common sense of an epoch."[5]

This is not to imply that either ontologies or paradigms are necessarily complex and pervaded with multiple layers. On the contrary, normally only a few features, such as the identity of major actors and the essential attributes of their activities, are selected out as crucial structures of governance that serve to explain how and why polities move in one direction rather than another. The prevailing ontology prior to World War II, for example, focused on the balance of power as the common sense of that epoch; in the subsequent period the Cold War with its superpower rivalry served to organize thinking about the world; today neither of these perspectives pertains to the order that has emerged since the beginning of the 1990s. In other words, ontologies are so thoroughgoing and paradigms so all-encompassing in their empirical scope, so capable of accounting for all the developments that are perceived to be relevant to the maintenance or alteration of the political world, that people can summarize their understanding of complex phenomena by reference to a few organizing principles. They do not need to go back and forth between paradigms with the rationale that it all depends on the issue. For ontologies and paradigms are cast at a level of understanding where the sources of behavior in world affairs are presumed to derive from roots more fundamental than those associated with issue differences.

How, then, do ontologies and paradigms, those specifications of the common sense of an epoch, undergo change? In two ways: either the conditions of peoples' existence are so profoundly transformed that people are led by the cumulation and normalization of anomalies to alter the way they intersubjectively experience them, or their awareness of their existing conditions shifts in response to new technologies that enable them to perceive their prevailing circumstances in a new context.

In the present era, both sources of ontological transformation seem likely to operate and reinforce each other. The globalization of national economies, the emergence of a worldwide consumerist culture, the advent of global norms pertaining to human rights and the environment, the challenges of AIDS, the fragmentation of some societies and the integration of others, the drug trade, international crime syndicates, currency crises, and the ozone gap are only the more obvious changes that have become central features of people's condition today. At the same time, the continuing spread of global television and many other features of the unending microelectronic revolution have greatly facilitated an intensified awareness of these new conditions with which they must cope.

However the altered conditions and the awareness of them may combine to foster new intersubjective experiences, a more appropriate ontology and its concomitant paradigms will be slow to evolve and difficult to frame. As previously implied, ontologies are so deep-seated and so rooted as the bases of analytic habits, that they do not readily yield to evidence of obsolescence. The concept of regimes is a good case in point. Conceived originally as an issue area in which the relevant actors share the rules, norms, principles, and procedures through which decisions are made and implemented, the preponderance of the literature that has since mushroomed lays emphasis upon states as comprising the members of regimes.[6] Little attention is paid to those other than governmental actors despite considerable evidence that in many regimes—such as oil—firms, NGOs, and other types of actors play crucial roles. If it is the case that regimes are a major institutional form through which global governance is carried forward, then it is virtually impossible to assess their contribution to governing processes if their ranks are conceived to consist exclusively of national governments. Nonetheless, analysts using the regime approach have yet to update their inquiries by allowing for NGOs and other types of actors to play major roles in the conduct of regimes.[7]

Stated more generally, faced with the case for an ontological shift, many people may acknowledge that changes are occurring in the territorial, temporal, and organizational underpinnings of governance, but in the same breath they are likely to insist that states and national governments nevertheless continue to retain the primary authority and power they have possessed for several centuries.[8] Yes, they would agree, the Cold War is over, but it is still an anarchical world of states where national governments and their power balances predominate. Understandable as it may be to presume that history has resumed from where it left off in 1939, such a reaction can only perpetuate and heighten the limits of our grasp of governance in a turbulent and transformative age. At the same time, the necessity of an ontological shift may seem less ominous and more palatable if it is appreciated that the ensuing formulation does not dismiss states and governments as secondary and peripheral; rather it posits them as central to and consequential for the course of events along with a host of other actors. In other words, a fine line needs to be drawn between treating states as the only players on the global stage and as unimportant and aged players that have long since passed their prime. Given the necessity of not devoting exclusive attention to states and acknowledging that a wide range of nongovernmental actors increasingly need to serve as foci of intensive analysis, it follows that states and governments should be posited not as first among equals, but simply as significant actors in a world marked by an increasing diffusion of authority and a corresponding diminution of hierarchy. Yes, states retain their sovereign rights, but the realms within which these rights can be exercised has diminished as the world becomes ever more interdependent and as state boundaries become ever more porous. With the increasing diffusion of authority, states can no longer rely on their sovereignty as a basis for protecting their interests in the face of increasingly complex challenges.

As will immediately be seen, new ontologies require new labels to clearly differentiate the common sense of the new epoch from its predecessor and to facilitate the development of a widespread intersubjectivity as to the ways in which it breaks with the past. It must be stressed, however, that the label used here is offered tentatively, that it may prove too technical to generate broad usage, and that in all probability a less complex and more compelling terminology will evolve. Indeed, the label used here is not the first to be suggested; among others, for example, are *polyarchy*,[9] *panarchy*,[10] and *collibration*,[11] all three of which highlight the degree to which the world has undergone decentralization since the end of the Cold War. Whatever labels may eventually be adopted, in other words, they are likely to point incisively to the key arrangements that distinguish the epoch from its predecessors. It is not sufficient to designate the new epoch by the label of *post-Cold War*, since this is a term that conveys no image of what the core dynamics of the new epoch involve. The Cold War label, like the "balance of power" epoch that preceded it, did point to substantive phenomena. It was a label that served to summarize the superpower rivalry and the structures thereby imposed on the rest of the world, whereas to speak now of the post-Cold War period is merely to highlight that the earlier period has ended. Awkward as the label used here may seem, it does capture the essential dynamic wherein the new epoch is marked by the simultaneity of continual tensions and interactions between the forces propelling the fragmentation of communities and those conducing to the integration of communities.

GLOBALIZATION, LOCALIZATION, AND FRAGMEGRATION

It seems clear that powerful tendencies toward globalization not only underlie the shifting of boundaries, the relocation of authorities, the weakening of states, and the proliferation of NGOs, but they also provoke equally powerful tendencies toward localization that give rise to further consequences of this sort. If the interactions of sovereign states in an anarchical world lie at the heart of the old ontology, at the center of the new one are the interactions of globalizing and localizing forces, of tendencies toward integration and fragmentation that are so simultaneous and interactive as to collapse into an erratic but singular process to which I have attached the label of *fragmegration*.[12] Grating as this term may be, it has the virtue of capturing the inextricably close and causal links between globalization and localization, highlighting the possibility that each and every increment of the former gives rise to an increment of the latter, and vice versa.

It follows that we live in and study a fragmegrative world that cascades events through, over, and around the long-established boundaries of states and, in so doing, relocates authority upwards to transnational and supranational organizations, sidewards to social movements and NGOs, and downwards to subnational groups. It is a world in which the logic of governance does not necessarily follow hierarchical lines, in which what is distant is also proximate, and in which the spatial and temporal dimensions of politics are so confounded by fragmegrative dynamics as to rid event sequences of any linearity they once may have had. Today's chains of causation follow crazy-quilt patterns that cannot be adequately discerned if one clings to an ontology that presumes the primacy of states and governments.

At the very least, a more appropriate ontology will highlight the large extent to which the erosion of state authority and the proliferation of NGOs has resulted in a disaggregation of the loci of governance. Notwithstanding the overriding power of globalizing forces in the economic,

communications, and cultural realms, and despite the signs of expanding integration to be found in Europe and other regions today,
fragmegration has been accompanied by a dispersion of the sites out of
which authority can be exercised and compliance generated. The weakening of states has not been followed by authority vacuums (although
there may be situations where this is the case) so much as it has resulted
in a vast growth in the number of spheres into which authority has
moved. Fragmegration points to a redistribution of authority and not to
its deterioration.

In short, if a map of the world based on the new ontology were
drawn, it would depict global governance as highly disaggregated even
as many of its spheres are overlapping. Global governance is not so
much a label for a high degree of integration and order as it is a
summary term for highly complex and widely disparate activities that
may culminate in a modicum of worldwide coherence or that may
collapse into pervasive disarray.[13] In the event of either outcome, it
would still be global governance in the sense that the sum of efforts by
widely disaggregated goal-seeking entities will have supplemented, perhaps even supplanted, states as the prime sources of governance on a
global scale. And whichever outcome eventually predominates, both
will surely be sufficiently cumbersome to prevent either from amounting
to an effective arrangement for addressing the need for decisive and
equitable policies that ameliorate the large problems comprising the
global agenda.

Of course, the present era is not the only moment in history when
disaggregation has marked the loci of governance. In earlier eras, for
example, considerable authority was exercised by members of the
Hanseatic League and the Medici and Rothschild families. Indeed, one
can doubtless find numerous historical circumstances that parallel any
examples that appear as central to the dynamics of boundary erosion
and change today. Just as AIDS moves quickly through national boundaries today, so did the Plague in the Sixteenth Century; just as the
Internet, fax machine, and global television render boundaries ever more
porous today, so did the advent of the printing press, the wireless, and
the telephone spread ideas independently of national borders in earlier
eras; and so on for all the channels whereby the processes of globalization and localization are presently expanding and contracting horizons.
The difference in the current period is that the processes of aggregation
and disaggregation are occurring and interacting so rapidly—more often than not instantaneously—to the point of being literally simulta-

neous. That is, the pace of politics at all levels of community has accelerated to the extent that reactions to events occur roughly at the same time as the events themselves, leaving actors as always in a mode of seeking to catch up with the consequences of decisions to which they were also parties. It is for this reason that the emergent ontology will doubtless include a new understanding of the temporal dimension of politics.

UNITS OF GOVERNANCE

It follows that the new ontology requires us to focus on those political actors, structures, processes, and institutions that initiate, sustain, or respond to globalizing forces as they propel boundary-spanning activities and foster boundary-contracting reactions. Approached in this way, states become only one of many sources of authority, only one of many organizations through which the dynamics of fragmegration shape the course of events. Stated differently, instead of initially positing a world dominated by states and national governments, the new ontology builds on the premise that the world is comprised of spheres of authority (SOAs) that are not necessarily consistent with the division of territorial space and are subject to considerable flux. Such spheres are, in effect, the analytic units of the new ontology. They are distinguished by the presence of actors who can evoke compliance when exercising authority as they engage in the activities that delineate the sphere. Authority, in other words, is conceived not as a possession of actors, nor as embedded in roles. Authority is relational; its existence can only be observed when it is both exercised and complied with. A new occupant of a position may acquire formal authority upon taking up the duties of the position, but whether his or her authority is effective and enduring depends on the response of those toward whom the authority is directed. If they are responsive, then authority can be said to be operative; if they do not respond compliantly, then the formal prerequisites of the position are quite irrelevant.

It follows that SOAs can differ in form and structure, depending on the degree to which their relational foundations are hierarchically arrayed. They can vary from those founded on hierarchical arrangements that explicitly allow for unexplained orders backed up by the capacity to coerce or dismiss those who do not comply (command authority), as is the case in military organizations, to SOAs that involve an implicit capacity to force compliance if persuasion proves insufficient to achieve it (bureaucratic authority), as is the case when nonmilitary governmental or nongovernmental officials exercise authority, to SOAs in which authority derives from expertise (epistemic authority), as is the case when people comply because specialists concur in a recommendation.[14]

It also follows that an SOA may or may not be coterminous with a bounded territory; those who comply may be spread around the world and have no legal relationship to each other, or they may be located in the same geographic space and have the same organizational affiliations. If the sphere involves the allocation of values through certifying and rating the reliability of bond issuers, for example, then its actors will include Moody's, Standard and Poor's, and a number of other credit rating agencies whose evaluations determine which firms, governments, and NGOs in various parts of the world get loans and which do not.[15] In contrast to these nonterritorial SOAs, on the other hand, are those in which the allocation of values remains linked to geographic space, thus enabling local, provincial, and national governments to achieve compliance when they exercise authority over taxes, parklands, police activities, and other domains wherein they have not experienced a shift and contraction of their jurisdictions.

The advent of nonterritorial actors and relocated authorities helps to explain the recent tendency to focus on processes of governance rather than those of governments as the instruments through which authority is exercised. While governments are concrete actors accorded formal jurisdiction over specified territorial domains, governance is a broader concept that highlights SOAs that may not be territorial in scope and that may employ only informal authority to achieve compliance on the part of those within the sphere. *Governance,* in other words, refers to mechanisms for steering social systems toward their goals,[16] a conception which is far more amenable to understanding a world in which old boundaries are becoming obscure, in which new identities are becoming commonplace, and in which the scale of political thought has become global in scope. Indeed, it might well be that the shift to the emphasis on governance will prove to be the first major indicator that a new intersubjective ontology for understanding world affairs is already in the process of taking hold in the awareness of people.

Still another sign of the emergent ontology can be discerned in the variety of new terms that have evolved to designate units of governance which are not instruments of states and governments. At least ten such units have achieved acceptance in (and in some cases pervade) the literature on world politics: NGOs, nonstate actors, sovereignty-free actors, issue networks, policy networks, social movements, global civil society, transnational coalitions, transnational lobbies, and epistemic communities.[17] While an intersubjective consensus has yet to shake this terminology down into a shared vocabulary, clearly the proliferation of such terms expresses a restlessness with the prevailing ontological preoccupation with states and governments.

HIERARCHY

In a disaggregated, decentralized world in which SOAs are relatively independent of each other, what might the new ontology specify as common sense with respect to the pervasiveness of hierarchy? Again it may be difficult to move on to new ways of thinking. Hierarchy involves power and the relative capability of actors, and we are so accustomed to positing pecking orders in these terms that it will not be easy to come to grips with a disaggregated array of actors whose power is limited to a particular expertise or set of issues, thus rendering them essentially autonomous and not dependent on where they stand in a pecking order. More specifically, the new ontology allows for within-sphere hierarchies, since actors with similar goals in a SOA are likely to have different capabilities that differentiate their degrees of influence, but there is no basis for presuming that a pecking order will develop among SOAs. Some credit rating agencies may be more influential than others, but there is no necessary basis for presuming either that the most high-status credit agency can achieve compliance from actors outside its sphere or that its compliance can be achieved by actors in other spheres. "Wait a minute," those wedded to the old ontology might exclaim, "what about the state's sovereignty? Surely that enables it to curb or override any credit agency operating within its borders!" Not at all, respond those who have adopted the new ontology, authority inheres in a sphere, and if a state or national government succeeds in curbing or overruling the actions of a credit agency, such an outcome will be a consequence of the circumstances of the sphere in which the two actors compete rather than stemming from the state having sovereign authority which the credit agency lacks. Put differently, what enables an actor to obtain compliance from another actor in a disaggregated world is an interdependent convergence of needs and not a constitutional specification that assigns the highest authority exclusively to states and national governments. In addition, the hierarchy that derives from the military power over which states have a monopoly and through which they exercise their sovereignty in the last resort can no longer, given the disaggregation of SOAs, be translated into leverage over credit agencies.

WHAT ABOUT BOUNDED SYSTEMS?

Given the widening porosity of conventional political boundaries, the shifting loci of authority, and the emergence of a nonterritorial, nonlinear politics, the question arises as to whether the foregoing analysis cannot also be applied to the governance of more circumscribed domains? If fragmegrative dynamics are as pervasive and significant as suggested here, are they not also operative within bounded societies? And if so, do they not also exert pressure for a new ontology to replace the one that has long served as the intersubjective basis for understanding domestic politics?

A positive answer to such questions can readily be asserted even if it may yet be premature to undertake specifying an ontology comparable to that organized around the notion of fragmegration. Certainly fragmegrative dynamics are no less relevant to societal systems than they are to the global system. Surely it is reasonable to think in terms of SOAs as units of governance within societies as it is between them. Doubtless the exercise of authority in societal processes is as likely as in global ones to cascade across space and time in an erratic fashion, flowing first in one direction, then in another, followed by still a third redirection, even a reversal to the point of origin, with the result that compliance cumulates, gets modified, or is terminated in nonlinear sequences. And given societies that are as disaggregated as the global system they comprise, they will in all likelihood increasingly be marked by an eroding between-SOA pecking order.

Indeed, given a conviction that "the governing capacity of political/administrative systems . . . either has crossed the threshold of the law of diminishing returns or is quite close to such a boundary,"[18] with the result that "*political governance in modern societies can no longer be conceived in terms of external governmental control of society but emerges from a plurality of governing actors,*"[19] signs of efforts to specify a new common sense of societal governance in the emergent epoch are already manifest. An entire symposium, for example, has been devoted to probing "new patterns of interaction between government and society" and thereby to "discovering other ways of coping with new problems or of creating new possibilities for governing."[20] It seems clear, in short, that this paper is part and parcel of a larger thrust to update our commonsense understanding of politics in a turbulent world.

NOTES

1. See, for example, a new journal, *Global Governance*, published by Lynne Rienner Publishers in cooperation with the Academic Council on the United Nations [ACUNS] and the United Nations University. The books and study commission reports on the subject include The Commission on Global Governance, *Our Global Neighborhood* (New York: Oxford University Press, 1995); The Commission on Global Governance, *Issues in Global Governance: Paper Written for The Commission on Global Governance* (London: Kluwer Law International, 1995); Meghnad Desai and Paul Redfern, eds., *Global Governance: Ethics and Economics of the World Order* (London: Pinter, 1995); Jan Kooiman, ed., *Modern Governance: New Government-Society Interactions* (London: Sage Publications, 1993); Mihaly Simai, *The Future of Global Governance: Managing Risk and Change in the International System* (Washington, DC: United States Institute of Peace Press, 1994); and Yoshikazu Sakamoto, ed., *Global Transformation: Challenges to the State System* (Tokyo: United Nations Press, 1994)

2. Lawrence S. Finkelstein, "What Is Global Governance?" *Global Governance*, vol. 1 (Sept.–Dec. 1995), pp. 367–72 (the quote is from p. 369).

3. This notion of paradigm extends, but does not contradict, the early specification of the concept set forth in Thomas S. Kuhn, *The Structure of Scientific Revolutions* (Chicago: University of Chicago Press, 1970, 2nd edition). For a discussion of twenty-one different ways in which the paradigm concept is employed, see Margaret Masterman, "The Nature of a Paradigm," in Imre Lakatos and Alan Musgrave, eds., *Criticism and the Growth of Knowledge* (Cambridge: Cambridge University Press, 1970), pp. 61–65).

4. Robert W. Cox, "Critical Political Economy," in Bjorn Hettne, ed., *International Political Economy: Understanding Global Disorder* (London: Zed Books, 1995), p. 35.

5. Cox, "Critical Political Economy," p. 34.

6. For examples of how regimes are conceived to consist primarily of national governments, see most of the essays in Stephen D. Krasner, ed., *International Regimes* (Ithaca: Cornell University Press, 1983), and Volker Rittberger, ed., *Regime Theory and International Relations* (Oxford: Clarendon Press, 1993), as well as Robert O. Keohane, *After Hegemony: Cooperation and Discord in the World Political Economy* (Princeton: Princeton University Press, 1984), pp. 98–106.

7. For an exception in this regard, see Virginia Haufler, "Crossing the Boundary between Public and Private: International Regimes and Non-State

Actors," in Rittberger, ed., *Regime Theory and International Relations*, pp. 94–111.

8. For written expressions of this ambivalent perspective, see Robert Gilpin, *War and Change in World Politics* (New York: Cambridge University Press, 1981), p. 7; Alan James and Robert H. Jackson, "The Character of Independent Statehood," in A. James and R. H. Jackson, eds., *States in a Changing World: A Contemporary Analysis* (Oxford: Clarendon Press, 1993), pp. 5–8; Stephen D. Krasner, "Sovereignty: An Institutional Perspective," in James A. Caporaso, ed., *The Elusive State: International and Comparative Perspectives* (Newbury Park: Sage Publications, 1989), chap. 4; Eugene B. Skolnikoff, *The Elusive Transformation: Science, Technology, and the Evolution of International Politics* (Princeton: Princeton University Press, 1993), p. 7; and Kenneth N. Waltz, *Theory of International Politics* (Reading, MA: Addison-Wesley, 1979), p. 94.

9. Seyom Brown, *New Forces, Old Forces, and the Future of World Politics* (New York: HarperCollins, Post-Cold War Edition, 1995), chap. 8.

10. James P. Sewell and Mark B. Salter, "Panarchy and Other Norms for Global Governance," *Global Governance*, vol. 1 (Sept.–Dec. 1995), pp. 373–82.

11. Andrew Dunsire, "Modes of Governance," in J. Kooiman, *Modern Governance*, p. 31.

12. This concept was first developed in James N. Rosenau, " 'Fragmegrative' Challenges to National Security," in Terry Heyns, ed., *Understanding US Strategy: A Reader* (Washington, DC: National Defense University, 1983), pp. 65–82, and has since been considerably elaborated in James N. Rosenau, *Along the Domestic-Foreign Frontier: Exploring Governance in a Turbulent World* (Cambridge: Cambridge University Press, 1997), chap. 7.

13. For a cogent discussion of the dynamics driving change in globalizing directions, see Philip G. Cerny, "Globalization and the Changing Logic of Collective Action," *International Organization*, vol. 49 (Autumn 1995), pp. 595–625.

14. For a useful discussion of the nature of authority and the forms it can take, see Bruce Lincoln, *Authority: Construction and Corrosion* (Chicago: University of Chicago Press, 1994).

15. Timothy J. Sinclair, *Guarding the Gates of Capital: Credit Rating Processes and the Global Political Economy* (Toronto: Ph.D. Dissertation, York University, 1995).

16. James N. Rosenau, "Governance in the 21st Century," *Global Governance*, vol. I (Winter 1995), p. 14.

17. I am indebted to Ken Conca for this listing.

18. Jan Kooiman, "Social-Political Governance: Introduction," in J. Kooiman, ed., *Modern Governance*, p. 1.

19. Quoted from the back flap of B. Marin and R. Mayntz, *Policy Networks*, in Jan Jooiman, "Findings, Speculations, and Recommendations," in J. Kooiman, ed., *Modern Governance*, p. 258 (italics in the original).

20. J. Kooiman, "Social-Political Governance: Introduction," p. 1.

Contributors

M. MARK AMEN is Associate Professor of International Studies and Associate Dean for Academic Affairs (College of Arts and Sciences) at the University of South Florida. His research program focuses on the political economy of credit.

EDWARD A. COMOR is Assistant Professor at the School of International Service, American University. He is the editor of *The Global Political Economy of Communication* (1994 and 1996) and is the author of *Communication, Commerce, and Power: The Political Economy of America and the Direct Broadcast Satellite, 1960-2000* (1998).

YALE H. FERGUSON is Professor and Chair, Department of Political Science, and Faculty Associate, Center for Global Change and Governance, Rutgers University-Newark. His numerous publications include *Contemporary Inter-American Relations, Continuing Issues in International Politics,* and with Richard W. Mansbach: *The Web of World Politics; The Elusive Quest; The State, Conceptual Chaos, and the Future of International Relations Theory;* and *Polities: Authority, Identities, and Change.* In recent years he has twice been a Visiting Fellow at the University of Cambridge, Fulbright Professor at the University of Salzburg, and Senior Fellow at the Norwegian Nobel Institute.

MARTIN HEWSON is a researcher at the Center for International and Security Studies, York University, Toronto, and teaches at McMaster University, Hamilton, Ontario. He specializes in international relations theory and global information and communication.

ROBERT LATHAM is Program Director with the Social Science Research Council-MacArthur Foundation Program on International Peace and Security. He is author of *The Liberal Moment: Modernity, Security, and the Making of Postwar International Order,* published by Columbia University Press (1997). He is currently coediting a book titled *Global Reconfigurations of Power: International Intervention and Local Governance in Africa.*

RONNIE D. LIPSCHUTZ is Associate Professor of Politics and Associate Director of the Center for Global, International, and Regional Studies at the University of California, Santa Cruz. He is editor of *On Security* (Columbia, 1995) and author of *Global Civil Society and Global Environmental Governance* (SUNY Press, 1996).

KAREN T. LITFIN is Associate Professor of Political Science at the University of Washington. She is author of *Ozone Discourses: Science and Politics in Global Environmental Cooperation* (Columbia, 1994) and editor of *The Greening of Sovereignty in World Politics* (MIT Press, 1998). Her current research is on the political implications of the use of satellite data by nonstate actors.

RICHARD W. MANSBACH is Professor of Political Science at Iowa State University. Professor Mansbach's field is international political theory, and he is the author, co-author, or editor of ten books, including *Polities: Authority, Identities, and Ideology; The Elusive Quest: Theory and International Politics;* and *In Search of Theory: Toward a New Paradigm for Global Politics.* He has also published numerous articles and book chapters.

RONEN PALAN is Lecturer in International Relations and Politics at the University of Sussex and, during 1998/99, Visiting Professor in the Department of Political Science, York University, Toronto. He is the coeditor of the *Review of International Political Economy.* Recent publications include (with Jason Abbott, *State Strategies in the Global Political Economy* (Pinter, 1996), and (with Barry Gills, eds.) *Transcending the State-Global Divide* (Lynne Rienner, 1994).

TONY PORTER is Associate Professor of Political Science at McMaster University, Hamilton, Ontario. He is the author of *States, Markets, and Regimes in Global Finance* (Macmillan, 1993) and coeditor, with A. Claire Cutler and Virginia Haufler, of *Private Authority in International Affairs* (SUNY Press, 1999).

JAMES N. ROSENAU is University Professor of International Affairs at the George Washington University. His recent writings include *Along the Domestic-Foreign Frontier: Exploring Governance in a Turbulent World* (1997), *Turbulence in World Politics: A Theory of Change and Continuity* (1990), and coauthorship of *Thinking Theory Thoroughly: Coherent Approaches to an Incoherent World* (1995).

MICHAEL G. SCHECHTER is Professor of International Relations at James Madison College of Michigan State University. His research focuses on global governance and teaching pedagogy. His most recent publications include *Historical Dictionary of International Organizations* (1998) and editing and contributing to *Innovation in Multilateralism* (1998) and *Future Multilateralism: The Political and Social Framework* (1998).

TIMOTHY J. SINCLAIR is Lecturer in International Political Economy at the University of Warwick in England. His publications include (with Robert W. Cox) *Approaches to World Order* (Cambridge University Press, 1996) and articles in *Policy Sciences* and *Review of International Political Economy*. A former economic and financial analyst in the New Zealand Treasury, Dr. Sinclair is a member of the governing council of the IPE section of the International Studies Association. He is currently writing a book on bond rating agencies and the global political economy.

Index